Articulating Dissent

Articulating Dissent

Protest and the Public Sphere

Pollyanna Ruiz

PlutoPress

www.plutobooks.com

First published 2014 by Pluto Press
345 Archway Road, London N6 5AA

www.plutobooks.com

Distributed in the United States of America exclusively by
Palgrave Macmillan, a division of St. Martin's Press LLC,
175 Fifth Avenue, New York, NY 10010

British Library Cataloguing in Publication Data
A catalogue record for this book is available from the British Library

ISBN 978 0 7453 3306 9 Hardback
ISBN 978 0 7453 3305 2 Paperback
ISBN 978 1 8496 4885 1 PDF eBook
ISBN 978 1 8496 4887 5 Kindle eBook
ISBN 978 1 8496 4886 8 EPUB eBook

Library of Congress Cataloging in Publication Data applied for

10   9   8   7   6   5   4   3   2   1

Typeset by Stanford DTP Services, Northampton, England
Text design by Melanie Patrick
Simultaneously printed digitally by CPI Antony Rowe, Chippenham, UK
and Edwards Bros in the United States of America

This book is dedicated with much love to my parents,
Elizabeth and Tony.

Contents

Acknowledgments

I would like to acknowledge the loving support of my immediate family; my partner David who has faithfully read every word I have ever written, and my children Benji, Mira and Chela who have joyfully distracted me from writing many more. And my extended family; Elizabeth, Tony, Mathew, Thomas and Katie who have cooked, shopped, cleaned and made tea with such constancy and care.

I would also like to acknowledge the support of my friends who have provided encouragement and solace in equal measures. I'd particularly like to thank Janice, Kate, Caroline and Ben for their invaluable academic advice, Beck and Louise for their activist insights, and Iseult, AnneMarie and Kathy for their absolute confidence in my ability to carry on writing.

Preface

As the daughter of politically active parents, much of my childhood was spent going to demonstrations, making human chains and holding candlelit vigils. These were hugely enjoyable events which usually culminated in a shared picnic. After each demonstration I would go to bed fully expecting to wake up to a brand new dawn. My faith in the democratic process was rooted in the belief that public opinion was a force capable of holding those in power to account. I presumed that my role, as a small but active citizen, was to inform the world in general and my government in particular, of previously unnoticed injustices and inequalities. The gradual realisation that the relationship between the will of the people and the actions of the state was far more complex led me to ask a number of interrelated questions.

Firstly it has prompted me to ask whether the flow of information from my world to the wider world is somehow being impeded. As I grew older I began to think about why our demonstrations were so often ignored by the mainstream media. I thought about the ways in which the communication strategies of the protest organisations I knew seemed to be structured by ideological, rather than communicative considerations. I reflected upon our failure to adequately articulate our shared political ends. I asked myself whether these internal frictions contributed to the mainstream's tendency to dismiss the radical left as unrepresentative, irrelevant or irrational.

As time went by the single-issue campaigns which had characterised the late 1970s and early 1980s were gradually replaced by more fractured multi-issue campaigns. Class, which had for so many years been perceived to be the defining binary of radical politics, was unsettled by a plethora of alternative identity positions. There seemed to be a growing recognition that individuals' 'material interests' were complicated by a far wider 'sense of themselves and their place in the world' (Gilbert, 2008, p. 153). This shift in radical politics was initially constructed around the politics of gender, race and sexuality but was soon further complicated by the rise in political groupings around issues such as environmentalism, global inequality, and the need to protect civil liberties. This proliferation of positions was politically productive but also exacerbated the radical left's pre-existing problems with the management of difference.

The need to negotiate a route within and between these different political positions led me to ask a second series of questions. I began to think again in more detail, about the ways in which different protest groups communicate with each other as well as the mainstream. I asked myself how individuals, who held very different and sometimes even entirely contradictory protest positions, could communicate (productively) across political difference. In short, I began to think about the ways in which this fracturing of radical politics impacted on the movement of alternative ideas from the margins to the mainstream. I asked myself how protest coalitions could communicate a position of both solidarity *and* difference to a mainstream homogenised by commercial imperatives.

These pages will reflect in detail on some of these questions. This book examines the organisational systems which structure alternative and mainstream public spheres and explores the ways in which protest coalition movements communicate *across* political difference. It seeks to examine the ways in which different activist groupings interact with each other and the various protest repertoires they employ in their attempts to engage with a frequently hostile mainstream. Thus it attempts to develop a more interconnected understanding of 'the public sphere' and focus upon the ways in which political ideas can travel through the complex system of connections which both bind and separate the margins and the mainstream.

Articulating Dissent offers complex critical insights into the communicative strategies of coalition protest movements and rigorously analyses their impact on the movement of ideas from the margins to the mainstream. It is unique in that it foregrounds the connections that exist between the aspirational certainties of Habermas' classical approach to the public sphere with the fluctuating political potential inherent in more rhizomatic media models. In doing so this book combines two very different critical approaches and offers new insights into themes that have, until recently, been consistently neglected by social movement theorists and alternative media scholars.

The first part of the book will challenge the theoretical boundaries that have traditionally contextualised debates surrounding protest and the public sphere and suggest an alternative understanding of the way in which multi-issue protest contributes to wider political debates. This section will use the work of Jürgen Habermas as a springboard into more contemporary understandings of the public sphere. I will focus in particular on radical democratic interpretations of the public sphere such as those proposed by Curran, Mouffe and Dahlberg as well as formulations rooted in an explicitly activist tradition such as those suggested by Castells, Benkler and Hands.

The second part of the book will be grouped around original research into the innovative communication strategies and protest repertoires of particular coalition movements. The emphasis in all these chapters will not be on producing an anthropological account of each particular coalition movement but on drawing out the interconnections between a wide variety of protest movements in order to say something about the nature of protest coalition as a developing political force. The chapters in this section will establish and then develop a clearer understanding of the ways in which coalition movements have adapted new technologies in order to evolve through time and space. Chapters 3 and 4 will be concerned with the intra and inter communicative relations of protest coalitions while Chapters 5 and 6 will engage with the communicative relations between coalition movements and the mainstream.

Introduction

This intercontinental network of resistances, recognising difference and acknowledging similarities, will strive to find itself in other resistances around the world.

Second Declaration of La Realidad for Humanity and against Neoliberalism (2001, p. 125)

A media environment which is perceived to discourage the articulation of dissent is deeply problematic. Jürgen Habermas claims that 'a portion of the public sphere comes into being in every conversation in which private individuals assemble to form a public body' (1974, p. 49). In this way the public sphere mediates between society and state enabling the individual, via the articulation of rationally debated opinion, to exercise a degree of political power. According to liberal models of the public sphere the media therefore represent a forum in which all views can be collectively articulated, discussed and evaluated in order to arrive at a consensus about what best serves the common good.

This model aspires to be a 'utopia of transparency', a space in which 'pure publicity and full disclosure' (Johnson, 2001, p. 97) protects private individuals from the insidious influence of money and power. In principle the media in such a model not only accommodates but actively welcomes the articulation of dissent. Thus the liberal bourgeois public sphere aspires to be an all inclusive space in which power inequalities are carefully bracketed off creating a zone of neutrality in which political communication can flourish. However this understanding of the public sphere as a transparent and inclusive space is deceptive. As Fraser points out: 'Declaring a zone neutral is not enough to make it so and consequently deliberation can all too easily become "a mask for domination"' (Fraser, 1990, p. 64).

There has long been a feeling amongst the radical left that the mainstream media fails to adequately articulate and sometimes even actively misrepresents activist issues and debates (Donson et al. 2004). Coalition protest groups who frequently find their polyvocal position difficult to articulate in an arena accustomed to a single and unified narrative feel this sense of injustice particularly acutely. The frustration felt by activists is exemplified by the words of an anonymous protester who complained that the mainstream coverage of Orange Alternative[1] 'happenings' was 'a veil that missed or minimised every substantive issue' (cited by Bruner, 2005, p. 148). According to this view the media actively impeded, rather than facilitated, the flow of information from the political margins to the mainstream.

An understanding of the mainstream media as a communicative barrier, which stands between the public and the articulation of dissent, has led protest coalitions to experiment with alternative communication forms. Conventional protest forms such as leafleting the public and gathering signatures still play an important role in many protest groups' campaign strategies. However this approach is increasingly combined with attempts to create a groundswell of public opinion by public acts that exert pressure on government and business. Other protest organisations are relatively uninterested in the cultivation of public opinion and prefer to target the business activities of 'culpable' individuals by engaging in more confrontational forms of direct action (Rootes, 2000, p. 35). This book will endeavour to explore the protest repertoires of coalition movements that encompass elements of all three of these positions.

Protest groups in general, and their communicative strategies in particular, have recently been highlighted by a number of interrelated events. The ongoing financial crisis has enabled protest organisations challenging the global neo-liberal hegemony to gain traction. Our awareness of this resistance has been intensified by innovations in communicative technologies, which allow individual protesters and organisations to share information through their online networks. At the same time these communicative technologies are also challenging the power of the nation state to determine the parameters of resistance by facilitating outbreaks of civil unrest in Europe and revolutionary uprising in the Middle East. This creates an atmosphere of economic and political uncertainty that is as frightening as it is exhilarating. Consequently *Articulating Dissent* is a timely book. It engages with a dynamically interconnected set of real world processes and is therefore situated within an unusually interdisciplinary field.

---

1. The Orange Alternative originated in Wroclaw Poland in 1981 and organised 'happenings' designed to outwit and embarrass the authorities. It made no explicit demands and enjoyed huge popular support. More information about the Orange Alternative can be found at www.pomaranczowa-alternatywa.org/orange%20 alternative%20overview.html.

This book builds upon the work of scholars from a number of fields. Firstly it engages with scholarship from a radical democratic tradition drawing upon the work of Curran, Mouffe and Hands, in order to develop a more nuanced and flexible understanding of the public sphere. In doing so it explores the theoretical implications raised by the communicative strategies of protest coalitions attempting to express both political solidarity and ideological difference. It is innovative in that it also draws upon the work of post-structural theorists such as Deleuze and Guatarri in order to construct a model of the public sphere that can accommodate the articulation of a multiplicity of intertwined, and sometimes contradictory, dissenting positions. It is particularly interested in the significance of the us/them distinction (both within and beyond individual protest movements) and the ways in which the need to maintain agonistic relationships impacts upon the communicative strategies of protest coalitions.

This research also develops the work of social movement scholars. Authors such as McKay and Doherty have studied the protest culture of DiY movements and the anti-roads movement respectively. More recently Marianne Maeckelberg has written about the alter-globalisation movement and Jeremy Gilbert has analysed the relationship between the anti-capitalist movement and radical theory. However *Articulating Dissent* differs from these approaches in that, rather than taking a protest-specific viewpoint, it seeks to examine the issues that overarch the articulation of political dissent. As a result, while it inevitably dwells in detail on the communicative implications raised by particular political moments, it tries to address the problems and potentials inherent to the polyvocal articulation of dissent as a genre. Consequently these pages focus on a range of different political moments – the women's peace movement, the anti-Criminal Justice Bill movement, the anti-globalisation movement, the anti-war movement and anti-austerity movements – in order to reflect on the problems faced by coalition movements attempting to engage with the wider public.

Finally this book contributes to work being done by researchers in the field of media and communications, particular those studying alternative forms of media and the communication practices which bring them into being. It extends the work of scholars such as Chris Atton and John Downing who have examined the production of alternative media forms such as newssheets by exploring the move from printed to online spaces. These issues are developed on an international level in Ford and Gil's examination of the Zapatistas[2] in Mexico (2001), and Bailey et al.'s exploration of the Movimento Sem Terra[3] in Brazil (2008). This book therefore seeks to contribute to this body of work by tracing the articulation of dissent through a range of differently organised alternative and mainstream spaces; the online and the offline, the actual and the textual, the local and the global.

Articulating Dissent combines these three fields in order to reflect upon protest movement's construction of alternative spaces. While radical movements have always been shiftingly heterogeneous (Calhoun, 2012) I argue that contemporary protest movements are newly and acutely aware of these frictions. There are many interrelated and sometimes contradictory interpretations of 'alternative', 'radical', 'counter-hegemonic' and 'oppositional' organisational spaces. Atton makes a distinction between alternative and oppositional spaces by arguing that 'alternative culture seeks a place to coexist within the existing hegemony, whereas oppositional culture aims to replace it' (McGuigan cited in Atton, 2002, p. 19). I argue that the need continually to grapple with very differently orientated protest clusters blurs these distinctions and therefore alters the movement of ideas from the margins to the mainstream.

The protest coalitions in this book are all rooted in what one could describe as a socialist-anarchist tradition. As such they refuse to 'offer a fixed body of doctrine based on a particular world view', proffering instead a 'complex and subtle philosophy, embracing many different currents of thought and strategy' (Marshal 1993, p. 3). While there are many differences between coalition movements stemming from this tradition, they are similar in that they share a commitment to not taking control over the decisions of others. As a result of this imperative, the organisations under consideration, like the anarchist organisations of the 1800s, endeavour to capture spaces in which to construct social systems capable of tolerating horizontal communication structures and the autonomous articulation of dissent.

The development of such spaces across time is very uneven for as Woodcock points out 'because anarchism is in essence an anti-dogmatic

---

2.   The Zapatistas are a revolutionary group whose use of the internet and international attention has contributed to their successful articulation of dissent in and beyond Mexico. (www.zapatistas.org).

3.   The Movimento Sem Terra is an agricultural reform organisation which has utilised mass occupations of uncultivated land in order to redefine the political terrain in Brazil. (www.mstbrazil.org).

cluster of related attitudes, which does not depend for its existence on any enduring organisation, it can flourish when circumstances are favourable and then, like a desert plant, lie dormant for seasons, and even years, waiting for the rains that will make it burgeon' (1962, p. 452).

However it's important to note that this book does not attempt to offer a comprehensive or historical account of the protest movements under consideration. Rather than focusing extensively on a limited number of organisations, I have chosen to investigate tactics and strategies that inter-connect a wide range of very different protest movements. In this way I hope to say something accumulative about the nature of coalition movements as a developing political force. *Articulating Dissent* is therefore primarily concerned with the connections that lie between the protest coalition movements and the way in which these connections continue to unsettle the boundaries between alternative and mainstream spaces.

I am primarily concerned with the production of textual and actual protest spaces which stand in an explicitly contestatory relationship to the mainstream. A protest group's choice of 'agitational activities' (Fraser, 1990, p. 68) depends largely upon the way in which activists perceive the protester/public distinction. Despite the emphasis on consensus in mature western democracies, I follow Curran and Mouffe in arguing that a fully functioning democracy requires contestation and confrontation. However, and as Mouffe points out, the tensions inherent in this agonistic friend/opponent relationship are perpetually in danger of tipping over into an antagonistic friend/enemy distinction (2005, pp. 35–63). As an ongoing consequence of this friction, protesters' position on the legitimised side of the 'citizenship line' is constantly (and sometimes retrospectively) being negotiated (Waddington, 1999, p. 61). This book is therefore primarily concerned with protest repertoires which exist on the very brink of the agonistic/antagonistic divide.

As a result it is concerned with two interrelated lines of tension that challenge the us/them distinctions defining the parameters of the public sphere. While protest organisations rooted in a communist tradition have been riven by factional disputes, organisations from a socialist-anarchist tradition seem to be more able to maintain a sense of collective purpose without 'squelching particularistic identities' (Bartholomew and Mayer, 1992, p. 144). Despite the diversity of political identities and associated protest repertoires available to activists, contemporary new social movements seem to have side-stepped the ideological divides which characterised the inter-organisational relationships of the traditional left.

They have done so by foregrounding an organisational methodology which prioritises pragmatic and flexible forms of political allegiance (Kingsnorth, 2003, Graeber, 2004). This position is most succinctly summed up by the anti-globalisation movement which sometimes describes itself as 'a movement of movements' (Klein, 2004, p. 220) or a movement with 'one no and many yeses' (Marcos cited in Klein, *Guardian*, 3 March 2001).

I begin by examining the way in which protest groups manage difference. Consequently this book is concerned with the frictions that exist between the different elements of a protest coalition movement such as those dedicated to non-violent direct action and those who advocate more confrontational forms of intervention. It investigates whether activists who advocate radical confrontations, tend to be assimilated into more generally cautious and reformist political movements or whether differently orientated activists can manage their communicative strategies in such a way as to maintain solidarity *and* difference. In short this strand of the book asks how protest clusters combine into an articulate polyvocal whole.

The second line of tension developed in these pages relates to the classification and representation of public demonstrations. The relationship between protesters and police is of central importance to the formation of wider public opinion. Waddington points out that during public demonstrations the police become 'the de facto arbiters of citizenship' and determine the legitimacy of protesters' 'insecure' position (1999, p. 41). This has particularly important implications for those mainstream organisations, such as the local media, charged with mediating coalition movements' multiple protest strategies. I suggest that the overtly disordered nature of polyvocal protest is frequently used to legitimise their 'exclusion and subordination . . . through the process of criminalising' (1999, p. 41) and that protest coalitions are therefore particularly susceptible to being 'publicly connected with extreme violence and criminality' (Donson et al., 2004, p. 9).

Coalition movements tend to include agitational activities that range from the quietly supportive to the violently committed. The heterogeneous nature of coalition demonstrations is such that 'plurality of meanings and orientations' (Martin, 2004, p. 35) cannot easily be classified. Protest spaces produced by such organisations remain 'infuriatingly impossible to classify' (Hollingsworth, 1986, p. 195), which can provoke a reaction of panic in a mainstream accustomed to hierarchy and order (Graeber, 2004). As a result, I am particularly concerned with the frictions that exist between protester groupings and mainstream organisations such as the police and the media. I therefore ask how protest clusters' communication with each other impacts on the ways in which they are represented in the mainstream.

This book is an attempt to answer some of the questions that perplexed me as a very young activist. It is concerned with the communication flows, which exist in between different political spaces. As such it will foreground and then blur the boundaries between different organisational structures and systems. In doing so it will examine the ways in which activists attempt to negotiate and override these tensions in order to occupy a deliberately in-the-middle position. In this way I hope to explore the parameters of polyvocal dissent and arrive at a more complex and nuanced understanding of the ways in which the political margins, 'my world', are both separated from and connected to the mainstream, 'the wider world'. It examines the ways in which different organisational systems can occasionally overlap, creating temporary spaces of political engagement that contribute to the renegotiation of the boundaries which both separate and connect the political margins to the mainstream. It will conclude by suggesting that the creation of this type of space facilitates the movement of ideas from the margins to the mainstream and in doing so contributes to democratic public life.

1

Unmasking Domination

So, in sum: the media are not the holders of power but they constitute by and large the space where power is decided.

(Castells, 2007, p. 242)

The mainstream media have traditionally been hostile to polyvocal articulations of dissent (Hollingsworth, 1986). I argue that an explanation for this sense of distrust can be found in Jürgen Habermas's influential model of the public sphere. As Habermas points out, the eighteenth-century bourgeois public sphere precipitated, and most successfully embodied, this aspirational ideal. Crucially this understanding of the public sphere depends upon a notion of an educated, coherent and, perhaps most importantly, an explicitly exclusive group of individuals. Unsurprisingly contemporary commentators have been highly critical of Habermas's delineation of the boundaries which constitute the public sphere and have tried to address the exclusionary implications raised by his original conception.

Despite these serious reservations, Habermas's model has generated much academic debate and is considered by theorists such as Fraser to be 'indispensable to critical social theory and to democratic political practice' (1990, p. 57). Garnham points out that the debates concerning the public sphere have focused on two particular problems. Firstly 'on the nature of the public sphere (in particular was it one or many)' and 'secondly on the validity of Habermas's concept of discourse ethics and communicative rationality as a normative test of "undistorted" communications' (2007, p. 207). I discuss and develop these issues in relation to the media strategies of contemporary coalition protest movements. In doing so, I seek to re-examine some of the 'binary fault lines' which underpin the notion of the public sphere (Goode cited by Garnham, 2007, p. 208) and explore the ways in which they stifle articulations of polyvocal dissent.

The need to re-conceptualise the parameters which define the public sphere becomes particularly pressing when one considers the way in which Habermas ascribes so many of the problems traditionally associated with the erosion or disintegration of the public sphere to the movement of structures and systems *across* these boundaries. Thus, for example, the refeudalisation or 'colonisation' thesis outlined in Habermas's later work states that the movement of instrumental rationality and information based communication forms from the systems world to the lifeworld will lead to the eventual corruption of the liberal bourgeois public sphere. However, as radical democratic commentators point out, declaring the public sphere to be a space of uncontaminated neutrality is not enough to make it so (Fraser, 1990). Moreover, such a declaration can belie the complexities and contradictions of the actual existing terrain and in doing so, obscure the power imbalances which structure supposedly universal discursive arenas. In these circumstances it can be argued that, rather than being of protective value, carefully demarcated boundaries may contribute to the preservation of an already corrupted power dynamic and therefore actively prevent potentially positive consequences.

The rise of coalition movements requires intellectuals from the radical left to reflect again upon the way in which different groups of protesters communicate with each other, and with a mainstream accustomed to more unified expressions of dissent. Whereas single-issue campaigns frequently pivot upon a grand ideological refusal, coalition campaigns tend to formulate around a series of smaller, more immediately achievable acts of resistance. Coalition activists therefore tend to foreground methodology in such a way as to enable groupings from very different ideological backgrounds to coalesce into fractured but generally united whole. These shifts have impacted upon the communications strategies of coalition movements in such a way as to require a re-conceptualisation of the theoretical models that traditionally frame our understanding of the public sphere.

This book argues that the need to combine solidarity and difference is of central importance to a notion of coalition politics and draws upon the work of radical democratic scholars such as Curran, Mouffe and Dahlberg to explore the complex network of us/them relationships that characterise both the intra and inter group communications of protest coalitions. Consequently this chapter extends and develops Habermas's focus on communicative procedure and combines it with more rhizomatic understandings of the media environment. This synthesis creates a theoretical space in which coalition movements' use of innovative and challenging protest methods can be better understood. As such *Articulating Dissent* will add to arguments that have appeared in recently published works such as @ *is for Activism* by moving beyond the notion of activism as a digitalised endeavour and engaging with a broader range of technological, cultural and political practices.

I will build on the work of scholars of alternative media such as Chris Atton (1999, 2002) and John Downing (1984, 1995, 2001) who argue that organisational differences underpin the relationship between alternative media and the political 'mainstream'. These organisational differences will be explored within the context of rhizomatic media models first introduced by commentators such as Landow (1994) and Moulthrop (1994) in relation to the internet and then developed by authors such as Bailey, Cammaerts and Carpentier (2008) to include other alternative media forms.

This book aims to go beyond the 'particualrism' (Epstein, 1993, p. 241) of specific movements without losing the sense of fractured harmony that is so characteristic of coalition protest movements at the start of the twenty-first century. In doing so it also builds on the work of social movement scholars. Epstein points out that these theories emphasises the 'diffuse, fragmentary quality' of social movements at the turn of the twentieth century (p. 241). As such these movements are reluctant to impose a shared agenda upon the fragmentary multiplicity of elements through which they are constituted. Instead of prioritising agreed unity, there is a celebration of diversity and difference. This is not an entirely new phenomenon. As Calhoun points out, the commentators of today have a tendency to 'vastly underestimate the diversity of earlier social movements' (2012, p. 3)

This book therefore recognises that activists today, like activists in the past, can pose radical challenges to the status quo while also and at the same time being 'moved by contradictory values and beliefs' (Calhoun, 2012, p. 6). However it also suggests that contemporary coalition movements demonstrate a particular awareness of the need to manage difference in such a way as to make the inevitable conflicts politically productive. I would suggest that such awareness of the risks associated with coalition is typical of self-reflexive risk societies (Beck, 1992) in which the individual is acutely aware of their (in)ability to influence the worlds in which they live and distinguishes coalition protest movements from the social movements which have gone before.

In his review of the social movements, protest and mainstream media McCurdy (2012) argues that work in this field draws upon sociology, social movement studies, political sciences and media and communications, and can be divided into two approaches. The 'representational' which focuses on the way in which protest movements are framed in the mainstream media and the 'relational' which explores the media strategies of protest movements as they contest their media representations. This book brings together these two strands of scholarly interests into a single line of enquiry.

In doing so it develops elements taken from the study of alternative media, social movements in two interwoven directions over the next two chapters. Firstly, it extends rhizomatic models of media organisation to include the emergence of protest coalitions such as the anti-globalisation movement and the anti-war movement. Secondly, I follow Habermas in making a connection between methodological systems and structures (such as rational consensual deliberation) and ideological spaces (such as the liberal bourgeois public sphere). In this way I will argue that a rhizomatic understanding of political communication can be developed into a model of the public sphere, which accommodates rather than laments the nature of contemporary public spheres.

This chapter begins by exploring the ways in which dominant/subordinate binary pairings have shaped the liberal bourgeois model of the public sphere. It questions Habermas's emphasis on the strict separation of the lifeworld and the systems world and examines the ways in which Fraser's notion of overlapping 'dual aspect activities' (1987) complicates many of the theoretical divisions which constitute the liberal bourgeois model. Thus, it foregrounds the possibility of movement between both the different elements of contemporary protest coalitions, and between those coalitions as a whole and the mainstream. In this way it begins to suggest that a re-conceptualisation of the parameters which define the liberal bourgeois public sphere may create a model of the public sphere more able to accommodate the fractious and fractured boundaries which characterise the postmodern political environment.

Sections two and three of this chapter offer a contextualised and detailed account of some of the 'binary fault lines' (Goode, 2005, p. 113) which are particularly significant to the media strategies of multiplatform or coalition protest organisations. Both of these sections are structured around a number of binary opposites such as inclusion/exclusion, consensus/conflict, reason/passion and artifice/authenticity. I have chosen to focus on these boundaries in an attempt to illustrate the usefulness, both academically and politically, of an approach which foregrounds the blurring of binary distinctions. Therefore, while these two sections retain their theoretical focus they also seek to examine the issues raised in far greater detail than a purely abstract debate could allow. In this way I endeavour to demonstrate the usefulness of a public sphere model which could accommodate the articulation of polyvocal dissent.

In 'The Pressure of the Streets' I will examine the way in which Jürgen Habermas's emphasis on a single overarching arena can be particularly problematic for political activists and will explore the way in which a more contemporary reworking of the classical liberal model allows for a more flexible understanding of the public sphere. I argue that the International Encounter for Humanity and Against Neoliberalism which took place in 1996 in Chiapas, Mexico can be understood as a model of the ways in which coalition protest movements establish a 'common space' (Mouffe, 2005, p. 52) away from the 'supervision of dominant groups' (Fraser, 1990, p. 66) in which a diversity of consensuses can be reflected upon.

Section three, 'Public Frictions', then focuses on the relationship between differing forms of discourse within and between spheres. It suggests that traditional public sphere theory's tendency to privilege conversation and the written word not only fails to accommodate the needs of a mass democracy but actively excludes modes of address which could – potentially – reinvigorate political debate. These arguments are contextualised by examining the place of demonstrative events within the public sphere, focusing in particular on the way in which these communicative forms blur the distinction between reality and unreality, substance and surface. This sense of duality contributes to, rather than detracts from, the development of contemporary public spheres. Finally this section combines a theoretical understanding of communicative discourses with a historical approach which examines the ways in which changing technologies have contributed to contemporary understandings of the public sphere. These two strands interweave to create a model in which emotion and non-verbal forms of political communication, such as those employed by contemporary protest coalitions, can be effectively accommodated.

Divide and Rule

Those that seek to dominate and rule our lives rely on keeping us apart. If you think you're alone in your desires, you're less likely to act. Divide and rule. Tolerate single issues but don't let them join up.

Wat Tyler (protester pseudonym), 2003, p. 195

Public sphere theory has 'a long history and deep roots . . . within Western post-enlightenment thought' and is therefore structured around a series of complex and interrelated binary oppositions such as feelings/reason, freedom/power and action/structure (Garnham, 2000, 174). John Durham Peters (1993) argues that these categorisations developed the earlier threefold models of civil society established by philosophers such as Hegel and created a space in which a more flexible understanding of the public sphere could be conceived. This enabled theorists to 'schematically locate the bourgeois public sphere in a fourfold table' and, in doing so, neatly map out some of the (many) borders which circumscribe the classical liberal public sphere (p. 557). Peters illustrates the benefits of such an approach in the following grid which maps out the relationships between Habermas's concept of the lifeworld (characterised by lived everyday human experiences) and the system world (characterised by the media of money and power).

The lifeworld/systems world binary is then further dissected by the introduction of a private/public divide which distinguishes between the particular interests of the individual and those of society as a whole. In this way the 'fourfold scheme' illuminates the lifeworld/systems, public/private nuances which underpin the notion of the bourgeois public sphere with 'more subtlety' and to greater 'effect' than previous models (Peters, 1993, p. 557).

	Life World	Systems World
Public	Public Sphere	State
Private	Family	Economy

Taken from Peters (1993), p. 557.

The carefully demarcated boundaries outlined in the table serve two primary functions. Firstly, they create an empty space within the lifeworld which private individuals occupy in order to organise themselves as 'the bearer of public opinion' (Habermas, 1974 p. 50). Secondly, they preserve and protect this space from the insidious and infectious influences of money and power in the systems world beyond. However there are problems inherent to this formulation of the public sphere. These problems are acknowledged by Peters and further explored by Garnham who argues that, far from being a neutral zone, the concept of a public sphere necessarily foregrounds our 'deep unease' over the 'conceptual difficulties' raised by binary pairings such as feeling/reason, personal/political and freedom/power (2000, p. 174). Thus while the liberal bourgeois model clearly offers more subtle theoretical inflections, its dependence on the strict maintenance of boundary definitions creates a new series of problems.

Garnham describes binary pairings such as the private/public distinction as 'value vectors' (2000, p. 174). His use of the word 'vector' is significant because it highlights the way in which the relationship between the two elements of any pairing – as well as the definition of each individual element – is liminal and in flux. This sense of ambivalence seems to exist on both a historical and a philosophical level. Thus Garnham describes how the term 'private' has changed and developed historically from feudal to modern eras. He also describes the way in which 'classical liberal' theorists and theorists from a 'classic civic republican tradition' have deployed the term 'private' in fundamentally differing ways (2000, pp. 175–6). In both instances it becomes clear that the parameters, which define and delineate the 'private realm' are neither static nor exact but constantly evolving. Consequently the theoretical terrain that underpins the neat and tidy constitutive boundaries of the analytic grid reveals itself to be both uncertain and unstable.

A number of scholars have sought to disrupt the boundaries and borders of classical public sphere theory by focusing on historically subordinated social groupings such as women (Benhabib, 1992) and the proletarian (Negt and Kluge, 1993). Fraser's work on the 'masculine subtext on the citizen role' (1987, p. 45) and her critique of 'actually existing democracy in late capitalist societies' (1990, p. 77) has been particularly influential within this field. Moreover her more recent work on the implicitly Westphalian nature of the public sphere (2007) has highlighted a previously unconsidered series of 'tacitly assumed' boundaries which 'frame' the notion of that sphere. The sustained emphasis on the need to 'expose the limits of the specific form of democracy we enjoy in contemporary capitalist societies' makes Fraser's work of particular relevance to this book (1990, p. 77).

In 'What's Critical about Critical Theory?', Nancy Fraser re-examined the way in which Habermas's classical model cleanly allocates symbolic and material production to isolated quadrants of the fourfold structure, arguing that symbolic and material reproduction – like many other constitutive elements of the public sphere such as 'socially integrated' and 'systems integrated' action contexts, 'normatively assured' and 'communicatively achieved' outcomes – are in fact dual activities. She concludes by maintaining that 'Habermas misses important cross connections among the four elements of his public-private schemata' and maintains that feminine and masculine gender identity run like pink and blue threads through . . . all arenas of life' (1987, p. 45). Despite these reservations Fraser maintains that 'public sphere theory is in principle an important critical-conceptual resource that should be restructured rather than jettisoned, if possible' (2007, p. 9).

Consequently in 'Re-thinking the public sphere: a contribution to the critique of actually existing democracy' Fraser rejects Habermas's notion of a single, reason-based public sphere in favour of a multiplicity of themed spheres standing in a contested relation to each other. This creates a theoretical space for the notion of subaltern spheres which Fraser describes as 'parallel discursive arenas where members of subordinated social groups invent and circulate counter discourses' (1990, p. 67). Fraser goes on to argue that the subaltern spheres have two functions. Firstly 'they function as spaces for withdrawal and regroupment' which enable countercultural groups to 'formulate oppositional interpretations of their identities, interests and needs' (1990, p. 68). She illustrates the functions of subaltern public spheres in stratified societies by discussing the way in which the 'intra public' relations of the American feminist movement in the mid to late twentieth century enabled them to both create and disseminate alternative viewpoints. Secondly, subaltern spheres 'function as bases and training grounds for agitational activities directed towards wider publics' (1990, p. 68). Fraser highlights this argument by describing the ways in which discourses formulated within feminist subaltern spheres went on to influence and alter the debates surrounding issues such as spousal abuse and date rape in the 'official' public sphere. As a result of these interactions between official and subaltern spheres, Fraser argues that in stratified societies it is possible for subaltern discourses eventually to find a place within the official public sphere.

While the notion of a subaltern public clearly has much to offer an understanding of alternative politics and activism, it should be noted that in attempting to create a more flexible and nuanced account of the spaces in which differing cultural and political discourses may flourish, Fraser creates another binary pairing in the form of subaltern and official public spheres. Fraser is careful to stress that the boundaries between subaltern and official publics – unlike the boundaries which structure classical models – are characterised by a 'porousness, outerdirectedness and open endedness' which facilitate rather than block 'communication across lines of cultural difference' (1990, pp. 70, 69). Her account of 'inter public communication' in 'hypothetical multicultural egalitarian societies' even acknowledges that 'people participate in more than one public, and that memberships of different publics may partially overlap' (1990, p. 70). However while she concedes that 'in principle' inter sphere communication is 'conceptually conceivable' she does not extend this discussion to reflect upon the actual movement of people and ideas between different subaltern publics.

Moreover, while Fraser's work on inter sphere communication in stratified societies acknowledges the fact that 'cultural identities are woven of many different strands' (1990, p. 69) and allows for the movement of individuals and ideas between differing subaltern publics, she tends to confine her analysis to the relationship between subaltern and official publics. Consequently she tends to focus on the subordinated side of a binary pairing, without reference to other subaltern spaces of resistance. I would therefore argue that her work on the ideological subordination of women occupies a theoretical terrain which Soja and Hooper would identify as producing 'parallel, analogous, but rarely intersecting channels of radical consciousness each designed and primed to change their own discrete binary world of difference' (1993, p. 186).

In other words, while feminism has had a profound effect upon the official public sphere its relationship with other subaltern identity positions has been less thoroughly developed. For example, the African-American civil rights movement did not extend its challenge to power by re-evaluating the role of women in society. In this way the work of activists and academics has, until recently, confined itself to single channels of resistance. Furthermore, it could be argued that it is precisely these neglected elements of connection and conflict that lie at the root of the coalition protest organisations' success.

More recently Hands has celebrated Fraser's refusal to submit to the notion of a single or official public sphere as well as her emphasis on the need for *actual* equality of access (2011). However he also recognises that Fraser's conceptualisation of the public sphere may be problematic in so far as it confines the individual within the discretely limited parameters of identity specific counter publics. Thus he argues that the 'need to have boundaries drawn somewhere in order to be defined as a sphere' does not reflect the realities of our contemporary networked context (2011, p. 103). While Benkler's influential formulation of the public sphere, *The Wealth of Networks*, appears to address these issues, it lacks the nuanced understanding of power that Fraser brings to bear upon the subject. Indeed, and as Hands points out, 'Benkler doesn't at any point recognise that the legitimacy of actual existing democracy is in question' (2011, p. 104).

In subsequent chapters I will challenge the 'infatuation with clean orderly binary opposition; the intolerance of ambiguity, disordering, multiplicity and fragmentation' (Soja and Hooper, 1993, p. 188). However I do so without losing a nuanced sense of the power dynamics which inevitably structure the relationship between different counter publics. Moreover, and unlike Hands, I will do so without losing the notion of the boundary. This book argues that while the loss of the clearly demarcated boundaries offers a more fluid and resilient understanding of the public sphere, it also means that the political traction required for resistance can become dissipated or lost. It suggests that it is therefore necessary to think about how one can keep the conflictual dynamic that underpins the notion of resistance whilst also accommodating the flux and flow which characterises the contemporary public sphere. This understanding of the boundary as threshold rather than barrier will be returned to in chapter 2.

The Pressure of the Street

Laws which obviously have come about under the "pressure of the street" can scarcely still be understood as arising from the consensus of private individuals engaged in public discussion.

Jürgen Habermas – 'The Public Sphere:
An Encyclopaedia Article' (1974, p. 54)

Habermas famously defines the public sphere as a 'sphere which mediates between society and the state, in which the public organises itself as the bearer of public opinion' (1974, p. 50). A crucial element of this understanding lies in Habermas's belief that 'access to the public sphere is open in principle to all citizens' (Fraser, 1990, p. 63). Moreover, according to Habermas, those who participate in the public sphere 'set aside such characteristics as difference of birth and fortune and speak to one another as if they were social and economic peers' (Fraser, 1990, p. 63). This emphasis on temporary equality is an attempt to guard against coercion and to guarantee both the 'freedom of association and assembly' and the 'freedom to express and publish their opinions' (Habermas, 1974, p. 49). In this way one can understand Habermas's classical interpretation of the public sphere as a universally accessible space in which individual differences are set aside in order to facilitate reasoned debate and achieve a consensus in public opinion.

However, as critics have pointed out, many voices were (and still are) routinely excluded from the public sphere (Fraser, 1990; Curran, 1991; Mouffe, 2005). Whilst very few groups are overtly barred from taking part in public debate, more covert influences often conspire to prevent these voices from being heard. As a result it has been argued that the public sphere today – as in the past – supports, rather than challenges, the distribution of power within society. This gap between the theoretical ideal and practical reality of the public sphere undermines many of the arguments put forward by Habermas and has encouraged other critics to develop their own interpretations of the public sphere.

Many contemporary public sphere theorists from what Curran describes as a 'radical democratic perspective' (1991, p. 27) question the assumptions behind Habermas's work and argue that the existence of a single non-partisan sphere is as undesirable as it is impossible. For example, Fraser maintains that it is more appropriate to 'unbracket inequalities in the sense of explicitly thematising them' creating spaces in which marginalised groups can withdraw in order to define their politics both to themselves and to others (1990, p. 64). Curran maintains that the media are – and by implication should be – a 'battle ground' in which 'contending forces' meet in order to 'redress the imbalance of power in society' (1991, pp. 29–30). Similarly Mouffe advocates the notion of a 'vibrant "agonistic" public sphere of contestation' (2005, p. 30) arguing that while 'consensus is no doubt necessary . . . it must be accompanied by dissent' (p. 31). In this way Habermas's classical notion of a single unified public sphere is replaced by the notion of a multiplicity of themed spheres standing in a contestatory relation to one another.

Subaltern Spheres: Spaces for Withdrawal and Regroupment?

As discussed, Fraser argues that subaltern public spheres combine two essential qualities. While Fraser's article is concerned primarily with the implications raised by feminist subaltern spheres, her thesis can clearly be adapted to accommodate other oppressed and resisting groups and organisations. I argue that the International Encounter for Humanity and Against Neoliberalism called by the Zapatistas in 1996 created a similar space for the anti-globalisation movement. Moreover I suggest that this initial contact led to the creation of a plethora of similarly organised subaltern spheres across the world which have gone on to influence and shape the formation of contemporary anti-war movements.

It is difficult to overestimate the significance of the International Encounter for Humanity and against Neoliberalism in La Realidad, Chiapas. Activists arrived from all over the world expecting to be taught strategies by the Zapatistas and found themselves instead being left to invent new ways of articulating dissent and organising protests. Academic and anti-globalisation activist David Graeber describes this as a '"new language" of civil disobedience' which includes and combines elements of street theatre, festival and non-violent warfare within a decentralised, non-hierarchical consensus based democracy (2004, p. 208). Authors such as Klein (2000) and Kingsnorth (2003) have suggested that these alternative ways of doing things have dispersed across the globe like some sort of benign viral infection. For example, Naomi Klein describes the way in which these ideas have 'spread through activist circles, passed along second and third hand' in an eight-page article for a liberal but mainstream, UK-based newspaper (*Guardian*, 3 March 2001).

I am not in any way suggesting that the emergence of the Zapatistas in Mexico led to the formation of the anti-globalisation movement or any of the coalition movements which followed. There is a long history of protest coalitions, such as the women's peace movement, the anti-roads movement and environmental movements, which preceded the uprisings in Chiapas and in Seattle. I am, however, claiming that the *encuentro* highlights many of the theoretical issues raised by the resurgence in, and development of, protest coalitions more generally. This is a view shared by academics and activists alike (Hands, 2011; Mackelbergh, 2009; Kingsnorth, 2003; Mertes 2004). The *encuentro* created a physical and metaphorical space to which activists could withdraw – far from the attentions and distractions of mainstream life – to 'formulate oppositional interpretations of their identities, interests and needs' (Fraser, 1990, p. 67). This enabled activists from more than 50 different countries, each focused on their own particular national agendas, to regroup and position themselves as 'an intercontinental network of resistance against Neoliberalism, an inter-continental network of resistance for humanity' (Second Declaration of La Realidad, 1996).

One could interpret the anti-globalisation movement as an empirical example of Fraser's faith in an 'overarching' (1990, p. 69) public sphere within an egalitarian multi-cultural context, albeit a counter-cultural one existing in opposition to globalised neoliberalism. According to this view, the anti-globalisation movement acts as a 'comprehensive arena' in which 'participants can deliberate as peers across lines of *difference* about policy that concerns them all' (my italics, Fraser, 1990, pp. 69–70). Chantal Mouffe describes such an arena as being characterised by a sort of 'conflicting consensus providing a common symbolic space among opponents who are considered as "legitimate enemies"' (2005, p. 52). In this way the multiplicity of perspectives brought together by the *encuentro* (and by implication in other protest coalitions) was able to coexist, despite differences and antagonisms, both within and beyond the actual encounter in the rainforest.

Fraser's delineation of an egalitarian, multicultural public sphere rests not upon the bracketing of personal or group differences, but upon the 'multi-cultural literacy' of participants. I would argue that in the anti-globalisation movements' case, 'multi-cultural literacy' is engendered by the creation of new and experimental organisational structures that prioritise methodology over ideology. These structures flow continuously from those that came before (for example from the women's movement and from the socialist-anarchist traditions) however they are also new in that they focus self-consciously on the issues raised by the need to manage the intra group conflicts that inevitably arise out of diversity.

Despite the anti-globalisation movement's description of itself as 'a movement of one no and many yeses' (Kingsnorth, 2003; Mertes, 2004) it is frequently chastised by establishment figures (Abel, 1997; Vidal, *Guardian*, 1 May 2001) for its lack of anything even remotely resembling a coherently unified ideological position. In response, writers from the Notes from Nowhere collective point out the anti-globalisation movement, unlike most previous international left groups, is not interested in creating 'a new ideology to impose from above'. It is instead attempting to create 'a new participatory methodology from below' (Notes from Nowhere, 2003, p. 506). The belief that 'the means are the ends' (Subcomandante Marcos, 2004, p. 11) has created an important shift in radical politics by taking attention away from what is said and focusing on how it is said.

Marcos describes the way in which the Zapatistas 'became conscious of language – not as a means of communicating but of constructing something' (p. 12). As a result, while the rebel fighters in Chiapas refused to lead the anti-globalisation movement in any ideological sense, they did implement various organisational structures designed to create an inclusive and accessible communicative space. These organisational strategies enabled 'groups with diverse values and rhetorics' (Fraser, 1990 p. 69) to participate fully and equally in the *encuentro*. This removed the potentially divisive need for dichotomised consensus, enabled conflict 'to take a form that does not destroy political association' (Mouffe, 2005, p. 20) and, in doing so, created a communicative space in which a diversity of consensuses could flourish.

This emphasis on new ways of talking is curiously similar to the stress Habermas traditionally places on the importance of reasoned discourse within the classical public sphere. Habermas's insistence on 'procedural rationality' (McLaughlin, 1998, p. 603) within an 'ideal speech situation' is pertinent because, while the anti-globalisation movement clearly does not share Habermas's view of reasoned argument as the only 'worthy form of discourse for a democratic culture' (Peters, 1993, p. 562), the movement does prioritise certain forms of discourse over others, in the belief that alternative ways of communicating produce alternative ways of thinking. In this way some activists within the anti-globalisation movement go one step further and claim that 'those new forms of organisation are its ideology' (Graeber, 2004, p. 212).

Subaltern Spheres: Spaces for Agitational Activities

Atton maintains that the creation of an alternative or counter-cultural public sphere is a valid and politically empowering act in itself (2002). To a certain extent this is true but, as Habermas points out, 'however limited a public sphere may be in its empirical manifestation at any given time, its members understand themselves as part of a potentially wider public' (Fraser, 1990, p. 67). In a similar way Dahlberg argues that while counter discourses 'provide an important step in building alternative visions' they should also contribute to 'opening the boundaries of dominant discourse through explicit forms of contestation' (2007, p. 837). As a consequence of the need to 'open [. . .] up possibilities for transformative forms of resistance' (McLaughlin, 1998, p. 615) textual and actual protest spaces are as concerned with external as well as internal communication practices. For example, Subcomandante Marcos argues that while the 'free spaces' reclaimed and occupied by the Zapatistas are important as autonomous zones in themselves, they are more significant in that they 'create counter powers to the state simply by existing' (Klein, *Guardian*, 3 March, 2001).

The relationship between the margins and the mainstream is complex. Jim Walch argues that alternative spaces are an 'integrated utopia . . . part and parcel of the mainstream: its unutilised or under-utilised component' (1999, p. 2). This interpretation allows it to be occupied by individuals who are actively 'choosing marginality' (Hooks cited in Soja and Hooper, 1993, p. 103) instead of, or indeed as well as, those who have been relegated to the fringes of public life. This rather optimistic view is supported by commentators such as Lefebvre who see an enormous political potential in places of difference. For Lefebvre these utopias are a way of linking 'that which is near and far, here and there, actual and utopian, possible and impossible' (1996, p. 27). Thus I argue that the boundaries between the subaltern and official publics can be usefully understood as connecting as well as separating the political margins to the mainstream. This conceptual move enables one to move away from a binary model of the public sphere and towards one which explores the smooth and varied relationships between multiple spheres.

Fraser argues that in stratified societies such as ours, alternative or 'subaltern' counter publics 'stand in a contestatory relationship to dominant publics' (1990, p. 70). Her use of the word 'agitational' is particularly significant because it reveals the inevitable tensions between even the most inextricably connected marginal and mainstream spaces. This friction is particularly problematic for classical public sphere theorists who tend to see 'violence and hostility...as an archaic phenomenon to be eliminated' by 'the advance of individualism and the progress of rationality' (Mouffe, 2005, pp. 3, 5). I would argue that the anti-globalisation movements' capacity to accommodate conflict internally enables them to adopt similarly 'agonistic' but not 'antagonistic' positions in relation to the mainstream or official public sphere.

Unlike classical liberal theories which rely heavily on Habermas's notion of a calm and reasoning public sphere mediating between the government and private individuals, the radical democratic approach sees the media as a battle site (Curran, 1991, p. 29). This view is developed in 'Further Reflections on the Public Sphere' when Habermas appears to recognise the contestatory nature of globalised democracies and acknowledges a model in which a 'battle is fought' (1992, p. 437) by 'competing public spheres' (p. 425). While Habermas does not dwell in detail on this point it lends weight to the notion of a contestatory relationship, enables it to be developed one stage further and become a relationship based on conflict. The introduction of a conflict-based discourse into the public sphere has enormously liberating implications for coalition movements in so far as they offer activists a communicative strategy which can accommodate the expression of political difference.

James Curran maintains that '[a] basic requirement of a democratic media system should be . . . that it represents all significant interests in society. It should facilitate their participation in the public domain, enable them to contribute to the public debate and have an input into the framing of public policy' (1991, p. 30). Unfortunately, many marginal political groups feel excluded from public debate, maintaining that the mainstream media fail to articulate their views fully or fairly and prevents them from influencing or framing public opinion (Stein, 2001). While mediated cultural debates frequently dismiss accusations of bias as paranoia ('Inside Stories', BBC, 29 September 2008) academic studies of demonstrations and protests, such as those conducted by James Halloran et al. (1970) and Todd Gitlin (2003), seem to confirm this viewpoint.

This excluding movement is often exacerbated by the tabloid press who caricature anti-globalisation activists as either mad or bad ('Anti-war girl "silly" – judge', *Sun* 3 May, 2003; 'Anti-war yob jailed for attack' *Daily Mirror,* 24 October, 2006). As D. H. Downing points out, movements from what he describes as a socialist-anarchist tradition are invariably 'associated in the public mind with a love of disorder and creating chaos, even with sanctifying terroristic actions against public figures' (2002, p. 245). According to commentators such as Hollingsworth (1986) the radical left are therefore frequently ridiculed, vilified and finally excluded from the public spheres of parliamentary democracy, the legal system and, of course, the media. In this way the impassioned voices of anti-globalisation groups tend to be characterised in the mainstream media as both unreasoned and unreasonable (Donson et al., 2004).

Habermas's work is invariably highly critical of social movements which 'associate themselves with the expressive, the romantic and the local rather than with the communicative and the value-rational' (Hetherington,

1998, p. 33), arguing that their emancipatory potential is dulled by their rejection of a more neutral discourse ethic. However, as Curran points out, as a consequence the radical left's contributions to the public sphere have frequently been dismissed out of hand as little more than an 'ideological pollutant' (1991, p. 40). The way in which non-conforming voices are excluded from public conversation is well illustrated by Hollingsworth when he says, 'it is as if these radical views have intruded into a private dinner party where the hosts and guests have already arranged the terms of their discussion and anything that might threaten the presupposed agenda is . . . deemed "loony" or "extreme" or "power mad"' (1986, p. 288).

Critics from a radical democratic perspective would argue that the tendency to exclude protesting voices from the official public sphere is particularly rooted in liberal rationalism's propensity to 'ignore the affective dimension' and dismiss 'supposedly "archaic" passions' (Mouffe, 2005, p. 6). However, as Fraser points out, Habermas's misplaced faith in the efficiency of 'bracketing' (1990, p. 64), like his confidence in universal accessibility, rests upon the notion of the mainstream public sphere as a perfectly neutral, rather than reason based discursive arena. Fraser challenges this understanding of the public sphere and argues that the classical liberal traditional reliance on a 'space of zero degree culture' (Fraser, 1990, p. 64) disguises, rather than eliminates the inequalities inherent to the system and actually legitimises the under-representation of some political voices.

Many cultural theorists maintain that 'emotion as well as cognition' (McGuigan, 1998, p. 92) should become defining features of the public sphere. This is a view developed by Hetherington who questions the validity of Habermas's emphasis on rationality by pointing out that the symbolism of revolt calls upon feeling as well as reason. He goes on to argue that 'the privileging of the faculties of reason by the Enlightenment and the alignment of the expressive with the world of unreason' (1998, p. 51) has led to the marginalisation of many radical left groups. This is a view developed by Mouffe who argues that democracy ought to 'mobilize passions towards democratic designs' (2005, p. 6) thereby harnessing its energising potential.

If reason is no longer the sole legitimate means of communication then the angry, distressed and despairing voices articulated by the anti-global-isation movement can no longer be dismissed as 'spurious' (Blair cited by Vidal, *Guardian*, 1 May 2001) or hysterical, but must be acknowledged. Moreover, the acceptance of a conflict-based relationship between multiple public spheres such as the mainstream and anti-globalisation movements is theoretically liberating in that it opens up the political realm to a variety of previously excluded voices, opinions and protest repertoires. The acknowledgement of conflict as an inevitable and beneficial element of wider public communications transforms alternative organisations' relationships with the mainstream and creates the possibility of alternative sites and modes of connection between the margins and the mainstream.

Public Frictions

Public fictions, once believed, can become public facts.

McGee, 1975

While much has been written concerning the way in which certain individuals are excluded from the public sphere, less critical energy has been spent analysing the reasoning behind Habermas's exclusion of groups per se. Habermas argues that the Chartist movement in England and the February revolution in France led to an unsustainable expansion of the public sphere which in turn led to the 'violent' introduction of group interests. As far as Habermas is concerned, the introduction of any 'public body of organised private individuals' intent upon appealing to 'the court of public opinion' erodes and eventually refeudalises the public sphere (1974, pp. 54–5). In this chapter I argue that this grouping of private individuals is in fact an inevitable and entirely necessary consequence of an ever-expanding public sphere. Moreover, I suggest that the articulations of special interest groups and their use of 'public relations work' furthers, rather than destroys, the democratic potential of a fully functioning contemporary public sphere.

As Mouffe (drawing on Schmitt) points out, 'every consensus is based on an act of exclusion' (2005, p. 11). Thus while Habermas's original notion of the ideal speech situation (which also draws on Schmitt) guaranteed theoretical access to all citizens, in actuality it depended upon an exclusion of the problematic masses. The gradual expansion of the franchise during the late nineteenth and early twentieth centuries created a hugely enlarged public sphere and forced politicians and critical theorists alike to engage with the notion of the massed population. In his article on Habermas and the public sphere Peters points out that basic economies of scale prevent conversation from fulfilling its prescribed role within the contemporary public sphere and argues that other forms of representation must therefore be developed (1993, p. 565). This emphasis on shifting modes of mediation has important implications.

Peters argues that, in order for an inclusive democratic community to function in the contemporary political arena, some form of 'aesthetic representation' (1993, p. 565) must be allowed. Similarly McNair points out that, 'greater emphasis on "image and style" is . . . the price of mass democracy in a late capitalist, post-cold-war environment, whether one likes it or not' (1998, p. 54). Simons moreover argues that the 'intellectual distrust of popular culture' has led cultural elites who are heavily invested in print culture 'to overlook the possibility that popular culture is actually a hospitable terrain for democratic politics (Simons, 2003, p. 172). I would go further and argue that not only should 'aesthetic representation' be permitted, it should also be respected as an entirely valid, even desirable means of political communication.

Habermas's championing of the individual's role within an exclusive public sphere is part of a more general critical distrust of 'the masses'. These suspicions are evident in the work of conservative and radical intellectual traditions alike (Williams, 2003). Thus while commentators as politically diverse as Theodor Adorno (1979) and F.R. Leavis (1930) allow for the possibility of an authentic mass culture from below, they invariably focus on the ways in which mass culture has been administered from above. Consequently they tend to view any mass intervention in public life as somehow inevitably hollow and manufactured. This view is perhaps most clearly articulated by Lippmann who describes the American population's participation in the democratic process as no more than the 'trampling and roar of a bewildered herd' (Lippmann cited in Chomsky, 1997, p. 12). According to this notion, a placidly bovine population may be gently prodded by their political masters into supporting any number of previously selected causes. The massed public, as opposed to individual members of the public, are frequently viewed as peculiarly unreflecting spectators passively content with their paltry 'walk on part' in the democratic process (McNair, 1998, p. 62).

Mouffe argues that this view of the crowd, like the distrust of emotion discussed above, is rooted in the 'rationalist approach's incapacity to come to terms with political mass movements which they tend to see as an expression of irrational forces or a 'return to the archaic' (2005, p. 24). Crucially, the manipulation of the masses by the media in general, and the public relations industry in particular, takes place 'without public awareness of its activities' (McChesney, 1997, p. 15, my italics). However activists' use of communicative strategies which deliberately foreground the use of artifice enables them to foreground (rather than disguise) the persuasive nature of their appeal and thus side-step the 'sense of deceitfulness' which Corner identifies as being at the core of both propaganda and spin (Corner, 2007, p. 673). In this way their symbolically demonstrative (and therefore explicitly unreal) forms of protest allow protest groups to distinguish themselves from the 'self-interested strategizing . . . and vapid slogans that are customarily imputed to candidates for governmental office' (Feher, 2007, p. 13). Coalition activists utilise a wide range of protest repertories, many of which are not rooted in dispassionate discursive modes. In the following section I focus on the ability of demonstrative events in particular to contribute to formation of the public opinion.

Demonstrative Events in the Public Sphere

The role of demonstrative events within the public sphere is an ambiguous one. Habermas's emphasis on 'conversation, reading and plain speech as worthy forms of discourse', combined with his open hostility towards the 'theatre, courtly forms, ceremony, the visual and to rhetoric more generally' (Peters, 1993, p. 562), clearly make creating a space for 'aesthetic representation' within the public sphere difficult. Indeed Habermas's refeudalisation thesis argues that special interest groups who go through 'the process of making public' their arguments contribute to the structural disintegration of the public sphere (1974. p. 55). Peters points out that Habermas's distrust of spectacular politics is rooted in his 'lifelong struggle against fascism' (1993, p. 565). However, while he acknowledges the historical pertinence of this position, Peters goes on to use the more-or-less neutral term 'aesthetic representation' to describe the ways in which such a process could be realised (1993, p. 565).

Interestingly, many contemporary pressure groups such as environmental and anti-globalisation organisations are also rooted in a subcultural ethos which distrusts spin and spectacle. This position is articulated by activist (and journalist) George Monbiot in his online 'Activists' Guide to Exploiting the Media' when he describes the 'suspicion' felt by activists forced to engage with the commercial media. Thus activists often go to great lengths to emphasise the way in which direct actions go beyond mere surface and constitute 'an act of non-compliance, an act of authenticity to one's own beliefs' (Corrine and Bee cited in McKay, 1998, p. 5). Consequently even sympathetic academic commentators such as George McKay express concern over the way in which direct action movements are invariably dominated by a 'culture of immediacy' (1998, p. 12) which prioritises spectacle and confrontation at the expense of more traditional qualities such as 'reflection, history [and] theory' (1998, p. 13).

It therefore could be argued that both liberal public sphere theorists and radical left activists' share an emphasis on the ways in which communication *form* contributes to the political effectiveness of its *content*. Neil Postman argues that 'every technology has a prejudice. Like language itself, it predisposes us to favour and value certain perspectives and accomplishments' (1998). According to Postman, linguistic communication forms require sustained attention and create propositions which 'can be assessed rationally in terms of truth or falsity' (Simons, 2003, p. 177), while visual communication forms rely on rapid pictorial skills which 'appeal to the emotions to support a sense of reality' (Simons, 2003, p. 177). This conceptualisation of medium theory clearly privileges verbal and textual communicative forms and therefore has much in common with Habermas's notion of the liberal bourgeois public sphere.

In *Orality and Literacy* Walter Ong, following McLuhan, argues that 'technologies are not mere exterior aids but also interior transformations of consciousness' (1982, p. 82). However unlike Postman, Ong, who is careful to distinguish between verbal and textual communicative forms, highlights some of writing's more problematic qualities. Thus Ong maintains that, 'Writing fosters abstractions that disengage knowledge from the arena where human beings struggle with one another. It separates the knower from the known. By keeping knowledge embedded in the human lifeworld, orality situates knowledge within the context of struggle' (1982, p. 43).

Ong goes on to suggest that the 'mind set' of print culture, as opposed to spoken or conversational culture, is characterised by a sense of distance, 'closure' and 'completion' (Ong, 1982, pp. 132–3). I would argue that it is these qualities, which are characteristic of modernist conceptualisations of the public sphere, that have contributed to the liberal bourgeois public sphere's inability to accommodate polyvocal articulations of dissent.

Mainstream political commentators have been quick to point out that the printed word 'has lost its monopoly' in the public sphere, arguing that reasoned argument has been 'supplemented by the politics of carnival and theatrical protest' (Barker, R., *Guardian* 25 September 2001). However, academic commentators such as Van Zoonen (2004) argue that the almost elegiac nostalgia of seminal authors such as Habermas, Postman and Boorstin inevitably hinders attempts to engage with the public sphere as an actual, rather than as an already lost, ideal. This view is developed further by Jon Simons who argues that the academic tendency to overlook the 'risky arena[s]' where visual and political cultures coincide is rooted in a 'lament' for the 'loss of effective cultural capital' (2003, p. 187) traditionally invested in the written word rather than the visual image.

Boorstin, like Habermas and Postman, takes the view that the mass media has created a 'pseudo public sphere' (Simons, 2003, p. 176) in which the individual has become a passive and uncritical being. In his book *The Image: A Guide to Pseudo-Events in America*, Boorstin examines the relationship between spontaneous and fabricated events arguing that the 'graphic revolution' (1992, p. 13) has left citizens vulnerable to political manipulation. He maintains that manufactured images (as opposed to raw ideals) are 'more interesting and attractive than spontaneous events' (p. 37) and therefore seduce us away from the more mundane 'truth' of reality. Consequently he comes to the conclusion that the artifice of sought-after publicity can achieve little of substance in the real world.

Boorstin employs the negative term 'pseudo-event' to describe the fabricated performances manufactured by the public relations industry in order to gain maximum publicity and win public approbation within a public sphere corrupted by the effects of market forces. However a more sympathetic understanding of the same political practices is articulated by commentators who support and encourage marginalised groups' attempts to capture mainstream attention. These activists and academics take a bottom-up perspective and interpret the expansion of political discourses as a means of empowering traditionally resource-poor grassroots movements. According to this view, demonstrative events can be both fabricated and authentic. This position is exemplified by Monbiot who ends his online guide with the words 'the revolution will be televised but that doesn't mean it won't also be live'.

Moreover Boorstin's emphasis on 'pseudo-events' which have an 'interesting ambiguous relation to underlying reality' (1992, p. 21), forces him to acknowledge that a pseudo-event can become a type of self-fulfilling prophecy. Ironically this is a line of thinking also developed by Baudrillard when he asks the question, 'since the simulator produces "true" symptoms, is he ill or not?' (1983, p. 7). Unlike Baudrillard, Boorstin makes very clear distinctions between the binary of reality and unreality, although even he accepts that 'the power to make a reportable event is [also] the power to make experience' (1992, p. 10).

Academics such as Brian Doherty who examined environmental protesters' use of confrontational but non-violent direct action in the 1990s, argue that such protest repertoires are essentially 'dual' in their purpose (2000, p. 70). On the one hand they function by 'making power visible by prolonging its exposure' and on the other they function by 'attempting to change government policy (p. 70). He argues that tactics which expose activists to physical danger create a sense of 'manufactured vulnerability' and place 'the responsibility for the protester's safety in the hands of the authorities' (p. 70). According to this view, fabricated forms of political communications are not automatically inauthentic and content free. Instead, they are a communicatively legitimate means of demonstrating 'the contrast between the force used by authorities and protesters' moral superiority' (p. 70).

The way in which substance and image, political content and aesthetic representation can exist in combination rather than conflict during demonstrative events can be exemplified by the way in which activists protested against the Newbury Bypass.[1] A coalition of environmental activists used two 30ft tripods with spectacular efficiency to block the Highways Agency's access to the land (Doherty, 2000, p. 70). This manoeuvre achieved both a practical and a symbolic end. It stopped clearance work for the day and prompted the papers to run valedictory headlines the following day ('The Newbury Roundhats Outflanked', Telegraph, 10 January 1996 and 'Tripod Tactics Halts Work on Bypass', Guardian, 10 January 1996). This blurring of boundaries between the 'real' and 'unreal' means that it is often difficult, if not impossible, to say exactly where direct action ends and aesthetic representations begin.

In this book I use the term 'demonstrative event' to describe acts of protest which are *demonstrative* in that they are designed to reveal inequalities of power within the public sphere and *events* in that they are knowingly produced by activists and consumed by audiences. As such, demonstrative events are frequently practical interventions designed to stop or at least delay 'undesirable' state activities (such as passing repressive laws, surrendering to global economies or destroying local habitats and communities). However, demonstrative events are more than action-based responses to the policies of the day in that they also

---

1. The Newbury Bypass became a focal point in the anti-roads protests of the mid to late 1990s. While the coalition of protesters failed to prevent the construction of the A34 they did force the government to re-evaluate its existing road policy.

involve the production of activities (such as mobilising protesters, land occupations and street parties) which follow Bahktin in attempting to embody alternative organisations' resistance (1941). Thus they are, as activists Corrine and Bee put it, 'propaganda of the deed', authentic acts of resistance which *also* aim to capture the media's attention and win public support (cited in McKay, 1998, p. 5).

Organisations such as Amnesty International have a long and honourable tradition of coordinating demonstrative events which highlight the existence of what they perceive to be morally reprehensible acts. They do so in the belief that public awareness of these wrongdoings will somehow force perpetrators to modify their own behaviour. This strategy's ideological roots lie in the work of philosophers such as Jeremy Bentham and John Stuart Mill and their belief in the ethically purifying qualities of publicity.[2] Groups such as Greenpeace have developed this witnessing strategy one step further by videoing themselves attempting to stop (or at least impede) what they see as ethically dubious actions and events, such as the killing of minke whales in the North Atlantic Ocean. This forces 'everybody [to] bear witness – through news dispatches, voice reports, press releases, columns and of course photographs' (McKay, 1998, p. 10). Such acts of 'bearing witness' (Doherty et al., 2000, p. 2) are of particular relevance here because they are rooted in a tradition which endows the act of seeing (rather than listening or reading) with a peculiar moral force.

I would argue that this notion of an ethical publicness is inextricably bound to our understanding of demonstrative events in an era of mass communications. Peters maintains that 'witnessing presupposes a discrepancy between the ignorance of one person and the knowledge of another' (Peters, 2001, p. 710). This is a view that has informed much alternative news production and hinges on the notion that knowledge implies a certain degree of responsibility which will in turn lead to action. Thus Atton cites Sam Beale, editor of *Squall*, as saying that his motivation lies in ensuring that MPs cannot 'say they don't know' about a particular issue or problem (2002, p. 92).

---

2. Of course, Foucault's work on surveillance and the disciplining of publics complicates this position and the question of whether the public sphere acts as 'an instrument of domination or a utopian ideal' is one which will be returned to in Chapter 5.

According to Chatterton, individuals who have been 'confronted, challenged and even shamed' (McKay, 1998, p. 29) by demonstrative actions enter an 'uncommon ground' between actors and spectators and create connections which can unsettle the essentialisms between 'activist and public, the committed and the caring' (2006, p. 272). Thus activists' use of demonstrative events can open up 'a moment of hope' which 'undermines dominant understandings of what is possible and opens up new conceptual spaces for imagining and practising possible futures' (Fournier, 2002 p. 184). The ways in which such acts disrupt the boundaries which characterise liberal bourgeois models of the public sphere will be returned to in Chapter 5.

It ought to be noted that the use of demonstrative events is not in itself a new phenomenon. Even in the late eighteenth century when, according to Habermas, the public sphere was functioning at its historical best, special interest groups were employing visual metaphors in order to illustrate and publicise their cause. Thus the dumping of British tea in Boston Harbour was a symbolic act which scandalised drawing rooms across England: 'captured the imagination of the rebels' and precipitated America's battle for independence (Downing, 1995, p. 240). Indeed one could argue that the workers of Boston Harbour foreshadowed contemporary globalised forms of resistance in that they posited a 'local solution to globally produced problems' (Bauman, 1998, p. 6).

In her article on the transnational public sphere, Fraser points out that 'the ground rules governing trade, production and finance are set trans-nationally by agencies more accountable to global capital than any public' (2007, p. 17). Consequently there has been a disconnection between efficacious communicative power of a public and the sovereign state's ability to express the will of its citizenry. This has important implications for activism. Not only is it no longer clear *who* activists should address with their concerns, it is no longer clear *where* those concerns should be articulated. Many grassroots organisations have responded to these circumstances by directing their activities towards business as well as governments. For example activists at Newbury lobbied businesses involved in the construction of the bypass such as Costain and Tarmac as well as the local council and the Houses of Parliament.

This is particularly pertinent in an environment in which the authorities are reasserting geographical control of previously contested processes and places. Anti-road activists at Newbury were able to occupy the woodlands earmarked for destruction. However, activists engaged in a contemporary globalised world are denied such place-bound protest positions and this has important implications for protest strategies which have traditionally employed direct action tactics. In the aftermath of 11 September 2001, anti-globalisation protesters could not establish permanent protest sites around the centres of global capital. Not only do they rarely take place, but when summits are called they tend to be in *deliberately* geographically inaccessible places. Similarly anti-war activists cannot physically demonstrate their opposition to Guantanamo Bay because the military base exists in a place beyond the boundaries of international transport networks.

The gradual erasure of protest sites in a globalised world requires protest coalitions to strengthen and foreground the symbolic aspect of demonstrative events. As a result of these developments, protest coalitions such as the environmental, anti-globalisation and anti-war movements occupy protest spaces which deliberately blur the boundaries between action and representation. In this book I argue that demonstrative events could provide an opportunity (albeit limited) for ordinary people to take active control of their globalised circumstances and produce their own outcomes. The space for this understanding is created by Habermas's rather grudging distinction between democratically unacceptable and almost respectable communicative processes. Unacceptable processes are those defined as being 'promoted by organisations intervening in a public sphere under the sway of the mass media to mobilise purchasing power, loyalty or conformist behaviour' (1992, p. 437). These communicative processes are contrasted with '[S]elf-regulated, horizontally interlinked, inclusive, and more or less discourse-resembling communicative processes' (p. 437) which are, somewhat reluctantly, tolerated.

This theoretical chink allows for what has been described as the 'sluice-gate' model of the public sphere to exist (Herbert, 2005, p. 107). The sluice-gate enables the movement of issues from the lifeworld to the systems world through the enactment of high profile action such as national boycotts or infringements of particular laws. This model is clearly far more tolerant of grassroots organisations that use demonstrative events in order to introduce marginal issues into the public realm.

Demonstrative Events as Symbolic/Material Interventions
This tension between reality and unreality opens up demonstrative events to a wider complex set of interpretations. As a journalist covering the

Palestinian intifada points out, all conflicts are characterised by a crucial symbolic dimension. There is:

> a struggle over symbols expressed in flags, in slogans, in calls and even in curses. Even the rocks are in a sense symbols, it is also a weapon that could kill someone, but its primary use is as a symbol of protest. They must send these symbols to the outside world and not just their enemy. And they are very aware of the need for the media to send these messages to the world. (Cited in Wolfsfeld, 1997, p. 205)

According to this view, direct actions combine 'social criticism' with 'cultural creativity in what is both a utopian gesture and a practical display of resistance' (McKay, 1998, p. 27). However demonstrative actions, unlike direct actions, necessarily go beyond physically responding to the governmental policies of the day. They also involve the production of 'symbolic challenges' (Melucci, 1989, p. 75) at a cultural level which attempt to embody alternative organisations' resistance to the status quo.

The pertinence of this discussion can best be illustrated by pausing very briefly to highlight a spate of differently motivated but similarly designed demonstrative events. In September 2008 three men charged with plotting to bomb transatlantic airliners were found not guilty at Woolwich Crown Court. Despite having manufactured homemade bombs and martyr videos, the jury accepted that the men involved had wanted to create 'a political spectacle' and aimed to 'frighten rather than kill the public' ('Three Guilty of Bomb Conspiracy', BBC News, 8 September 2008). Similarly, loyalist paramilitary leader Michael Stone claimed that his 2003 attack on Sinn Fein leadership was 'an act of performance art' and that each item he carried (including a replica gun and explosives) had 'symbolic significance' ('Stormont Bomb was Art says Stone', BBC News, 22 September 2008). While Stone's defence was eventually thrown out of court, I suggest that in both these instances the boundary between the real and the unreal, symbolic and actual, violence and art is, to say the very least, problematic.

I argue that this potentially troubling rather postmodern blur and ambiguity could be best exploited by turning to the work of Michel Foucault. Foucault rejects many of the modernist concepts that underpin the work of Habermas. He does not see power as dialectical or negative in essence, arguing that it can actually be a positive and enabling force (Kripps, 1990). He also dismisses the classical model of consciousness and reality as vulnerable entities that can be seized and abused by those with power. Instead he claims that subjectivity and reality are actively produced – rather than represented – by discourse, and exist within the ever changing 'web of fragments' (Plant 1992, p. 116). This interpretation of power allows for the possibility of promotional forms of political resistance, albeit within the confines of the existing discursive regimes.

Foucault might argue that if signs and images are used as a means to establish a particular view of reality, and their production/representation in the media causes them to become the dominant version of 'reality', then demonstrative events have succeeded in conflating their dual purpose. The theoretical possibilities opened up by Foucault's arguments are made concrete in Wolfsfeld's observation that 'challengers who obtain significant amounts of media coverage usually enjoy a significant rise in political status. Those who are recognised by the news media as serious players become serious players' (1997, p. 67). In this way the nebulous and contradictory relationship between binary opposites such as 'reality' and 'unreality', 'substance' and 'image' enables protesters to actively promote their cause without the manufactured nature of public relations as a discourse undermining the validity of their actions.

Journalist/activists such as George Monbiot claim that by feeding journalists certain types of events, pressure groups like those at Newbury can exert a certain degree of control over the type of material that frames the representation of a political debate. This view is supported by academics such as Wolfsfeld, who reminds us that, 'one of the first lessons in journalism is to construct news stories as a pyramid by leading off with the most important part before spreading out to give background and details' (1997, p. 51). There is little doubt that the most important part of most mainstream news stories is the event that is 'pre-cooked' (Boorstin, 1992, p. 19) into news. However, while the pseudo-event may well be the point of an article, it can never be the whole story. Therefore it could be argued that the issues which inspired the event's creation will inevitably make an appearance, even if they are relegated to the broad base of the story's background detail.

Supporters of traditional democracy and the classical public sphere such as Boorstin and Habermas would argue that demonstrative events distract from, or disguise, the real issues. There is an element of truth in this assertion. Demonstrative events probably do create an image that is more entertaining and less meaningful than the complex reality of life as a political activist. However, this glamorisation of reality does not necessarily undermine its value as a tool for democracy. Demonstrative events that also entertain and give pleasure are not automatically emptied of their political content. Furthermore, the consumer satisfaction engendered by demonstrative events increases circulation figures, which in turn makes them more attractive to editors. This ensures that any promotional material finally published gains as wide an audience as possible. Therefore one could argue that pressure groups use demonstrative events as a Trojan horse in order to access an audience made susceptible by pleasure.

This is a view that John Purkis hints at in his analysis of the cultural implications of direct action. Purkis argues that by eschewing the public realm and '"colonising" private spaces' such as shopping malls, banks and superstores, activists are able to jolt an unsuspecting public out of their political lethargy and prod them into re-evaluating the discourses that surround them (1996). McKay makes a similar point when he describes the 'subversive, funny, daring' ways in which guerrilla gardeners smuggle 'small images of small wilderness . . . into the patrolled urban zone' (1998, p. 33). Here I too want to explore how demonstrative events disguised as entertainment might be able to slip into private spaces 'in a manner which fuses the real with the symbolic, and transcends normal notions' of how the world works (Purkis, 1996, p. 205). In short, demonstrative events allow people 'to think differently, instead of legitimising what is already known' (Foucault, 1985, p. 9)

While organisations such as Amnesty International and Greenpeace are clearly attempting to mobilise mass support for their particular ideals, they have been accused of elitism. Doherty points out that the tactics employed by these groups require the acquisition of very specific technical skills and a high degree of personal commitment. This creates a situation in which a 'clique' (McKay, 1998, p. 26) of professional activists can quickly dominate an organisation and exclude alternative means of communication. However this view is directly contradicted by activists such as John Purkis who argue that non-violent direct action actually 'requires very little training' and attempts to deconstruct the idea of the environmental protester as part of a protest elite (1996, p. 206).

I would argue that the professionalism/amateurism of protesters becomes a moot point if one accepts Kant's view that progress is characterised not by the expertise (or even the ethics) of particular players but by the level of enthusiasm engendered in the population at large. Donald and Donald argue that Kant's position foregrounds 'the attitude of the onlookers' (2000, p. 116) and go on to suggest that this understanding of political discourses 'prefigure[s] media critique' in that it 'turns away from the event and focuses on its representation and its spectators' (Donald and Donald, 2000, p. 116). Thus they maintain that, via the 'work of representation', 'spontaneous events' are translated into 'spectacle or drama' for 'an audience of distant spectators' (2000, p. 116).

In 'The Contest of Faculties', Kant argues that while the French revolution was not necessarily evidence of human progress, the way in which people perceived and judged it as a revolutionary event was 'a form of improvement in itself' (Kant, 1991, p. 182). He describes the attitude of those observing the French revolution as 'sympathy' bordering on 'enthusiasm' and goes on to pair 'enthusiasm' with 'passion' (1991, p. 183). However this attitude towards enthusiasm should not be equated with an unqualified acceptance of emotion. Indeed Kant is quick to reiterate his commitment to reason as the source of enlightenment by stating that 'all passion as such is blameworthy' (1991, p. 183).

However Donald and Donald argue that Kant's conceptualisation of publicness 'requires and even demands' a new understanding of the ways in which one can participate in the public sphere. Moreover they suggest that these new forms should be based on explicitly 'aesthetic judgement' (2000, p. 116). This approach creates a space within the public sphere in which spectators of demonstrative events are neither passive nor marginal but dynamic and vital elements of the democratic process. I argue that this interpretation of the public sphere is of particular relevance to contemporary protest coalitions because it creates a space in which both the construction of spectacular events and the role of the spectator can be understood as potentially politically worthwhile. I would go on to suggest that activists' sophisticated and contextualised use of demonstrative events deliberately unsettles preconceived understandings of political situations and thereby contributes to the invigoration rather than erosion of the twenty-first-century public sphere.

Simons claims that contemporary political discourses require a new series of skills which would enable activists and publics to communicate in ways which disrupt without necessarily destroying Habermas's aspirational ideal (2003). Clearly this understanding of the visual within the public sphere requires a more generous interpretation of the role that spectators have to play in politics. Thus, as Donald and Donald argue, it 'implies a different way of living in the social and cultural present: not an ethic of self-formation through public participation, but distraction, diffusion and anonymity' (2000, p. 118). As Simons goes on to say, Walter Benjamin offers just such an interpretation when he argues that the masses are not 'wretched, worn out creatures' (1982, 240.1) but entirely capable of critical – if somewhat distracted – examination.

2

The Paradox of the Frontier

This is the paradox of the frontier: created by contacts, the points of difference between two bodies are also their common points. Conjunction and disjunction are inseparable in them. Of the two bodies in contact, which one possesses the frontier that distinguishes them? Neither. Does this amount to saying: no one?

de Certeau, 2004, p. 127

Unlike the writings of their compatriots, the work of Deleuze and Guattari has not impacted heavily on the field of political communications. Thus, for example, Mark Poster's *The Mode of Information: Poststructuralism and Social Context* (1990) dedicates a chapter each to Baudrillard, Foucault, Derrida and Lyotard but only comments in passing on the work of Deleuze and Guattari. However their book *A Thousand Plateaus* has influenced the development of research into the use of the internet and is beginning to appear more consistently in accounts of the alternative media. Thus in the second half of the 1990s there was a flurry of publications (Landow, 1994; Aronowitz, 1996; Shields, 1996) which fruitfully explored the ways in which cyberspace could be conceived in terms of both the rhizome and the nomad. During this period some attempts were also made to expand rhizomatic communication models in order to include other resisting uses of the media such as the radio (Sakolsky, 1998).

Another separate but not entirely unrelated field in which metaphors of the rhizome have emerged is that of political theory. In the unexpectedly successful *Empire* (2000) Michael Hardt and Antonio Negri reflect upon the move away from modern concepts such as sovereignty, nation and peoples and towards what they described as a new postmodern global order of 'continuous movement and absolute flows' (Hardt and Negri, 2000, p. 28). This book was followed in 2004 by *Multitude* which focuses on the 'living alternative that grows within Empire' (Hardt and Negri, 2004, p. xiii) and the ways in which the multitude could 'construct [. . .] a counter-Empire, an alternative political organisation of global flows and exchanges' (Hardt and Negri, 2000, p. xv). Both books rely heavily on the works of Deleuze and Guattari in general and on *A Thousand Plateaus* in particular. However, while these books remain influential in activist circles, there is a growing consensus within academia that despite the 'messianic desire' (Moreiras, 2001. p. 224) of *Multitude* 'its basic theses do not stand scrutiny' (Mouffe, 2005, p. 107). This position is most succinctly summed up by Gilbert when he says: 'Beyond shutting our eyes and wishing very hard, it's never very clear how Hardt and Negri imagine that the prophetic character of their work is going to manifest itself in some new political reality' (2008, p. 165).

These books were written by what I would describe as politically committed academics during a time of great technological and political optimism. The unanticipated success of the anti-globalisation demonstrations against the World Trade Organisation in Seattle in 1999 was attributed in part to activists' innovative use of new communication technologies. The internet quickly became seen as having an 'affinity with new forms of protest' (Couldry and Curran, 2003, p. 8) which contributed to the 'global imagining of those events' (Bennett, 2003, p. 31). Needless to say this almost euphoric sense of possibility and hope was gradually eroded by the grinding realities of every day political life. This is evidenced by more recently published books such as Curran, Fenton and Freedmans' *Misunderstanding the Internet* which questions a perception of the internet as the 'alpha and omega of all technologies' (2012, p. 3). The anti-globalisation slogans 'we are winning' which had appeared on the walls of Seattle, Washington and Genoa began to fade until, following the attack on the World Trade Center, they disappeared completely. Moreover governments across the globe used legislation introduced after September 11 (such as the Patriot Act in America, the Terrorism Act 2000 and the Anti-Terrorism, Crime and Security Act 2001 in the United Kingdom) to reassert state control in cyberspace.

There followed a period in which rhizomatic interpretations of the media quietened. This slightly chastened silence was recently broken by Olga Bailey, Bart Cammaerts and Nico Carpentier in their 2008 publication *Understanding Alternative Media*. This volume uses Deleuze and Guattari's work to conceptualise various approaches to map out four interrelated and overlapping approaches to media studies which seek to combine 'essentialist and relationist positions' (Bailey et al., 2008, p. 30). The first approach sees alternative media as serving the community, the second as an alternative to community and the third as linking alternative media to civil society. The fourth approach conceptualises alternative media as rhizome. Bailey et al. argue that rhizomatic approaches foster an understanding of marginal organisations which foregrounds their ability to breach the 'rigid separations' (2008, p. 33) imposed by more traditional models. Thus, according to this view, rhizomatic models 'highlight the role of alternative media as the crossroads of organizations and movements linked with civil society' (2008, p. 27). Several more recent publications have developed this more rhizomatic approach to the conceptualisation of both alternative media and social movements. For example Maeckelbergh's book *The Will of the Many* (2009) draws heavily on the work of Deleuze and Guattari.

The notion of the rhizome is drawn from *A Thousand Plateaus*, a book which introduces a myriad of interrelated and sometimes analogous concepts, including the notion of rhizomatic and arborescent structures. According to Deleuze and Guattari rhizomes are: 'a-centred, non-hierarchical, non-signifying in communications which runs from any neighbour to any other, the stems or channels do not pre-exist and all individuals are interchangeable, defined only by their state at any given moment – such that the local operations are coordinated and the final global result synchronised without a central agency' (Deleuze and Guattari, 2004, p. 19).

Bailey et al. argue that alternative media can be, but do not have to be, rhizomatic. Such media organisations and outputs are characterised by the 'elusiveness and contingency' of the rhizome which allows them to 'cut across borders and build linkages between pre-existing gaps' (2008, pp. 27–8). This 'elusiveness' has many advantages. For example it makes alternative media 'hard to control . . . to encapsulate in legislation' (Bailey et al., 2008, p. 29). These qualities enable coalition protest movements to survive in times which are particularly hostile to dissent in even its mildest of forms. However while this ungraspable, unstoppable notion of relational structures offers alternative movements distinct advantages, it also requires both practitioners and theorists to let go of many of the essentialist binaries and boundaries which have traditionally structured our understanding of the political process.

All the interpretations of alternative media forms, global powers and civil society outlined above have used ideas gleaned from the work of Deleuze and Guattari. Thus they focus on the ways in which rhizomatic technologies, social movements and international organisations both structure and alter the expression of political opinion. In doing so, I would suggest that they depend implicitly, and to varying degrees, on the notion of the public sphere as a common communicative space in which ideas relating to the common good are debated and discussed. In the following section I foreground and theorise the connections between these very different bodies of research.

Smooth and Striated Space

In 'Rhizome and Resistance: Hypertext and the Dreams of a New Culture' Stuart Moulthrop argues that while *A Thousand Plateaus* 'arrives as a print artefact, it was designed as a matrix of independent but cross referential discourses which the reader is invited to enter more or less at random' (1994, p. 300). *A Thousand Plateaus* stands in a similarly eclectic but loosely interconnected relationship with the wider academic community. The authors leap from historical epoch to intellectual paradigm, from renowned academics to obscure but distinguished commentators without explaining or justifying their movements. While this sense of chaotic momentum can be exhausting it is also exhilarating. Moreover it actively encourages the reader to emulate Deleuze and Guattari's gleeful tendency to 'steal' from other scholars and disciplines and therefore repeatedly invites one to 'lift a dynamism out of the book entirely' and to 'incarnate it in a foreign medium' (Massumi, 2004, p. xv).

In this spirit I will 'steal' the notion of smooth and striated space and attempt to re-incarnate it in a field more traditionally occupied by public sphere theorists and political communication scholars. *A Thousand Plateaus* begins with a chapter on rhizomes, it develops this (and other) refrains in a variety of contexts and then (almost!) concludes with a chapter on smooth and striated spaces. This penultimate chapter (there is actually a fifteenth chapter which acts as a partial and purposefully incomplete coda to the book as a whole) examines 'the various aspects of the two spaces and the relationship between them' by describing six smooth and striated spatial models – the technological, the musical, the maritime, the mathematical, the physical and the aesthetic (Deleuze and Guattari, 2004, p. 524). While each model further develops previously established concepts – such as rhizomatic structures, assemblage or nomadolgy – they also introduce an array of subtle variations. In an attempt to avoid being caught in this entanglement of models, concepts and variations, I will confine myself to a discussion of the technological model which lends itself particularly well to an analysis of alternative media and organisational forms.

Arborescent and rhizomatic systems and striated and smooth spaces are abstract concepts. According to Deleuze and Guattari, arborescent systems and, by implication, striated spaces are characterised by the 'binary logic . . . of the root tree' (2004, p. 5). Such systems are therefore 'linear, hierarchical and sedentary and could be represented as the tree like structure of genealogy' (Wray 1998, p. 3). In this way we can imagine a tree trunk dividing into smaller and smaller branches until they become twigs or then the stems of leaves. Each element is different and yet constitutes part of a schematised and integrated whole.

Patton further clarifies this point when he argues that boundaries between points (trunk, branch, twig, stem) in striated space tend to be 'clearly defined and their parts connected according to an invariant principle of unity' (2000, p. 43). Such systems create striated spaces in which 'one closes off a surface and "allocates" it according to determined intervals, assigned breaks' (Deleuze and Guattari, 2004, p. 530). These very clearly delineated, static and standardised hierarchical structures tend to be occupied by those who champion 'order, purpose and control' (Moulthrop, 1994, p. 303). Thus Deleuze and Guattari maintain that arborescent systems and striated space exists in 'the most perfect and severest of forms' (2004, p. 543) within the confines of the capitalist nation state.[1]

Rhizomatic systems in contrast reject systems in which 'the tree imposes the verb "to be"' embracing instead 'the fabric of the rhizome, the conjunction "and . . . and . . . and . . ."' (Deleuze and Guattari, 2004, p. 27). In this way, rather than extending in an ordered way from trunk to branch to twig, the rhizome multiplies like a bulb; oddly, apparently at random and in any direction. These systems give rise to spaces which are 'in principle infinite, open and unlimited in every direction . . . [have] neither top nor bottom nor centre . . . [do not] assign fixed and mobile elements but rather distribute a continuous variation' (2004, p. 524). Thus smooth spaces are, according to Deleuze and Guattari, characterised by movement and are uncertain and constantly threatened but never the less perpetual 'becoming' (2004, p. 27).

In *A Thousand Plateaus* Deleuze and Guattari use these terms in order to identify two different types of space. Thus they argue that, 'in striated space, lines or trajectories tend to be subordinated to points: one goes from one point to another' while 'in smooth space it's the opposite: the points are subordinated to the trajectory (2004, p. 528). Whilst both

---

1. Paradoxically they also maintain that global capitalism, as opposed to localised capitalism, constitutes a smooth space.

spaces are therefore characterised by multiplicities, the way in which these multiplicities are conceptualised offers significantly different political scenarios.

Perhaps unsurprisingly, Deleuze and Guattari's technological model does not deal with technology as a whole. Instead it focuses upon the smooth and striated qualities of different types of fabric. Deleuze and Guattari maintain that woven fabric is striated (2004, p. 524). Thus 'in the simplest case' it is characterised by four basic principles. Woven fabric is constructed by parallel 'vertical and horizontal elements' which 'intertwine' and 'intersect' (the warp and the weft). These two elements each have a different function; one is fixed (the warp yarn is stretched over the loom) and the other is mobile (the weft yarn is threaded onto the shuttle). And finally the woven fabric/striated space is 'necessarily delimited' and has 'a top and a bottom' (set by the width and structure of the loom). According to Deleuze and Guattari, it is these four qualities which enabled Plato to employ the notion of weaving as a metaphor for the arborescent 'art of governing people or operating the state apparatus' (2005, p. 525).

Partly as a result of Plato's extended use of the weaving metaphor in the *Statesman* (in which Socrates and a stranger discuss the art of politics) society is often discussed metaphorically in terms of fabric. Thus for example threats to the social order are frequently depicted as 'straining' or 'unravelling' society ('Archbishop of Canterbury: UK Debt Culture Straining Fabric of Society', *Telegraph*, 25 April 2008; 'Off Side', Spiked Online, 7 April 2005) while state institutions such as the army are described as being essential (or not) to the 'fabric of society' (Heater Roy MP, 'Speech to Rotary', 11 September, 2008; John Redwood, political blog, 10 October 2007). Similarly fabric metaphors can also be found throughout the literature on classical liberal models of the public sphere. Habermas talks about the 'interweaving of the public and private realm' (1974, p. 54) while Fraser discusses the ways in which 'cultural identities are woven of many different strands' (1990, p. 69). More recently Garnham has reflected on the notion of new social movements as having arisen at 'the seam between lifeworld and system world' (Garnham, 2007, p. 204).

I would suggest that the 'analytic grid' discussed in the previous chapter (Peters, 1993, p. 557) can also be read using fabric metaphors. According to this view the classical liberal model of the public sphere can be understood as a woven and therefore striated space. Thus it is 'constituted by two kinds of parallel elements' which have each been allocated 'different functions'

(Deleuze and Guattari, 2005, p. 524). Moreover the use of dominant/subordinate binary pairings such as public/private, state/economy ensures that is has a top and a bottom thereby creating a 'delimited, closed [and] determined space' (Deleuze and Guattari, 2004, p. 524). In this way I would argue that the lifeworld/systems world, public/private distinction create a frame in which the domestic sphere stands in an ancillary relationship to the public sphere while the domestic economy is thought of as subsidiary to the state economy.

This rather static model is unsettled by Garnham's description of the binary oppositions which underpin the classical liberal view as 'value vectors' (2000, p. 174). This description echoes Deleuze and Guattari's emphasis on directional movement in smooth space and begins to disrupt the relationship between points and trajectories. This shift in emphasis is further developed by Fraser's use of 'pink and blue thread' metaphors which highlight the trajectories which run between points rather than the predetermined points themselves. According to this view the distinctions which define the public sphere constitute a conceptual loom across which different discourses and activities interweave. I would suggest that Fraser's model of the public sphere has much in common with the 'technological model' of embroidery. Thus Deleuze and Guattari argue that while 'embroidery's variable and constant, fixed and mobile elements, may be of extraordinary complexity', this type of space is nevertheless structured by essentially striated 'rhythmic [i.e. striated] values' (2004, p. 425). Therefore while Fraser's model begins to subvert a woven understanding of the public sphere, with what Deleuze and Guattari describe as 'the harmonies of embroidery' (2004, p. 526), she does not actually replace the striated structures which underpin the fabric.

Deleuze and Guattari go on to contrast woven or striated fabrics with 'supple solid products' or 'anti-fabric[s]' such as felt and patchwork. Unlike the woven spaces produced by sedentary societies such as those discussed in the *Statesman*, felt and patchwork are associated with nomadic or migratory societies such as settlers from Europe to the New World and the nomadic tribes in Africa. Thus, according to Deleuze and Guattari, these societies create a technological model which imply 'no separation of threads, no intertwining, only an entanglement of fibres obtained by fulling'[2] in the case of felt (Deleuze and Guattari, 2004, p. 525) and blocks

---

2. Fulling – a technique for the production of felt which creates [anti-]fabric by rolling a mass of fibres back and forth.

arranged in an 'amorphous collection of juxtaposed pieces that can be joined together in an infinite number of ways' in the case of patchwork (2004, p. 526). I will return to the possible ways in which the technological models of felt and fabric might usefully contribute to an alternative understanding of the public sphere in Chapters 3, 4 and 5. However before doing so I would also like to establish what Deleuze and Guattari describe as the 'many interlacings' (2004, p. 525) between different types of spaces.

The De Facto Mix

While there is a growing body of work which uses the abstract distinction between arborescent and rhizomatic structures (and therefore by implication smooth and striated spaces) to illuminate the relationship between subaltern and official public spheres, it is important to note that Deleuze and Guattari create *de jure* dualisms in order to overcome them, arguing that 'mental correctives are necessary to undo the dualisms we have no wish to construct but through which we must pass' (2004, p. 220). Thus they maintain that 'there are knots of arborescence in rhizomes, and rhizomatic offshoots in roots' (2004, p. 22) and that 'the two spaces in fact only exist in mixture: smooth space is constantly being translated and transversed into striated space, striated space is constantly being reversed, returned into smooth space' (2004, p. 524). As a consequence of this – and in keeping with A *Thousand Plateaus'* deliberately rhizomatic qualities – the notion of movement or 'passage' between different types of structures and spaces is central to their work.

Following this line of thought and further developing the arguments discussed in Chapter 1, I would like to further consider the constitutive boundaries of the classical public sphere. In his critique of Fraser's work on actually existing democracy Hands maintains that her emphasis on identity based counter publics necessitates the existence of boundaries that do not accurately reflect the realities of contemporary networked contexts (2012). However, and as Epstein points out, social movements are predicated upon a celebration of difference (1993) and as such I would suggest that the boundary is of central and defining significance. Indeed one could argue that it is precisely this emphasis on boundaries that enables Fraser to succeed where Benkler fails in offering an account of the public sphere in which the power differentials that constitute the public sphere are fully articulated.

Consequently rather than denying or eradicating the concept of the boundary within the public sphere I would suggest that there is a need to reconsider the nature of the boundary, going beyond thinking of the boundary as a barrier and to begin to conceptualise the boundary as a transformative threshold between different types of identities, organisations and space. Such a move enables one to begin to develop a more sophisticated understanding of identity and power within the public sphere.

This point can be illustrated by returning briefly to Fraser's discussion of dual aspect activities and her assertion that 'gender identity run[s] like pink and blue threads through . . . all arenas of life' (1987, p. 45). Consequently one could argue that the coloured threads of identity politics also begin to bleed into another and that this sense of threading and blurring between boundaries and borders inevitably undermines a classical understanding of the public sphere. Thus the notion of 'dual aspect' activities which not only straddle and subvert 'the weft and warp' of the classical model but do so freely and with impunity, begins to suggest a model of the public sphere which foregrounds movement or trajectories and overlays the clear divisions of classical models with a far more postmodern 'entanglement' (Deleuze and Guattari, 2004, p. 525) of spheres and activities, systems and spaces.

Deleuze and Guattari's definition of smooth space emphasises the *de jure* or abstract refusal of both hierarchy and boundary. Moreover, while much of *A Thousand Plateaus* (and all of Chapter 14) is spent elaborating on the distinguishing minutiae of *de jure* space, Deleuze and Guattari are adamant that in all cases and according to all models, 'We are always . . . brought back to a dissymmetrical necessity to cross from the smooth to the striated, and from the striated to the smooth' (2004, p. 536).

Deleuze and Guattari's repeated return to the 'rich and complex operations' required to 'translate' one type of space into another (2004, p. 536) inevitably and explicitly foreground the many binary dualisms – arborescent/rhizomatic, striated/smooth, nomadic/sedentary – which both shape and structure *A Thousand Plateaus*. Indeed, as with the binary oppositions which shape and structure public sphere theory – public/ private, reason/passion, reality/unreality – the constitutive identity of each element 'depends upon contrast and avid opposition' of its partner (Hartley, 1996, p. 79). In this way one could argue that, while Deleuze and Guattari may not wish to construct boundaries, they are inevitable and indeed necessary in order to relate one type of space into another. As a result the difficulties and continuing possibilities inherent in communication between the two types of space place these points of contact unexpectedly at the centre of their work.

The centrality of the *de facto* correlation or communication between smooth and striated space can be best illustrated by briefly examining a model or manifesto of civil society which does not fully accommodate the implications raised by differing spatial qualities. In both *Empire* and *Multitude* Hardt and Negri argue that 'in contrast to imperialism, Empire establishes no territorial centre of power and does not rely on fixed boundaries or barriers (2000, p. xii). Thus Empire, like the Multitude it begets, is essentially a smooth space which 'progressively incorporates the entire global realm' (2000, p. xii). In order to resist Empire, Hardt and Negri argue that the Multitude 'should be done, once and for all, with the search for an outside' and should instead 'enter the terrain of Empire and confront its homogenising and hetrogening flows in all their complexity' (2000, p. 46).

According to Hardt and Negri, immersion in the smooth space of Empire is potentially liberating in that it relieves political activists of the need to construct 'well structured communicating tunnels' between different types of space (2000, p. 58). Thus they argue somewhat optimistically that, freed from the need to dwell on the 'incommunicability' (2000, p. 54) of their separate struggles, the multitude will eventually leap 'vertically, directly to the centre' (2000, p. 58) and destroy Empire by creating a new unipolar order. This is a position which renders much of the research into horizontal communication flows entirely redundant!

However, this abstract conceptualisation of entirely isolated pockets of resistance grouped around a virtual centre fails to recognise the *de facto* relationship between different types of systems and structures. Thus, for example, Hardt and Negri frequently cite the Zapatistas' uprising in Mexico as one of many struggles which can in 'no respect be linked together as a globally expanding chain of revolt' (2000, p. 54). Yet protesters involved in the anti-globalisation demonstrations of the late 1990s frequently trace their inspiration back to the 1996 *encuentro* in Chiapas. For example Kingsnorth describes the way in which the 3,000 international delegates 'returned to their countries with new ideas, new ways of thinking about the future' (2003, p. 37). In this way the *de jure* distinction between smooth and striated spaces is immediately complicated and unsettled by the *de facto* mix which explicitly foregrounds the point of contact between these two spaces.

This desire to escape the tensions and frictions set up by binary dichotomies is recognised by Mouffe in *On the Political*. However, she argues that Hardt and Negri's vision of 'globalised smooth space . . . fails to appreciate the pluralistic nature of the world' (2005, p. 115) and that their associated refusal to address the issue of 'political articulation among different struggles' (p. 112) actually forecloses rather than extends the potentially liberating possibility of a more pluralistic order. Thus she maintains that, despite their use of 'Deleuzian terminology and the revolutionary rhetoric' (p. 108), Hardt and Negri's views exhibit a 'postmodern form of longing for a reconciled world' (p. 1150) which has much in common with more traditional critiques of our newly globalised post-September 11 world.

As a consequence of my focus on polyvocal dissent I do not intend to follow Hardt and Negri and 'celebrate the demise of boundaries as leading to emancipatory potential' (Passavant and Dean, 2004, p. 7). Rather I intend to actively foreground the notion of boundaries in an attempt to better understand the political contribution of coalition protest movements. By foregrounding the tensions and frictions inherent in the de facto mix between rhizomatic and arborescent systems and smooth and striated spaces I hope to highlight the self-reflexivity and awareness of difference that, I argue, distinguishes contemporary coalition protest movements from the ones of yesterday. In this way I hope to readdress the question of how movements – such as the anti-globalisation and anti-war movements – can communicate 'across [the] lines of difference' which both separate and connect the margins from the mainstream (Fraser, 1990 p. 71).

Conjunction and Disjunction
The 'disordering of difference' (Soja and Hooper, 1993, p. 187) that a multipolar world inevitably entails has particularly important consequences for less easily categorised, dissenting voices. Many traditionalists are struck by the 'horror of multiplicity' (Jameson quoted in Massey, 1993, p. 142) and are dismayed by the thought of all those 'web threads flung out beyond my situation into the unimaginable synchronicity of other people' (p. 142). However Graeber points out that protest cultures' deliberate and often gleeful 'scrambling of conventional categories' tends to 'throw the forces of order' and make them 'desperate to bring things back to familiar territory' (2004, p. 209). Consequently, dissenting voices which cannot be easily categorised within traditional binary structures tend to be dismissed from wider public consideration. Furthermore, as

George McKay points out, 'when the primacy of one binary is viewed as competing with the privileging of another, the prospects for flexible and co-operative alliances and empathy are likely to be dim' (1998, p. 186). Thus, while Fraser traces the skein of pink (and by implication blue) threads across the fabric of the public sphere she chooses not to become entangled in a plethora of other multicoloured identity options.

Protest coalitions frequently find themselves framed within official spheres as at best part of an 'unseemly' slide towards a mish-mash of 'competing –isms' (Smith and Katz, 1993, p. 77). Moreover, those on the political left frequently share this outlook tending to interpret any multiplicity of resistances as 'inevitably leading to a politically debilitating fragmentation and the abandonment of long-established forms of struggle' (Soja and Hooper, 1993, p. 188). Thus, for example, Tony Blair famously dismissed the anti-globalisation movement as 'a sort of anarchist travelling circus' ('Sweden Defends EU Summit Policing', BBC News, 17 June 2001) implying that the movement was chaotic, temporary and fundamentally unserious. In this way the relatively rigid categorisation systems imposed by most democratic nation states inevitably function at the expense of subaltern voices which are not linked into the mainstream by a binary pairing. As a result such voices frequently remain marginalised on the fringes of the political arena.

In contrast a rhizomatic or smooth conceptualisation of alternative spaces not only allows for a multiplicity of identities and spheres, but also foregrounds the flux and flow of both people and ideas between spheres. This conceptualisation of public space is helpful in that it goes beyond the binary opposition of categories such as 'hierarchical' and 'non-hierarchical', 'vertical' and 'horizontal' utilized by authors such as Downing and Atton and offers a theoretical framework which foregrounds the way in which 'the boundaries of discourse' are always necessarily 'intertwined with asymmetrical power relations and a struggle for domination' (Dahlberg, 2007, p. 835). In doing so it also creates a space for the development of a more sophisticated and nuanced understanding of the public sphere. As Bailey et al. point out, this not only creates a model of the alternative media which can 'cut across borders and build linkages between pre-existing gaps' (2008, p. 28), it also allows for the 'deterritorializing effect' of the rhizomatic systems and smooth spaces on the rigidities and certainties of political and economic mainstreams.

Whilst Fraser, Curran and indeed Habermas, in his later writings, question the concept of a single public sphere and introduce the notion of a plurality of publics, they do not fully develop the possibilities inherent in a multiplicity of public spheres. As a result, counter-cultural spheres are frequently conceptualised as that which the dominant sphere is not. This limits the political debate to arguments for and against any given issue, thereby excluding many less powerful dissenting voices. Benkler posits a more networked understanding of the public sphere, but like Habermas, he fails to distinguish between the normative and actual workings of democracy. While Hands's work goes some way towards synthesising the strengths of these competing models, his emphasis on the technological means that the equally significant socio-cultural dimension is almost inevitably downplayed. In this book I use Deleuze and Guattari's ideas to develop what I would call a more networked understanding of 'the public sphere' and focus upon the ways in which political ideas and discourses can travel through the complex system of connections which both bind and separate the margins and the mainstream.

The notion of a boundary between the public and the private, the real and the unreal, the reasoned and the impassioned depends upon 'contrast and opposition' (Hartley, 1996, p. 78). As has been discussed, such distinctions play a central role in the construction and development of classical models of the liberal bourgeois public sphere. However I would argue that a postmodern in-the-middle position also depends upon the implicit existence of such definable boundaries. Without these external parameters an in-the-middle position unravels and simply becomes a position in which the 'fabric of the rhizome', which Deleuze and Guattari maintain is constituted by the 'conjunction and . . . and . . . and' (2004, p. 27), has been replaced by the treelike verb to be.

Unravelling the Threads

> If on the one hand he actualises only a few of the possibilities fixed by the constructed order (he goes only here and not there), on the other he increases the number of possibilities (for example, by creating shortcuts and detours) and prohibitions (for example, he forbids himself to take paths generally considered accessible or even obligatory) He thus makes a selection. 'The user of a city picks out certain fragments of a statement in order to actualise them in secret'.
>
> De Certeau, 1984, p. 98

The approaches discussed above sit between various, very different theoretical and methodological fields. As such it is part of a wider trend within academia which aims to challenge, without dismissing, the boundaries which underpin modernist thinking. This position seeks to recognise, and even embrace, the changes wrought by the fracturing processes of globalisation, whilst also being reluctant to abandon the notion of a participatory and aspirational politics more commonly associated with the Enlightenment period. This awkwardly 'in the middle' position requires a methodological flexibility which moves away from what Foley and Valenzuela describe as the 'notion of an objective social sciences that produce value free ethnographies' (2005, p. 217) and towards an understanding which 'stresses the value of the lived experience' (Lovatt and Purkis, 1996, p. 264).

Andy Lovatt and Jonathan Purkis's article 'Shouting in the Street: Popular Culture, Values and the New Ethnography' explores some of the implications raised by this position which are of particular relevance to this book. They point out that ethnographical research has historically been concerned with producing scientific data in order to contribute to the progress of society as a whole and go on to discuss the way in which the work of the 'classical anthropological ethnographer' (1996, p. 257) has traditionally been imbued with a sense of the exotic and far away. However they argue that the clearly demarcated boundaries between the ethnographer and the 'other' are being evaporated by economic and social changes in both academia and the wider media environment. Thus they maintain that contemporary research is increasingly being undertaken by young academics whose intellectual engagement with the field is preceded by a more autobiographical involvement. They ask: 'In such circumstances, the role of ethnographic researcher becomes problematic, both in terms of their "tactics" and their identity – for example, are they a fan, an interpreter, a researcher, an essayist or all four?' (p. 250). In an attempt to resolve these issues they propose a new ethnographical approach which foregrounds values as well as facts in such a way as to better reflect 'the uncertainties of contemporary cultural developments' (p. 252).

This ethnographical approach is particularly concerned with what they describe as 'the background noise of the practice of everyday life' (p. 263). Within this context they are at pains to foreground the 'web of connections, tactics and identities' (Lee-Treweeck and Linkogle, 2000. p. 56) which comprise the ethnographic process and compose a 'thousand little stories' (Deleuze and Guattari cited in Lovatt and Purkis, 1996, p. 264). In doing so they go on to recognise and foreground the place of story-telling in popular cultural research and the ways in which stories constitute the 'rhizomatic, ephemeral cultures of the contemporary urban milieux' (p. 264). In many ways this book is just such a cluster of interrelated and overlapping stories. They have been gathered from the activists and ex-activists, lawyers and journalists, newspapers, newssheets and newswires, and create an entangled mass of narrative lines which both complement and contradict each other.

Stories do not simply reflect the unfolding of events, they constitute the construction of political reality (Lovatt and Purkis, 1996). They argue with De Certeau that 'story telling and story writing is not a substitute for reality' a mere theoretical or methodological move in the game but a way in which one can meaningfully contest hegemonic meanings and so 'create space out of place' (1996, p. 226). This view of storytelling has much in common with Boje's notion of the antenarrative as a messy, subterranean, highly interactive activity which constitutes and constructs 'evolving and shifting prestory connections' (2003). This is a position which echoes Deleuze and Guattari's notion of the rhizome and smooth spaces of ephemeral becoming and, as such, it is of particular relevance here.

In this chapter I unravel some of these narrative threads and to examine the ways in which stories are told within and between coalition movements. I also wish to explore the way in which these protest stories travel (some might say stagger!) towards the academic mainstream. Consequently I have traced the movement of stories from one type of alternative space to another as well as from activists' spaces to mainstream spaces. I have also explored the ways in which the same space, whether they are discussion spaces or demonstration spaces, can be told differently. However in the process of collecting and then arranging these fragments of experience I have inevitably constructed my own story and in doing so I have inevitably defined, framed and stilled what was, and still is, an ever changing political terrain. This is a process which recalls the work of Michele de Certeau.

In 'The Practice of Everyday Life', de Certeau describes the way in which Medieval or Renaissance painters represented the city from a perspective beyond their technical means. De Certeau goes on to argue that while such mapping practices make the complexity of the city/text 'readable' they are also problematic in that their 'opaque mobility' is immobilised into a 'transparent text'. As a result, resisting stories which once produced 'anti-text effects, effects of dissemination and escape' – such as the Zapatistas' uprising in Chiapas – are simplified into 'rumours propagated by the media' which 'cover everything and…wipe out' the possibility of resistance (de Certeau, 1984: 107–8).

According to de Certeau, the city seen from above in this way 'provides a way of conceiving and constructing space on the basis of a finite number of stable, isolatable and interconnected properties' (p. 94). In other words, it imposes order upon the 'ordinary practitioners' who live 'below the thresholds at which visibility begins' (p. 93). De Certeau likens himself to Icarus and describes the way in which the doomed boy's flight turned him into an all seeing, all knowing 'solar eye' and writes, 'His elevation transfigures him into a voyeur; it puts him at a distance. It transforms the bewitching world by which one was "possessed" into a text that lies before one's eyes. It allows one to read it, to be a solar eye looking down like a God' (p. 92).

Thus de Certeau argues that this elevated position enables him to read the city as if it were a text. However de Certeau is also careful to point out that this understanding of the city is a pleasurable 'misunderstanding' (p. 93) of the moving network which constitute city spaces. Moreover he suggests that by relinquishing the privileges offered by the solar eye and 'stepping in through proportions, sequences, and intensities which vary according to the time, the path taken and the walker' (p. 99) one can immerse oneself within a differently experienced city space. This requires one to adopt a far more uncomfortable in-the-middle position which entangles and enmeshes the walker within the 'murky intertwining daily behaviours' of city dwellers (p. 93). He goes on to suggest that their entangled routes through the urban landscape constitutes an 'intertwining unrecognised poem in which each body is an element signed by many others' but which eludes legibility (p. 93).

De Certeau's approach has been utilised by scholars in the field of movement studies to develop a 'third space' approach. In his influential article, Soja describes third space as an 'open ended set of defining moments' (1996, p. 260), a space that is 'creatively open to redefinition and expansion in new directions' (p. 2). This conceptualisation of space has been further explored by scholar activists such as Routledge. He uses the notion of third space to characterise the overlapping intersections between academia and activism and to reflect upon the 'coming and going in a borderline zone between different modes of action' (p. 406). As Moles points out, entering such spaces requires one to invent ways of crossing the borders which are momentarily brought into being by transformational dynamics of in-between space (2008). It is the borders between the actual and the textual, and the ways in which they overlap and interconnect, that I wish to focus upon here.

This topological view is further developed by the parallel between traversing textual space and actual space. De Certeau asserts that the 'act of walking is to the urban city what the speech act is to language' (1984, p. 97). In this way he makes a connection between seeing and reading, walking and writing. I would suggest that this notion of an elevated and God-like position is a particularly helpful way of thinking about how we experience the construction of both urban and textual public spaces. The city as a text viewed from above but experienced from within structures many aspects of this book and is synthesised with an analogous distinction between arborescent and rhizomatic thought. Arborescent thought has been described as 'taking a god's eye view of things' while rhizomatic thought has been described as requiring one to look at the world 'from the ground up' (Gilbert, 2008, p. 145).

Telling Alternative Truths

> The intent behind this radical postmodernism of resistance is to deconstruct (not destroy) the ebbing tide of modernist radical politics, to renew its strengths and avoid its weaknesses, and to reconstruct an explicitly postmodern radical politics, a new cultural politics of difference and identity that moves towards empowering a multiplicity of resistance rather than searches for the one 'great refusal', the singular transformation to precede and guide all others.
>
> Soja and Hooper, 1993, p. 187

Ethnographic research cannot be planned in advance or pre-programmed because its 'practice is replete with the unexpected' (Hammersley and Atkinson, 1995, p. 28). Hammersley and Atkinson point out the importance of remembering that 'the process of identifying and defining the case study proceeds side by side with the refinement of the research and the development of the theory' (1995, p. 43). This has certainly been the case in this instance and the research methods outlined below are ones which have unfolded and evolved over a period of years. I have been methodologically inspired by Hartley's explicit rejection of what he describes as a 'spurious unity or comprehensiveness in favour of a methodological approach which includes 'documentary, forensic, historical, argumentative, metaphorical and textual' (1996, p. 6). Following Amad, Hartley describes this approach as 'theory shopping' (Amad, 1994, p. 13) but is careful to point out that such a methodological approach should not be confused with an 'anything goes postmodernism' arguing that it should be understood as 'a scrupulous and responsible (albeit exciting and purposeful) model of intellectual work' (1996, p. 7).

Textual Spaces

This strand is underpinned by an analysis of four news sources from the radical left: *Socialist Worker*, Indymedia, *Circus Free* and *The Greenham Factor*. Hammersley and Atkinson maintain that 'the problem of obtaining access to the data one needs looms large in ethnography' (1995, p. 54). I would argue that the same can be said of accessing textual data. Thus while anyone can, in principle, access texts which have appeared in the public domain, in practice one tends to encounter a series of obstacles. Moreover, these obstacles and the means of overcoming them frequently highlight and reveal issues of wider methodological and theoretical relevance.

This viewpoint can be illustrated by briefly examining the obstacles which I encountered (or indeed failed to encounter) in accessing the texts analysed in Chapter 3. *Socialist Worker* is produced by the Socialist Workers Party and is supported by a formalised and permanent system of production and distribution which has enabled it to endure over the decades. Thus while there are some geographical locations in which accessing *Socialist Worker* remains problematic, it is relatively easy to access current issues of the publication. Any lingering distribution problems have been addressed by the fact that the weekly newspaper is now accessible in PDF format on the internet. At the time of writing, the *Socialist Worker* searchable online archive currently goes back as far as 1993 and is constantly being extended.

Indymedia's existence on the internet creates a similarly centralised archive of materials which enables activists (and academics) to utilise search engines which collapse the boundaries of both space and time and so circumvent the problem of access. Moreover, I would argue that it is the accessibility of Indymedia's online archive which has prompted much of the academic interest in alternative news sources and may have contributed to the elision between alternative media and computer-mediated technologies which characterises much of the research of the mid to late 1990s. Thus while *Socialist Worker* and Indymedia embody differing logics of collective and connective action (Bennett and Segerberg, 2012, p. 739) they are both examples of the ways in which communication structures, and in some cases becomes, organisation.

In contrast, print publications which preceded the internet are still difficult to access. Protest organisations rooted in a socialist-anarchist tradition tend to be characterised by a 'culture of immediacy' (McKay, 1998, p. 13) which makes them both structurally and temporally ephemeral. Consequently, material produced by them is seldom held centrally and tends to become fragmented as the individual(s) actively involved in its production drift away. This is particularly true of smaller protest organisations that are characterised by 'inclusive and diverse large scale personal expression rather than through common group or ideological identification' (Bennett and Segerberg, 2012, p. 744)

The dissipation of such publications exacerbates the sense of temporal and spatial distance between the researcher and the object of research. This tends to conceal and remove issues which could, if they were more fully examined, be of substantive significance. The elusiveness of such texts means that protest paraphernalia which some may think of as rubbish can be considered by others as archive. These routes to this sort of material are idiosyncratic and depend upon a certain degree of serendipity which supports Downing's assertion that material from a socialist-anarchist tradition tends to be 'accessible only in dusty back numbers of forgotten publications and in oral history interviews with aged political veterans' (Downing, 2002, p. 252).

Actual Spaces

As my research progressed I moved away from analysing the textual spaces produced by different alternative media forms and began to examine the actual spaces of resistance constituted by mass demonstrations, many of which I attended myself. This section is methodologically rooted in an analysis of mass demonstrations themselves as well as in the online and offline activist discourses which surround them. Much of this research was conducted as events unfolded and the data used in this chapter was gleaned from activist websites such as Indymedia, Urban75 and Alternet. It also draws on some of the many activist authored books which appeared in the years after the demonstrations. This chapter also utilises a small – and by no means comprehensive – amount of crossover mainstream coverage.

Whereas Chapters 3 and 4 were characterised by a spatial and temporal distance, the research process for Chapters 5 and 6 was defined by what

I would describe as a sense of closeness or proximity. This sense has manifested itself in a number of ways. Firstly, the temporal proximity of the anti-war movement means that, unlike the protest stories of the 1980s and 1990s, anti-war narratives are still in a state of historical flux. Secondly the spatial closeness of Save Omar, Smash EDO and Sukey means that there is no scarcity of material; there is an easily accessible abundance of rhizomatic and sometimes highly contradictory activity.

This reading of both textual and actual spaces has been underpinned by a series of personal interviews with activists, journalists and other interested parties within the field. Investigating groups which appear to be without hierarchy and which refuse to allocate roles such as 'leader' or 'spokesperson' raised a number of challenging issues. While mainstream organisations and indeed many alternative protest groups are happy for an individual to speak on behalf of the organisation as a whole, social anarchist movements tend to reject such an authoritative position and speak for themselves alone. As a result such protest milieus are characterised by various and often conflicting narratives which require one to ask important questions about the nature of power, anonymity and transparency within both the activist and the academic world.

As noted, Lovatt and Purkis argue that in order to avoid 'objectifying meta theories of culture', it is sometimes necessary to put empathy on a level with explanation. There are of course potential problems with this approach. Indeed authorities as well-established as Habermas have maintained that the public sphere will inevitably be undermined by any form of discourse to which one 'does not respond by arguing but only by identifying' (1964, p. 206). However I believe that, given the fluid and radically committed nature of both the subject matter and the wider theoretical context in which it is situated, a methodology which privileges the 'web of pre-existing historic or contemporary connection' (Lovatt and Purkis, 1996, p. 260) is appropriate and has much to offer the field. I have therefore attempted to adopt an ethnographic approach which accommodates 'the expressive, the romantic and the local' (Hetherington, 1998, p. 33) without entirely abandoning the communicative rationality favoured by Habermas.

Researching and then writing this book has been a journey through a terrain constructed by (often conflicting) activist narratives. Hetherington's description of travelling as 'a search for alternative truth' (1998, p. 118) implies that such a journey can have no predetermined destination and is therefore by definition an open ended search. The inevitable sense of doubt and uncertainty which accompanies such a search is identified by Patton who points out that the political philosophy of Deleuze and Guattari 'offers no guarantees: it is not a narrative of inevitable progress, nor does it offer the security of commitment to a single set of values against which progress can be judged' (2004, p. 8). Despite the difficulties inherent in such a muddled and intertwined position there is also an important and counterbalancing sense of optimism and abundance.

I feel that it is important to acknowledge that by picking out 'certain fragments' (De Certeau, 1984, p. 98) of the terrain and exposing them to an extended and rigorous analysis I inevitably unravel the tangled 'poem' constituted by the multiplicity of agitational activities I have encountered. I clean up the ambiguities and contradictions inherent in their intertwining behaviours and replace them with a single, coherent, unified academic narrative. Deleuze and Guattari point out that this sort of translation is a complex process which 'undoubtedly consists in subjugating, overcoding, metricizing smooth space'; however they go on to argue that such a process also creates a 'milieu of propagation, extension, refraction and renewal' (2004, p. 536). Thus, while one may sometimes resent the 'severe distortion' imposed by linearity (Rosello, 1994, p. 139) one must also embrace that 'good trick' of speaking from an omnipotent standpoint (Foley and Valenzuela, 2005, p. 218).

So it is important to point out that the paths I have taken 'actualise only a few of the possibilities' (De Certeau, 1984, p. 98) available to someone wishing to research the ways in which activists from protest coalitions communicate with themselves and the mainstream. The same elements could have been ordered and emphasised in such a way as to tell a different story. There are research routes which remain unexplored, waiting for someone else to find and follow them into entirely unexpected directions and in doing so to create an alternative patchwork of truths.

3

Networked Uprisings

We are the network, all of us who speak and listen.

Subcomandante Marcos, 2001, p. 125

At midnight on 31 December 1993 the North American Free Trade Agreement (NAFTA) was ratified. In an attempt to create a second 'Mexican Miracle' certain economic sacrifices had been deemed necessary. To secure a $300 million loan from the World Bank, the Mexican Government abolished Article 27 of the Constitution which (theoretically) protected indigenous lands from national and international agribusiness. The Salinas Government also deregulated coffee prices and disbanded the state agencies responsible for assisting small growers. As a result the indigenous share of the market fell from 16 per cent to 3.4 per cent in a single year (Carrigan, 2001). However, while the politicians in Mexico City were heralding a new and profitable era, the Zapatista National Liberation Army (EZLN) was stealing down from the mountains and occupying key areas within the state of Chiapas. By morning they had declared six large cities and hundreds of farms to be autonomous free zones.

The Mexican army's response was entirely expected – they immediately shelled the Chiapas mountainsides killing at least 145 indigenous people (Hansen and Civil, 2001, p. 445). However, by the second week of January, it became clear that the military were not going to go on bombing and shooting until every last insurgent was dead. Within a fortnight a unilateral ceasefire had been declared and the Zapatistas withdrew victoriously back into the mountains. It may seem odd to view not being killed as a successful political outcome. However the Mexican government has a long and brutal history of putting down indigenous uprisings. For example, the Party of the Poor's entire leadership, supporters and suspected supporters had either been shot or 'disappeared' 20 years earlier without particularly impacting on the national or international mainstream (Krøvel, 2008, not paginated). So what had happened? What made this uprising – and the many coalition uprisings that it has since inspired – so successful in comparison to those that came before?

Many commentators in the global south have argued that the answer to this conundrum lay in the Zapatistas' use of new communication technologies (Castells, 1996; Olesen, 2004; Cleaver, 1998). When the government dismissed the uprising, news of the conflict began to disappear from the national papers. However activists' enthusiastic use of alternative websites and mailing lists created an electronic 'lifeline' (Ponce de Leon, 2001, p. xxv) that prevented the story from dying. In this way the inflexible structures of both the government and the mainstream media were overwhelmed by rhizomatic forms of internet based communication.

Maeckelbergh points out that 'connectivity acts as security', protecting the vulnerable from the potential excess of the state (2009, p. 201). This was certainly the case in Chiapas. The ratification of NAFTA meant that Mexico was already in the global media spotlight. The Zapatistas use of the digitalised word enabled them to make use of this 'external public of onlookers' (Kant, 1991, p. 183) and led to the mobilisation of mass demonstrations in Mexico City and across the rest of the world. The realisation that Mexico's international reputation was being seriously damaged forced the government to suspend its military campaign and embark upon peace talks. In this way the global gaze could be said to have protected local activists from some of the Mexican authorities' more punitive measures.

As a consequence of the sophisticated use of such media strategies, the mainstream press began to position anti-globalisation movements within an increasingly technological narrative. Indeed global imaginings of the Zapatistas have become inextricably intertwined with its use of internet based communications strategies. For example by the beginning of January 1999 the *Guardian*'s environmental correspondent, John Vidal, referred to the Zapatista uprising as the 'first "cyber" or "net" war' (*Guardian*, 13 January). A mainstream media narrative was also constructed around the anti-globalisation movement as 'web-like . . . look[ed] like the internet and [which] . . . couldn't exist without it' (Viner, *Guardian*, 29 September 2000). These connections continue to be made in relation to the movements such as Occupy and have been represented as potentially utopic, such as in the case of the Arab Spring, or as disastrously distopic, such as in the case of the London riots.

Despite the use of such media frames, the authorities in the late 1990s appeared to remain unaware of the ways in which activists were using the internet to forge global connections (Graeber, 2004, Kingsnorth, 2003). Early anti-globalisation protesters exploited this gap between institutional and alternative organisations' use of new information technologies and their demonstrations therefore appeared to leap mysteriously from the mountainsides of Chiapas to the sidewalks of Seattle, Washington, Quebec and Gothenburg.

One could argue that the initial success of the anti-globalisation movement was partly rooted in technical expertise. However, as Lance Bennett points out, the importance of the internet goes beyond its ability to facilitate the organisation of simultaneous protests, it also contributes to the 'global imaging of those events' (2003, p. 31). Consequently it has been argued that the internet has become more than an organisational tool for coalition protest movements and that it has become a constitutive element of globalised protest movements. Thus alternative news wires aspire to become a space in which globally dispersed activists could both organise agitational activities and 'formulate oppositional interpretations of their identities, interests and needs' (Fraser, 1990, p. 67).

The many similarities between the networked spaces created socially by anti-globalisation movements and technically by the internet have been explored by activists and academics alike. The ways in which the internet enables the media-literate to articulate their oppositional identities and needs to a global community has been thoroughly documented by activists such as Sarah Berger (2005), Kate Coyer (2005) and David Graeber (2004). The more theoretical implications raised by these issues have been explored by academics such as Bennett (2003), John Downing (2003) and Stuart Moulthrop (1994). These important areas of work acknowledge and establish the importance of internet-based networked communication systems to protest coalitions. However in this chapter I question the extent to which the anti-globalisation movement's organisational successes have in fact been shaped by their use of the internet and to ask whether the anti-globalisation movement cannot be more usefully understood by separating the medium from the message.

This chapter argues that the smooth qualities of protest coalitions are rooted in ideological, rather than technological factors and is divided into two sections. The first section, Spaces of Resistance, begins by briefly outlining the arguments from the late 1990s, which suggested that the technological innovations offered by the internet created spaces which were inherently more political than print spaces. In the late 1990s it was argued that hypertext and hypermedia represented a 'revolutionary change' in the ways in which we read (Ess, 1994, p. 226) and might even lead to inherently new 'modes of thought' (Escobar, 1996, p. 124). The implications underlying this type of rhetoric were not only that the electronic word was a better version of the printed word, but that it heralded an entirely new era. These rather euphoric claims were countered by authors who considered 'cyberspace' to be nothing but 'a chaotic flux' in which political information quickly lost its 'coherent and cohesive value' (Thu Nguyen and Alexander, 1996, p. 103 and p. 110). While these debates are in many ways outdated, their influence over the perception of the internet as an alternative means of political communication remains formative.

The second section examines the ways in which radical politics has been, and continues to be, articulated in very traditional media forms. This argument is illustrated by an analysis of the way in which the arborescent organisational systems of the Socialist Workers Party lead to the creation of correspondingly striated editorial spaces in *Socialist Worker*. These systems are compared with the smooth online spaces produced by more rhizomatically structured political organisations such as Indymedia. It problematises the distinction between rhizomatic online and arborescent offline structures, smooth and striated spaces, by examining the smooth textual spaces produced by more rhizomatically structured political organisations stemming from what Downing describes as 'a socialist anarchist tradition' (2002, p. 245). Thus this section argues that smooth media forms, unlike striated media forms, enable protest coalition movements to publicly reflect upon their oppositional needs and identities (Fraser, 1990, p. 67) in a way which 'does not destroy . . . political association' (Mouffe, 2005, 20).

Spaces of Resistance

We employ a dualism of models only in order to arrive at a process that challenges all models. Each time mental correctives are necessary to undo the dualisms we have no wish to construct but through which we must pass.

Deleuze and Guattari, 2004, p. 22

As has been discussed, the printed word is accorded a particularly privileged position within liberal bourgeois models of the public sphere (Habermas, 1974, 1992; Peters, 1993; Garnham, 2000). Habermas argues that the emergence of daily political newspapers in the second half of the eighteenth century transformed the nature of power by establishing 'the principle of supervision' (1974. p. 52). As a result the principle of existing power, as an inherent right of the nobility, was infiltrated and then replaced, by the notion of shared power. The production and distribution of news via the printed word has been considered to be of central importance in 'the struggle for freedom and public opinion, and thus for the public sphere as a principle' (p. 53). This section focuses on activists' utilisation of newspapers, newssheets and newswires to inform the wider public on matters of 'general interest' and to instigate change (p. 53).

James Curran maintains that '[a] basic requirement of a democratic media system should be . . . that it represents all significant interests in society. It should facilitate their participation in the public domain, enable them to contribute to the public debate and have an input into the framing of public policy' (1991, p. 30). He goes on to point out that various socio-economic factors have created a media drift to the right and suggests that this has contributed to a tendency on the part of the mainstream press to stigmatise dissident voices (1991). Indeed, many activists point to the political economy of the media and argue, rather convincingly, that the mainstream press actively misrepresents their views in an attempt to prevent them from influencing or framing public opinion (George Monbiot, www.tlio.org.uk; Mary Black, www.alpr.org).

Many individuals and organisations have responded to this bias by attempting to create their own counter-balancing sources of news and views, a strategy best illustrated by alternative political organisations' production and distribution of monthly newsletters. Atton argues that this type of publication offers 'the most thorough going version of alternative news values' (1999, p. 52). He justifies this assertion by claiming that a grassroots periodical, 'produced by the same people whose concerns it represents, giving a position of engagement and direct participation', constitutes a forum for public debate in itself and therefore serves an all-important social function (p. 52).

This is a view shared by activists. Per Hergren maintains that 'by forcing a reaction, the whole of society, with its officials and citizens, is drawn into dialogue' and consequently suggests that the influence of such spaces extends beyond the boundaries of the subaltern (cited in McKay, 1998, p. 5). These mediated spaces are politically transformative in that their mere existence enables previously excluded political positions to be articulated. In this way many alternative publications aspire to create a subaltern space in which excluded voices can 'withdraw and regroup' away from the prying eyes and stunting influences of a hostile mainstream (Fraser, 1990, p. 68).

However, alternative publications are rarely read by anyone other than those who already subscribe to their political agenda and are therefore of limited value in terms of accessing wider publics (Landry et al., 1985). Therefore, despite Atton's belief that the distance of the alternative press from the mainstream is an 'essential component of media that seek to integrate themselves with the movement they are supporting' (1999, p. 69), various attempts have been made to formally transcend the boundaries of the counter-cultural realm. Moreover for a variety of reasons and with a few exceptions, these publications have never really thrived or, indeed, even survived.[1] The 1997 Royal Commission on the Press found that, of all the many disadvantages faced by grassroots journalism, 'distribution is the most difficult to overcome' (cited in Atton, 1996, p. 69). This is an observation supported by Herman and Chesney who point out that while 'anyone can produce a publication . . . the right to do so means little without distribution, resources and publicity' (1997, p. 125).

The rapid expansion of the internet in the late 1990s led many to believe that the advent of the internet could offer exciting new opportunities for activists to bypass the problem of distribution and communicate with a wider public. Rheingold argued that 'access to alternative forms of information and, most important, the power to reach others with your own alternatives to the official view of events, are by their nature political phenomena' (1994, p. 268). According to this rather optimistic view the internet would herald an era which echoed the political activism of the seventeenth century by enabling anyone 'with a modem' to become 'a global pamphleteer' (J. Markoff, *New York Times*, 20 November 1995). Thus it was hoped that the internet would succeed where print journalism has failed and 'make information flows more democratic, break down power hierarchies . . . circumvent information monopolies . . . and provide an effective counter-balance to trends in corporate control of the world's information flows' (Kling, 1996, p. 98).

The computer's ability to increase dramatically an organisation's readership through horizontal linkages is demonstrated by comparing the way in which print and electronic texts have attempted to bypass the estab-

---

1.   An excellent account of the radical left's forays into publishing can be found in *What a Way to Run a Railroad: An Analysis of Radical Failure* (1985) by Charles Landry et al.

lishment's distribution system. Copyright has always been a significant issue for alternative media organisations. The limited resources of counter-cultural organisations, combined with the inhospitable structure of print distribution networks, has led many grassroots authors to encourage the free circulation of their material. This anti-copyright ethos complements the ideology behind many radical left groups' anti-property principles and enables material to be disseminated through channels beyond the papers' own distributive networks. Thus newsletters like *Do or Die* are purposefully published in photocopy-friendly form and contain the slogan 'strictly @nticopyright – customise . . . photocopy . . . distribute' (cited in Atton, 1999, p. 67). This emphasis is repeated with even greater vigour on-line and almost identical imperatives can be found on the pages of websites such as Indymedia, Schnews and Squall.

The digitalisation of the printed word has fundamentally altered the way in which political texts reach their audience and accounts of these changes have been the subject of much scholarly research (Berry, 2008; Stokes, 2009). However internet scholar Stuart Moulthrop claimed that the advent of computer-mediated communication has changed more than the means by which texts are distributed. In doing so, Moulthrop drew on Deleuze and Guattari's work in *A Thousand Plateaus* to tease out the further possibilities offered by this interpretation. Moulthrop maintained that information technology in general, and the hypertextual link in particular, could alter the ways in which we actually think. Moulthrop justified this position by making a distinction between the printed word and the electronic word. Thus Moulthrop maintained that while the printed word is 'defined and supported' by striated space, the electronic word occupies smooth space (1994, p. 303).

According to Moulthrop, the word's existence on the electronic rather than the printed page alters the way in which it is read. Unlike the printed word which can be read from left to right, from to top to bottom, from start to finish, the electronic word requires one to choose to click this link or that link, to move forwards or backwards in order to progress through the document. In this way the familiar linear hierarchies of the traditional print as described by Ong are replaced by a sprawling ebb and flow of more rhizomatically printed clusters. Consequently Bolter claimed that electronic writing 'offers us a paradigm in which the text changed to suit the reader' (cited in Moulthrop, 1994, p. 304). Significantly this notion of information technology as a complex interlinked series of 'message pathways' (Cubitt, 1998, p. 22) depended on an understanding of the internet as being in a state of perpetual motion. The imagery used to describe people in relation to the World Wide Web provides an apt illustration of this point.

Smooth spaces rejection of hierarchy ensured that this plethora of unheard voices remains in an un-prioritised state of flux. As a consequence one could argue that smooth spaces tend to reject an understanding of society based on what Nancy Jay has described as the A/Not A dichotomy whereby 'the only alternative to the *one* order is disorder' (cited in Massey 1993, p. 147). In this way Moulthrop suggested that in accommodating unpredictable and perpetual change, smooth internet spaces enabled a continuous multiplicity of previously un-articulated political positions to be expressed. According to this view computer-mediated communications could be understood as being inherently 'more hospitable to alternative non-traditional points of view and more inclusive of cultural differences' (Burbules, 1998, p. 107).

However these empowering interpretations of hypertextual links have been countered by critics who commented negatively on the almost unbelievable speed with which individuals can move through virtual space (Virilo, 1995; Sardar and Ravets, 1996). In Sardar's opinion, the internet simply did not and does not grant users enough time to satisfactorily absorb the information it provides. Sardar articulates the 'unbearable lightness' (p. 26) which these critics maintain characterises much internet activity when he describes 'surfing the net' as a 'frenzied journey to nowhere' in which users are 'perpetually looking for the next fix, hoping that the next page on the web will take them to Nirvana' (p. 27).

Moulthrop's emphasis on movement and relativity also dismayed critics who perceive these qualities to exist at the expense of depth and stability of meaning. Thus while Sardar acknowledged that the internet offers those engaged in serious information retrieval, and equipped with the necessary skills, an 'excellent array of tools' (1996, p. 27), he also pointed out that the vast majority of activity on the internet lacks such clarity of focus. These critics tended to share a perception of the internet as being inherently more superficial than the book. This view is exemplified by Bryan and Tatam who found that there is a 'trade off between accessibility and depth of information' on the internet which means that 'information online is even more superficial than printed material' (1999, p. 165).

The sense of superficiality frequently associated with the internet existed in conjunction with a belief that the lightness of smooth space and the virtual world would somehow corrupt or even usurp the substance of striated space and the real world. Accordingly, critics such as Postman have suggested that the erosion of the public sphere is rooted in the gradual decline of the printed word (1998). Thus Iacono and Kling's suggestion that the rise of computer-mediated communications would lead to a situation where 'other media for learning, socialising, working or revitalising the community are treated as less important. Real life is life on-line. The physical world is relegated to IRL (in real life) or life off-line' (1996, p. 99). This view implied that hypertext's lack of organisational structure and multiplicity of options actually threatened the very existence of real world organisations and therefore the future of the liberal public sphere itself.

However, as Clay Shirky points out, the perception of 'cyberspace' as entirely separated and different from the 'real world' is a concept that is no longer recognised by a generation brought up in world where on and off line communication routinely overlaps (Shirky, *Observer*, 15 February 2009). More recently scholars have begun to emphasise the similarities and continuities which exist across the on/off line divide. They point out that while the qualities often associated with smooth space and electronic writing may be less familiar, they are nevertheless still disciplines (Burbules, 1998). Moreover they maintain that concepts commonly associated with smooth space, such as bricolage and juxtaposition, are not entirely lawless entities but exist peaceably within their own alternative regulating structure. According to this view, bricolage and juxtaposition should be seen as 'supplements' rather than 'replacements' for concepts more usually associated with striated space, such as outline and syllogism.

I would argue that these broader interpretations of hypertext enable one to embrace the opportunities generated by information technology without jettisoning the knowledge previously gained from previous forms of writing and thinking. According to this view the distinctions between the book and the web, the striated and the smooth, are less clear cut than they initially appeared to be. Indeed as Deleuze and Guattari argue, the rhizomatic and the arborescent, the smooth and striated, should not be set up in opposition to each other but examined in overlapping conjunction. This understanding creates a space in which counter cultural forms of organisation can offer an enlightening 'contrast to the dominant representations of social order' (Hetherington, 1998, p. 132) and contribute to our understanding of society as a whole.

In this section I have attempted to examine the ways in which both the printed and the electronic word contribute to the formation of the public sphere. I have reviewed debates from the 1990s which argued that the electronic page constituted a smooth space, understood by some critics as being particularly hospitable to the active articulation of political dissent. I have also reflected on the possibility of a theoretically overlapping position in which the apparently anarchic and chaotic qualities of smooth space supplement rather than undermine traditional forms of political discourse.

Space, Ideology, Technology

> Voyaging smoothly is a becoming, and a difficult, uncertain becoming at that.
>
> Deleuze and Guattari, 2004, p. 5320

Deleuze and Guattari maintain that 'all progress is made by and in striated space but all becoming occurs in smooth space' (2004, p. 357). I would argue that this distinction between 'progress' and 'becoming' is particularly problematic for activists and academics rooted in a modernist tradition. The postmodern willingness to abandon a linear and coherent narrative exemplified by 'progress' and 'the book', in favour of a fluctuating series of temporary connections exemplified by 'becoming' and 'the web', has been the source of much academic dismay (Jameson, 1984; Sardar, 1996; Virilo, 1995). In the section that follows I focus on how the organisationally rhizomatic 'becomings' of protest coalition movements structure the textual spaces they produce.

According to Perryman, papers such as *Socialist Worker*, are firmly rooted within an empiricist tradition which aims to 'expose the illusions of reform' (*Guardian*, 11 July 2000) through the force of rational argument. This position has much in common with traditional liberal models of the public sphere and echoes Habermas's belief in the purifying qualities of reason and transparency. Thus despite their rejection of reform through consensual debate, these publications mirror the liberal bourgeois aspiration to create an inclusive and egalitarian space in which reasoned challenges to the capitalist system can be examined and developed.

Papers such as *New Worker* (founded in 1977), *Weekly Worker* (founded in 1993) and *Socialist Worker* (founded in 1968) perceive themselves to be a 'modest' continuation of 'the revolutionary socialist tradition' established by Marx, Lenin and Trotsky. As such these papers offer a broadly Marxist interpretation of world news and current affairs and tend to foreground a political ideology rooted in the workplace, centred on a binary bourgeois/ proletariat class distinction. It should also be noted that many of these organisations and newspapers are (often acrimoniously) interlinked. I focus primarily on *Socialist Worker* as a representative of this genre as it has been the subject of much academic scrutiny[2] and is reasonably well known beyond an activist readership. In doing so I hope to provide a benchmark against which debates about the work of more rhizomatically organised protest coalitions can then be evaluated.

The Socialist Workers Party (SWP) began life in the 1950s (as the Socialist Review Group) and was an attempt to unite the multiple struggles of international socialism (Allen, 1985). It began with a membership of 33 and was, according to Peter Allen, 'federal' in its structure. However, as the organisation grew, this organisational principle became more and more unwieldy. As a result of a generally accepted decline in growth in the 1970s it was decided to reorganise the party according to a more Leninist concept of democratic centralism (Allen, 1985). This decision was not arrived at easily and many well established members of the SWP were forced out of the party.

According to the SWP website the paper strives to share 'the voices of those involved in the many efforts to try to change that world'. However, while the paper claims to respect a diversity of political opinion, it is also and at the same time seeking 'to persuade people of our revolutionary ideas'. Consequently, those outside the party, such as Howard Roake from the Communist Party of Great Britain, maintain that the whole culture of the SWP, like much of the rest of the left, precludes sharp and open clashes of opinion (www.cpgb.org.uk).

The SWP's tendency to at best minimise, and at worst actively discourage, dissent from the pre-determined 'political line' (Birchall, 1981, p. 19) frequently causes the bonds of wider 'political association' to splinter and snap. The rigidity of such an organisational structure tends to exclude the possibility of internal dissent, destroying the dream of a shared socialist 'symbolic space' in which activists can prepare for a fairer future (Mouffe, 2005, p. 20). In Deleuze and Guattari's terms the SWP might be

---

2. See Colin Sparks's 'The working class press: radical and revolutionary alternatives' (1985) for a more general review of Soviet inspired papers, and John Downing in *Radical Media* (2001) and Chris Atton in *Alternative Media* (2002) for an analysis of *Socialist Worker* in particular.

described as being characterised by the 'binary logic . . . of the root tree' (2004, p. 5), a logic characterised by hierarchical communication systems in which each point is predetermined and allocated.

Following the split, the triumphant faction decided to try and reverse declining circulation figures by establishing 'a closer relationship between the paper and its worker readers' (*Socialist Worker*, 13 April 1974). It was agreed that the collective aim should be to create a structure that was 'centralised with a full-time leadership' and 'able to make quick decisions on action' but which also allowed for 'full discussion and debate on the political line' (Allen, 1985, p. 221). Tony Cliff oversaw changes in the paper's tone and presentation intended to attract a new audience and encourage workers to contribute in greater volume to the newspaper. It was hoped that these organisational and editorial changes would lead to the development of more horizontal communication links, both within and beyond the confines of the newspaper.

Allen noted with a degree of pride '. . . we built up a network of people in industry [so that] it was largely written by industrial workers'. However he is quickly forced to qualify this statement by pointing out that many of these industrial workers 'had come from a middle class student background but . . . had gone into factories' (Allen, 1985, p. 211). Moreover while Cliff talked a great deal about seeking 'the abolition of the abyss between producer and consumer' (1974), he went on to discuss and promote workers' involvement with *Socialist Worker* in terms of the distribution rather than the production of texts. Thus he maintained that

A worker that buys one copy of the paper has a very different attitude to it than one who sells a couple of copies . . . it is not therefore only a quantitative change but a radical qualitative change in the relation of the individual to the ideas . . . we will therefore have to organise the transformation of the buyers of the paper into sellers. (Cliff, 1974)

While workers were encouraged to distribute the paper, significantly less organisational effort was put into encouraging workers to write for the paper. As a result 'the by-lines of the Paul Foots, Laurie Flynns and Tony Cliffs' (Cliff, 1974, p. 252) continued to appear regularly in the pages of *Socialist Worker*, while those of the workers failed to materialise at all.

Birchall described *Socialist Worker* as the 'mainline of the communication between the centre and the membership and the periphery' (1981, p. 19), although this use of the word 'centre' is misleading. It implies an organisational structure in which the leadership is surrounded by wider, intercommunicating tiers. However, what Birchall is actually describing is a traditional communication triangle where information is generated at the top and passed on, in an approved form, to the masses below. Thus the push to involve and expand its authorial base was undermined by the essentially one-way relationship which existed, between those who wrote for *Socialist Worker* and those for whom they were writing.

This top-down movement from the intellectual heart of the paper to its (pseudo) working-class periphery can best be illustrated by analysing the paper's letters page. Atton points out that selected and edited letters to the newspaper are the readers' only contribution to the paper. He maintains that the impact of these letters on the publication's contents or editorial policy is unknown but probably minimal and argues that as a result 'any comments from the general readership go against the flow' (Atton, 2002, p. 103). In this way political discussion is constrained by a hierarchical editor/supplicant binary which blocks the flow of potentially challenging horizontal connections, ensuring that the power to define *Socialist Worker*'s political position remains carefully controlled and centralised.

Thus, despite its publically avowed interest in the political position of others, *Socialist Worker* obliges its readership to follow the informational route established and approved by the SWP, requiring its readers to come to the same conclusions as those previously reached by its leadership. Furthermore this 'tendency to agree with party "orthodoxy" rather than seek out political challenges' (Roake, 2009, p. 5) is predicated on an us/them distinction which constantly teeters on the edge of antagonistic. Those who persist in articulating dissent or are perceived to threaten the friend/enemy distinction (Mouffe, 2005, p. 15) are required to be silent or leave the party. Consequently I would suggest that organisations and publications from this tradition tend to be riven with fractures and rifts which constantly undermine socialism's wider aims.

The failure to nurture and strengthen genuinely horizontal ties means that despite the creation of what even hostile critics acknowledge to be 'a hugely impressive organisational machine' (Perryman, *Guardian*, 11 July 2000), the SWP has never 'realized its aim to achieve a mass readership among the British working class' (Allen, 1985, p. 231). This failure seems to justify Downing's assertion that the revolutionary socialist media, despite 'their totalising claims against the monopolies of the capitalist mass media are hardly exemplars of media in action', arguing that they, like their mainstream rivals, are 'hierarchical, limiting and bound by authority' (Atton, 2002, p. 20).

Grassroots media are characterised by the desire to instigate social change and activate politically passive audiences (Atton, 1999; Downing, 1984, 2001). *Socialist Worker* attempted to achieve this end by inspiring the readership from above by creating a top-down communication flow. However an examination of the arborescent organisational and editorial structures employed by *Socialist Worker* reveals the way in which striated publication spaces can block the readership's active participation in the construction of communicative spheres. The advent of computer-mediated technologies appeared to offer a rhizomatic route out of these static and closed down political spaces.

As has been discussed, an understanding of the internet as a network of horizontal communication flows which were inherently supportive of the political left circulated through both mainstream and alternative media spaces. Consequently nascent protest coalitions took advantage of new communications technologies and a plethora of protest-specific sites sprung up across the internet. Such sites were deeply embedded within a pre-existing community ethos which was non-hierarchical and rejected any formal organising structures and editorial roles in favour of more informal horizontal communication flows. Thus the ideals of a particular ideological moment coincided with the technological capabilities offered by internet-mediated communications.

The most influential of these sites was Independent Media Centre or Indymedia. Indymedia was originally set up to cover the protest against the World Trade Organisation in Seattle. Since then it has established itself as the alternative news source for the radical left, describing itself as 'an evolving network of media professionals, artists and DIY media activists committed to using technology to promote social and economic justice' (www.indymedia.org). Indymedia continues to expand rhizomatically. As an organisation it strives to prevent a fracturing into incoherence by a shared commitment to three basic aims: 'generating alternatives to the bias inherent in the corporate media space'; 'furthering the self determination of people under-represented in media production' and 'empowering people through encouraging self publishing in all its formats'.[3]

Whilst material which appears in *Socialist Worker* is structured by editorial judgement, material which appears on Indymedia is structured

---

3. The quotes in this paragraph can all be found on the 'about us' pages of the Independent Media Centre's UK and USA sites.

by time. I would argue that this use of time creates a Riemann space. In these spaces,

> Each vicinity is [therefore] like a shred of Euclidean space, but the linkage between one vicinity and the next is not defined and can be effected in any number of ways. Riemann space at its most general thus presents itself as an amorphous collection of pieces that are juxtaposed but not attached to each other. (A. Lautman cited in Deleuze and Guattari, 2004, p. 535)

Each article appears under a timed and dated headline and introductory paragraph (a shred of Euclidean space) which is followed by a list of links to related posts and back stories (a Riemann collection of amorphous and juxtaposed linkages). This suggests that rhizomatic technology has enabled Indymedia to create a smooth public space in which content is shaped by an interwoven chronology of citizen uploads rather than top-down editorial judgements. Moreover these shreds of space are connected but not attached to an ever changing network of hyperlinks.

Burbules maintains that the hypertextual link is the elemental structure of hypertext and argues that links 'establish pathways of possible movement within the web-space' (1998 p. 105). He points out that 'links create signification themselves: they are not simply the neutral medium of passage from point A to point B' (p. 110). This fluidity creates a multiplicity of equally valid pathways through the internet. The link therefore provokes an unending series of choices or decisions, which must be acted upon if the journey is to progress beyond the current page. Thus, according to critics such as Moulthrop, 'the constantly repeated requirement of articulated choice in hypertext will produce an enlightened, self-empowered respondent' (1994, p. 304) who takes full 'political responsibility' (p. 304) for their chosen route through web-space.

The emphasis on interaction and production has always been an important element of alternative politics (McKay, 1998). In his analysis of zines, Stephen Duncombe comments favourably on the way in which the alternative press blurs 'the distinction between producer and consumer' (1997, p. 315). Duncombe's perspective is borrowed from Walter Benjamin who maintains that political writing should both inspire and enable others to produce, thereby compelling them to abandon mere 'contemplative enjoyment' of struggle. Benjamin suggests that writing of a 'truly exemplary character' is gauged by the 'consumers it is able to turn into producers, that is readers or spectators into collaborators' (1982, p. 216). However, while this distinction has always been a central concern of the radical left, it has been interpreted very differently. Whereas Tony Cliff maintained that readers' involvement in the distribution of *Socialist Worker* constituted production, the creators of Indymedia went further and defined collaboration as the production and publication of texts.

The political potential of this position can be illustrated by the open publishing software used by the Independent Media Centre. Many of the articles and audio/visual material found on Indymedia are followed by an 'add your own comments' button which enables those inspired by the pieces to publish their own response. In order to encourage ordinary people to participate in their own self-representation, the Independent Media Centre has designed a system which requires a minimal degree of technological knowledge and backs it up with additional online and off-line support. It could be argued that the Independent Media Centre has succeeded in creating an 'improved apparatus' (Benjamin, 1982, p. 216) which – through the act of collaboration – facilitates the transformation of consumers into producers. Such communication practices can be understood retrospectively as a form of mass self-communication: 'self generated content, self directed in emission and self selected in reception by many who communicate with many' (Castells, 2007, p. 70).

Such a system contrasts with the *Socialist Worker*'s letters page which requires all responses to be filtered through the editorial process. Sites such as Indymedia are completely accessible to all readers/writers and can fulfil *Socialist Worker*'s failed aspirations to become the movement's 'diary' (Cliff, 1974). However it is important to note that the technological ability to forge these routes does not guarantee their creation: there is always a 'gap between the theory and practice of social movement communication online' (Stein, 2009, p. 764). *Socialist Worker*'s website provides a good example of this gap and illustrates the way in which an online space can be shaped by a print-based mindset.

The online version of *Socialist Worker* simply reproduces material from the print edition and as such it necessarily shares many of its striated qualities. The articles are categorised and prioritised by both authorial status and political relevancy and are ranked accordingly. Moreover, should the reader choose to ignore this hierarchy and navigate their own way through the publication they will frequently be confronted by a prompt which reads 'this article should be read after . . . ' and a link re-connecting them with the route chosen by the editorial team. The passive role of the imagined reader is further illustrated by *Socialist Worker*'s 'comments' system which automatically sends comments to the publication's editors rather than uploading them straight on to the letters page. In this way, despite the technically smooth innovations offered by the internet, online readers of *Socialist Worker* are confined to a traditional and passive role.

Downing argues that 'the essence of the alternative media is the creation of horizontal linkages from the public's communication networks, to assist in its empowerment.' This point is developed by Atton who maintains that there are two ways in which radical organisations can mobilise against institutionalised society. The first method is modelled upon 'the example of the Communist media of the former Soviet bloc' whereby papers 'seek to enthuse its readership into action, whilst those writing remain above the readership' (Atton, 2002, p. 103). The second stems from a socialist-anarchist tradition and is concerned with a 'search for community, and the construction of alternative value systems' (M. Rau cited by Atton, 2002, p. 104).

Downing suggests that social anarchist media organisations have been 'largely eclipsed in the twentieth century' by the emphasis on communism and social democracy and claims that, as a consequence, activists from a socialist-anarchist tradition have become 'associated in the public mind with a love of disorder and creating chaos, even with sanctifying terroristic actions against public figures' (2003, p. 245). The mainstream media tendency to dismiss such protests, delegitimizes their opinions and excludes their position from public consideration. For these reasons Downing maintains that there are too few 'systematic studies of anarchist media' (p. 259) and argues that in the light of the success of the Independent Media Centre 'it makes sense to look again at what may be found in socialist anarchist tradition' (p. 245).

This need to look again at organisations from a socialist-anarchist tradition is made more urgent by recent changes in the socio-political environment. The financial crisis of 2008 has led to a resurgence of challenges to the neo-liberal hegemony and the reassertion of the politics of redistribution. These freshly invigorated movements frequently take the form of networked entities in which clusters of distinct but loosely connected activists mobilise around a particular event or situation before dissipating back into wider culture and society. Colin Ward describes anarchist organisations as 'small functional groups which ebb and flow according to the task in hand' (1972, p. 137-8). In my terms such organisations can be usefully understood as being constituted by rhizomatic structures, utilising horizontal linkages of otherwise 'unstructured clusters of related attitudes' (Woodcock, 1962, p. 453). This echoes Deleuze and Guattari's description of how 'a rhizome may be broken, shattered at a given spot, but will start up again on one of its old lines or on new lines' (2004, p. 10). Occupy and UK Uncut would be examples of horizontally-structured grassroots movements that are distinct but clearly connected to previous iterations of protest.

In order to further reflect upon the relationship between protest organisations rooted in a social-anarchist tradition and technological form I examine two rhizomatically structured print-based alternative media organisations; *Circus Free* and *The Greenham Factor*. *Circus Free* articulated the identities and needs of those opposed to the 1994 Criminal Justice Bill and *The Greenham Factor* expressed the thoughts and hopes of women opposed to the placement of cruise missiles being on the airbase at Greenham Common. While the anti-Criminal Justice Bill was initially understood as a single-issue pressure group, it actually addressed a plethora of issues connected to the rise of neo-liberalism and the corresponding erosion of civil liberties. Similarly, while the women's peace movement appeared to be a very specifically orientated grassroots movement, it was characterised by organisational structures which enabled it to accommodate a multiplicity of varied and sometimes contradictory protest positions. While neither of these two loosely aligned grassroots organisations was ever described as a 'movement', both can be understood as organisational precursors to the environmental movement, the anti-globalisation movement and the anti-war movement. This is because they were oddly rhizomatic inter-organisational, multi-modal organisations, and as such share the characteristics of contemporary protest coalition movements.

Circus Free was a monthly newsletter, published by the Leeds-based Babble Collective in the mid 1990s to campaign against the Criminal Justice Bill introduced in 1994. The Criminal Justice Bill attempted to use a single piece of legislation to criminalise a huge range of previously lawful activities. Consequently it was challenged by activists fighting for many disparate rights such as the right to squat in unused buildings, the right to live as a nomadic traveller, the right to hold parties in outdoor spaces and the right to organise and participate in previously legal forms of protest. Thus it had the unanticipated effect of consolidating opposition to the Bill and uniting many very different oppositional campaigns into a single (albeit fractured and perpetually shifting) movement.

One of the social areas specifically targeted by the Criminal Justice Bill was the 'free party' or 'rave scene'. As a result the public playing of rave music was effectively criminalised (Criminal Justice Bill, 1994). While most youth-orientated, counter-cultural movements (such as punk or hip hop) gain their credibility by antagonising the mainstream, few are actually criminalised. Consequently while the Babble Collective existed in an implicitly political subcultural milieu, it did not adopt a campaigning role until governmental policy began to threaten its continued existence. *Circus Free* has much more in common aesthetically, culturally, and in some ways politically, with the fanzines of the late 1970s than with the newssheets of the revolutionary left, such as the ecologically orientated *Do or Die*. *Circus Free*'s use of scissors, glue and the photocopier enabled it to be far more playful than the print-bound publications. Its pages were characterised by 'chaotic design', 'unruly cut 'n' paste' and 'uneven reproduction' which characterized the fanzines such as *Sniffin' Glue* and *Ripped and Torn* (Duncombe, 1997). Teal Triggs follows semioticians Kress and Van Leewen, maintaining that such publications mark a move away from 'the era of late modernity' and are multi modal in so far as they embrace a 'variety of materials and cross the boundary between art, design and performance disciplines' (Triggs, 2006, p. 69).

Such a production aesthetic mirrors *Circus Free*'s ideological position. The newssheet was produced by a small ever-changing group of individuals connected to the Babble Collective Sound System. Rebecca Tanyar, one of *Circus Free*'s many editors, describes the newssheet as an open conversation between a number of committed activists and the free party scene as a whole (2006, personal interview). Anyone from the wider anti-Criminal Justice Bill community could contribute by sending in copy to a PO Box, although contributions were far more commonly brought up to the DJs decks or handed in at the door of free parties. This material would then be literally cut and pasted into what Tanyar describes as a collection of 'snippets and thoughts' (Tanyar, 2006, interview). Thus while *Socialist Worker*'s letters page seek to inspire from above, *Circus Free* attempted to construct a 'smoothly' expanding patchworked space from within.

Circus Free's commitment to community and horizontal communication forms can be further illustrated by examining its monthly disclaimer. This usually formulaic element of the publication refused to adopt an authoritative top-down tone instead revealing a slightly anxious desire to emphasise the authors' embeddedness in the free-party scene. 'All efforts are taken to ensure accuracy and potency of the stuff written here.

However we're a bunch of sad lunch outs just like the rest of you so we're sorry for any fuck ups'. Thus its striated opening quickly dissolves into a far smoother refusal to adopt – even temporarily – a position of authority.

The title *Circus Free* offers a useful insight into the ways in which the fluidity of its rhizomatic organisational and editorial systems can constitute smooth political spaces. The word 'circus' speaks of pleasure and a temporary escape from the drabness of everyday life. Such carnivalesque notions of pleasure also contain an important political dimension (Bakhtin, 1941), in that they challenge hierarchy and allow 'a utopian glimpse of a community of plenty, freedom and creativity' (Conboy, 2008, 114). On an obvious level the word 'free' refers to the newssheet's rejection of the commercial ethos of mainstream society – it was a free publication. However, on a slightly more complex level it also signifies the desire to be free from the striated principles of organisation which characterise modern bureaucracies and 'all the central mechanisms of power' (Deleuze and Guattari, 2004, p. 19). In this way the newsletter's title encapsulates the free-party movement's utopian desire to construct new and alternative ways of living, thinking and being.

This emphasis on horizontal freedoms is further accentuated by the fact that *Circus Free*, like a circus ring, contains a multiplicity of acts. Thus 'snippets' (Tanyar, 2005) of information cut out from other organisations' publications, such as the Legalise Cannabis Campaign, Friends of the Earth and Festival Eye pass through the pages of *Circus Free*. The newsletter's refusal of striated editorial structures means that there is no single overarching narrative voice. Instead *Circus Free* is a patchwork of loosely-connected spaces of resistance all attempting, in different ways, to 'incite, to induce, to seduce, to make easy or difficult, to enlarge or limit, to make more or less probable' (Deleuze and Guattari, 2004, p. 70–1).

In many ways these rhizomatic linkages and relationships can be seen to foreshadow the inter-activist connections more commonly attributed to the advent of the electronic link. The rhizomatic editorial structures of both *Circus Free* and Indymedia enable different 'acts' or organisations to 'pass through' their pages. Thus cuttings, snippets or shreds are removed from arborescent publications and repositioned within the flux and flow of rhizomatic editorial structures. In this way one could argue that Euclidean spaces have been enveloped and overwhelmed by the Riemann spaces of politically smooth publications.

Moreover *Circus Free*'s use of informal activist connections collapses the editorial boundaries between key contributors and passing party-goers, creating a publication which attempts to create, rather than follow, pre-existing routes or channels. While the internet achieves this end by requiring the reader to choose links in order to progress through internet-mediated communications, *Circus Free* does so by surrendering many of the editorial controls utilised by publications such as *Socialist Worker*. In contrast, the pages of *Circus Free* are characterised by a vivid, kaleidoscopic quality which appears to anticipate the oddly speeded-up nature of (some) internet-based forms of communication.

However, despite the obvious pleasure *Circus Free* takes in being approachable and unpredictable, the newssheet necessarily contains elements of a more traditional or striated system. For example the exuberance of the newssheet's content is held together by various standardised features such as a tadpole ying-and-yang logo on the front cover, a Babble Collective editorial on the first page and a 'Love 'n' hugs' acknowledgements section with a Stonehenge Free Information Network logo at the end. These structural features, like Indymedia's much reproduced web format, establish the publication as an alternative media brand. Paradoxically, but perhaps not surprisingly, it is these standardised features – editorially and textually – which prevent the newssheet from spiralling smoothly out of control.

Circus Free's use of the photocopier appears to foreshadow many of the internet's rhizomatically smooth qualities. This is partly because creativity and innovation have been prioritised over structure and form. *Circus Free* came into being right on the cusp of the digital revolution. Indeed the 'pleasurably laborious' (Tanyar, 2005) task of cutting and pasting a movement's many voices onto a single sheet could almost have been achieved with a click of the mouse. However, while it is tempting to assume a causal relationship between networked forms of communication and the internet, *Circus Free*'s rejection of striated editorial systems within a print-based medium illustrates protest movements' technological independence. Consequently I would argue that the communicative systems employed by global protest coalitions are rooted in ideology rather than technology.

This idea can be developed further by stepping back historically and engaging with a publication produced by the women's peace movement on an IBM Selectric Composer. The IBM keyboard has been described as 'a sort of glorified typewriter' which enabled activists to reproduce the effects of traditional typesetting at minimal cost (Welch, 2007). Through this use of traditional typesetting methods, the women of Greenham

Common were able to produce a surprisingly smooth production aesthetic. In August 1981, 40 women who had been inspired by a women-led march from Copenhagen to Paris walked from Wales to Newbury and established a peace camp on Greenham Common. The women were protesting against the government's decision to site silos for American cruise missiles near common land. The occupation continued for 19 years and was supported by a surprisingly large and dedicated number of women.

Like the anti-Criminal Justice Bill movement, the women's peace movement articulated a multiplicity of oppositional positions to a single piece of governmental policy. The women's peace movement was also similar to the anti-Criminal Justice Bill movement in that it could be described as stemming from a tradition which advocated 'a set of notions about direct action, non-hierarchical organisation, even anti-organisation' (Landry et al. 1985, p. 8). Josephine Eglin maintains that the women's liberation movement equated means with ends. Whilst there are problems which arise from this equation, it nevertheless led the Greenham Women to reject 'the acceptance of leaders, hierarchies and bureaucracies' on the grounds that an acceptance of such systems would have 'implied a concern to seize power and to become part of the very dominant structure, which they were seeking to eliminate' (Eglin, 1987, p. 245). This refusal to reproduce the traditionally arborescent power structures of the mainstream created a space in which alternative organisational systems could – and did – flourish. Consequently the movement developed rhizomatically and, beyond the prerequisite opposition to war and nuclear power made few ideological demands upon its members. Thus it is very different both ideologically and organisationally from the Socialist Workers Party.

The rhizomatic nature of the women's peace movement had important editorial consequences for *The Greenham Factor*. Like *Circus Free*, the newssheet consists of a series of rhizomatically connected quotes, photos and facts, which appear to be printed more or less at random. Indeed *The Greenham Factor*'s rejection of traditionally arborescent editorial structures is so complete that the publication initially appears to be without structure. This gives the strong impression that the publication could be dismantled and put together again in a different order without any real damage being done to its form or content. The impression is compounded by the fact that the pages are all unnumbered and printed in a wide variety of typefaces and sizes. However as Deleuze and Guattari point out, smooth spaces 'are not without laws, even though their differences may be expressed in the guise of "anarchy"' (2004, p. 542). The apparent formlessness of *The*

Greenham Factor should be understood as more than a rejection of the objective, neutralised qualities of hierarchically structured and reasoned debate. Indeed *The Greenham Factor*'s adoption of deliberately rhizomatic linkages is evidently an attempt to foreground the personal and political diversity of its members by carefully, rather than recklessly, placing each voice on an entirely equal footing.

If *Socialist Worker* writes with a 'full blooded certainty' (Perryman, 2000), which depends upon a belief in an absolute truth beyond the confines of its pages, the truths posited in a social anarchist publication like *The Greenham Factor* are rooted in a world more open to a multiplicity of alternative perspectives. The Greenham Women's rejection of oppositional practices enables them to go beyond the 'logic of exclusive disjunction which is supposed to govern concepts' formation in the sciences and all rigorous thought' (Patton, 2000, p. 26). In this way the publication unsettles traditionally arborescent editorial structures, actively foregrounds its rejection of leaders and demonstrates its commitment to the creation of spaces which welcome the articulation of non-hierarchical, polyvocal dissent.

The significance of *The Greenham Factor*'s somewhat chaotic structure should not be underestimated as it allows concepts to change and metamorphose into new and perhaps more revealing insights. The ways in which *The Greenham Factor* aspires to be the teller of alternative truths can be most clearly illustrated through an example. The following quote and accreditation appears towards the middle of the newssheet:

> If a death occurs while you are confined to the fall out room place the body in another room and cover it as securely as possible. Attach an identification. You should receive radio instructions on what to do next. If no instructions have been given within five days, you should temporarily bury the body as soon as it is safe to go out, and mark the spot.
>
> From Protect and Survive, *the government handbook that 'tells you how to make your home and family as safe as possible under nuclear attack'.*

The Greenham Factor refuses to comment on the veracity of this statement. Instead it invites the reader to absorb this information in relation to the many other quotes which surround it and in relation to our own knowledge of the world. Within its own arborescent system (i.e. a government handbook) this quote is no doubt eminently sensible. However within the pages of *The Greenham Factor* and surrounded by anti-nuclear sentiment, the contrast between the clinical burial instruction and the reference to one's 'home and family' becomes both faintly ironic and rather disturbing. Thus in its new context 'Protect and Survive' serves to illustrate the ludicrously naïve nature of the government's response to the threat of nuclear war. Moreover it does so without having to resort to any particular ideological point of view.

The Greenham Factor serves as an example of the way in which smooth spaces can be constituted by the unexpected and sometimes contradictory relationship between a multiplicity of disparate elements. Deleuze and Guattari maintain that 'concepts are defined not by their relations to things or states of affairs but by their relations to other elements as well as their relations to other concepts' (Patton, 2000, p. 24). They argue that whereas arborescent concepts are set within their given systems, rhizomatic images 'are never stable but in state of constant flux as they are modified or transformed in the passage from one problem to the next', (p. 26). While this sense of flux and flexibility strips out much of the comforting security offered by *Socialist Worker*'s static and ordered pages, it also a model of political discourse in which a variety of alternative truths can comment and reflect upon each other.

Stuart Moulthrop follows Lefebvre and identifies similarly liberating implications in smooth spaces, arguing that because these spaces are in a constant state of becoming, they are 'by definition a structure of what does not yet exist' (Lefebvre cited in Moulthrope, 1994, p. 303). Such spaces enable elements of society to play with extremes, 'think about alternative possibilities' (1996, p. 21) and thus 'clarify [the] objectives and the consequences of choice' available to society as a whole (Levy quoted in Kofman and Lebas, 1996, p12). They are spaces which can accommodate perpetual change and therefore enable a continuous multiplicity of previously un-articulated political positions to be expressed. I would suggest that these powerful but undetermined spaces are central to the successful articulation of polyvocal dissent.

Scholars have argued that new information technologies enable activists to be empowered in ways that are beyond the means of traditional print-based alternative media forms (Bennett, 2003; Downing, 2003 and Moulthrop, 1994). However I have argued that *The Greenham Factor*'s refusal to prioritise or rank contributions, like *Circus Free*'s rejection of an authoritative editorial strategy and Indymedia's commitment to horizontal linkages, forces readers actively to navigate their way through a purposefully fragmented and ever-shifting text. Moreover I have suggested that these publications' occupation of printed space rather than cyberspace suggests that the desire to provoke a non-linear progression stems directly from their shared socialist-anarchist tradition and actively facilitates the articulation of polyvocal dissent.

Networked Uprisings: Challenging Mainstream Narratives

Rob Shields argues that spaces on the fringe of society illuminate, rather than corrupt, mainstream understandings of 'normality'. Thus he claims that while the margins are almost by definition places of exclusion, he maintains that they can also be 'a position of power and critique' in that 'they expose the relativity of the entrenched, universalising values of the centre' (1991, p. 277). According to this view, Indymedia, *Circus Free* and *The Greenham Factor* can be understood as 'spaces of freedom, resistance, alternative moral order and authenticity' (Hetherington, 1998, p. 129). Hetherington describes this distanced but connected vantage point as 'seeing through the prism of rejected knowledge' (p. 121). This is a reciprocal view which Walch develops further when he asserts that: '"Alternative" does not mean "outside" or cut off from the mainstream. On the contrary, the meaning of alternative, as integrated Utopia, is contained as part and parcel of the mainstream. Its unutilized or underutilized component' (1999, p. 2).

According to this interpretation, spaces of resistance, such as those created by the texts from a socialist-anarchist tradition, are an integral part of society as a whole and therefore have much to offer the political realm.

In this chapter, I have reflected upon the political implications raised by publications which are rooted in a socialist-anarchist tradition such as *The Greenham Factor*, *Circus Free* and Indymedia. I have argued that unlike *Socialist Worker*, these publications foreground fluctuating and rhizomatic relationships between concepts in an attempt to escape the striated 'dialectic of subversion and resistance' (Cubitt, 1998: 143). They create horizontal networks of communication which refuse to occupy a position of binary resistance and therefore exist outside the managed webs of globalisation. I have examined the ways in which rhizomatic systems characterised the communication structures of socialist-anarchist organisations creating smooth spaces which are particularly open to the articulation of polyvocal dissent. I also explored the ways in which these spaces encourage readers to take responsibility for their own route through political texts, blurring the traditional boundaries between media producers and consumers. By choosing to focus on publications which very clearly predate the widespread use of computer-mediated communications I have demonstrated the way in which socialist-anarchist organisations have adopted information systems which conformed to networked communication flows previously established by these protest movements.

Rhizomatic anarchist structures underpin the organisational systems of many contemporary polyvocal protest spaces such as the anti-globalisation and the anti-war movement. Moreover I would suggest that the uneven and unexpected communication flows between socialist-anarchist coalitions can be understood as a network of rhizomatically interlinked smooth spaces. Blunt and Wills point out that anarchist principles are finding currency in contemporary political protest. They argue that 'DiY culture and protest is reshaping the cartography of organised resistance, forging networks of activists across time and through space' (2000, p. 36). Consequently I would argue that protest coalition movements constitute a network of resistance across political time and space.

4

Into the Streets

It is not easy to see things in the middle, rather than looking down on them from above or up at them from below . . . .

Deleuze and Guattari, 2004, p. 25

The 1994 Zapatista uprising in Chiapas created politically autonomous spaces which privileged 'democracy, liberty and justice' in the belief that they would 'eventually create counter-powers to the state simply by existing as alternatives' (Klein, 2001, p. 14). The International Encounter for Humanity and Against Neoliberalism further developed this space by creating a subaltern sphere in which activists from around the world could gather and reflect upon their alternative political interests and needs. This meeting was enormously influential and culminated in the production of the *Second Declaration of La Realidad for Humanity and against Neoliberalism*. This declaration articulated 'a network of voices and resistance' (Subcomandante Marcos, 2001, p. 123) and in doing so revitalised the socialist-anarchist activist tradition which had previously been eclipsed by communist and social democratic models of political protest (Downing, 2002, p. 245).

These autonomous spaces in Chiapas enabled both the indigenous population of Mexico and anti-globalisation activists from around the world to 'undertake communicative processes' far from the 'supervision' of dominant groups (Fraser, 1990, p. 66). In 2001 the Zapatistas announced their intention to march from the mountainous fringe of their country to its symbolic and geographical heart: Mexico City. In this way Subcomandante Marcos attempted to move the Zapatistas from a marginal position on the edge of national debates and to occupy, albeit temporarily, the mainstream 'arena of power' (Subcomandante Marcos, 2004, p. 8).

The 3,000 km march covered twelve states and took insurgents and international observers two weeks. It followed the routes taken by the revolutionary heroes Emiliano Zapata and Francisco Villa in 1914 and culminated in the Zocalo. The Zocalo is a huge, empty square which covers the Aztec capital, Tenochtilian (razed to the ground by the Spanish conquistadors in 1519), and is fronted by the largest stone cathedral in the Americas and colonial-style governmental buildings. It is a significant political site as it symbolises the violent clash between indigenous and European cultures which continue to shape modern Mexico.

Michel de Certeau describes walking as 'the indefinite process of being absent and in search of a Proper' (1984, p. 103). I would argue that the notion of walking as both a 'lack of place' and the search for a socially and politically better 'place' can usefully be applied to political journeys from the margins to the mainstream (p. 103). When protesters converge on sites of national or global significance, they attempt to illustrate both their own lack of a place within the mainstream and to offer the wider public a glimpse of the view from an alternative political position. Consequently these city spaces become a site of both a physical *and* an ideological struggle, between those 'legitimising what is already known' (Foucault cited in Patton, 2000, p. 25) and those trying to offer the mainstream 'a glimpse of what is possible…a utopia defined not as a no-place but as this-place' (Notes from Nowhere, 2003, p. 182).

De Certeau contrasts an all-empowering solar-eye view over the city with the muddled, in-between experience of those who live within the city. This understanding of the city can be further developed through Deleuze and Guattari's notion of the city as a striated space. According to Deleuze and Guattari, the city can be experienced as a grid-like imposition of 'Royal science', a 'striated space par excellence' (2004, p. 531). Like the technological model of woven fabric, it can be conceived as a series of closed and allocated points. According to this view the capitalist city is a 'force of striation' (2004, p. 531) which uses the bureaucratic systems of money, work and housing to bind city dwellers into a governable mass.

However, Deleuze and Guattari maintain that the city also re-imparts smooth space in the 'sprawling temporary, shifting shanty towns of nomads and cave dwellers' (2004, p. 531). They suggest that the 'explosive misery secreted by the city' rises up from the striations of work and money and creates a patchwork of 'scrap metal and fabric' spaces which hold the possibility of counterattack (p. 531). Here they echo De Certeau's positon by arguing that it is possible to live smoothly even in the most striated of city spaces and to distribute oneself across the city through the uneven footsteps of the urban nomad. Indeed it is in these shreds of Riemann space, constituted by an 'amorphous collection of pieces that are juxtaposed but not attached to each other' (p. 535) that Hardt and Negri identify the potential of the Multitude.

While Deleuze and Guattari set up the abstract notion of striated city spaces and smooth nomadic occupations, they are also very clear that the two spaces can never be entirely separated. The de facto mix of space means that, 'Smooth space is constantly being translated and traversed into striated space; striated space is constantly being reversed, returned into smooth space' (Deleuze and Guattari, 2004, p. 524).

I begin by examining the way in which anti-globalisation movements have inflected notions of mass and militancy in order to position their protest strategies in relation to both each other and the mainstream. I suggest that in the build-up to a large international summit, demonstration affinity groupings can be understood as creating a patchwork of interwoven and overlapping smooth spaces. I also focus on the way in which affinity groupings develop non-textual organisational systems to structure protests, preserve difference and promote solidarity.

The final section of this chapter utilises Deleuze and Guattari's notion of smooth fabrics, such as felt, being constituted by an 'entanglement of fibres' (2004, p. 525). I go on to argue that during summit demonstrations these spaces merge and meld to become a felt-like 'entanglement of fibres' (2004, p. 525). I also focus on the frictions created by the points of contact between differently organised spaces and examine the implications raised by anti-globalisation protesters' refusal to be divided up into 'good' and 'bad' protesters. I will conclude this chapter by reflecting on the ways in which the chaotic and anarchic smooth spaces created by the anti-globalisation movements' summit demonstrations in Seattle, Washington and Genoa, were recaptured and re-enveloped by the striated systems constituting urban spaces.

Reading Demonstrations

I examine the ways in which activists physically occupy urban spaces in order to instigate 'agitational activities directed towards wider publics' (Fraser, 1990, p. 68). I focus on the ways in which the rhizomatic May Day protest structures unsettled, challenged and resisted the arborescent systems and structures of state. These arguments are substantiated by comparing the conventionally organised annual May Day march with the coalition Carnival Against Capitalism which took place on 18 June 1999.

The GLATC May Day demonstration is interesting because it represents a traditional and longstanding form of public protest, dating from the late 1800s when 1 May was set aside as International Workers' Day. However, in more recent years the class-based binaries which characterise this type of celebration have been unsettled by demonstrations, which articulate a plethora of identity-based protest positions. One such demonstration, Carnival Against Capitalism (or J18 as it is frequently known), is of particular significance because it preceded temporally, methodologically and ideologically the 'explosive' summit demonstrations which took place in Seattle, Washington and Genoa.

Traditionally organised demonstrations are invariably headed by a movement's most vocal and recognisable members. These leaders (in this instance the president of the Public and Communication Services Union, Janice Godrich, and the president of the TUC, Gloria Mills) usually carry a large banner which titles the demonstration and articulates activists' principal demands. This provides onlookers with a politically clear and unambiguous focal point. This group is usually followed by a mass of more anonymous protesters who are frequently organised into smaller subsections by banners proclaiming membership of a particular group or organisation.

These sub-sections tend to mirror the hierarchies of the demonstration as a whole. Thus they are invariably headed by the most committed local activists who are then followed by less active core supporters. This leaves non-affiliated individuals to demonstrate popular support, wave placards and generally bring up the rear. Thought of in this way, it could be said that traditionally organised demonstrations read very much like a book. They have a linear narrative, which has been carefully credited, titled and broken up into more or less discrete and manageable chapters. Moreover, as with a newspaper, their intent can be grasped by scanning the banners which head the columns of marchers.

Indeed, one could argue that traditionally organised demonstrations are remarkably text based. Political ends tend to be articulated via banners, placards and flyers which spell out the protesters' demands. Pamphlets and leaflets offering a more detailed account of the demonstration's aims are also distributed amongst the crowd in the hope that these text based forms of communication will initiate dialogue between activists and non-activists members of the community. The printed page is central to Habermas's conception of a well-functioning liberal bourgeois public sphere. Indeed, in the eighteenth century printed newssheets were the *only* 'specific means for transmitting information and influencing those who received it' (Habermas, 1974, p. 49).

Ong argues that the 'mindset' characteristic of print culture (Ong, 1982, p. 133) 'separates the knower from the known' (p. 43) and that this distance creates a sense of personal disengagement from 'the arena where human beings struggle with one another' (p. 43). Applying this idea to the march, an individual (who is, let's not forget, a potential activist) watching the demonstration pass by, is placed in a removed and excluded position. Like De Certeau on top of the World Trade Center (or like the person holding these pages) they read a pleasing, but in many ways 'fictional', account of the political terrain spread out before them (De Certeau, 1984, p. 93). Perhaps even more importantly, activists taking part in traditionally organised demonstrations cannot 'actualise' their own route through the 'constructed order' (p. 93). Instead activists are required/permitted to do little more that walk the pre-arranged route, echo the pre-chosen chants and listen to the prepared speeches.

Thus both the marchers and the observers occupy a politically distanced position. The arborescent structures and systems of traditionally organised demonstrations seem to encourage activists to be the passive element in the producer/consumer binary. For anti-globalisation activists this sense of closure has depressing political implications in that it removes the individual from the everyday struggles of the life-world, making politics appear both alien (it's nothing to do with me) and unalterable (I can't do anything about it anyway). As a result, many anti-globalisation protesters argue that traditional demonstrations are 'essentially' a form of 'lobbying en masse' (Black Bloc protesters, *Genoa Beyond the Hype*, http://flag. blackened.net).

The carefully ordered arborescent structures of conventionally structured demonstrations can be thought of as mirroring many of the hierarchies found in mainstream society as a whole. This enables/requires protesters to move harmoniously within the closed spaces constituted by a 'finite number of stable, isolatable and interconnected properties' (De Certeau, 1984, p. 21). The potentially smooth spaces of resistance are 'translated and traversed into striated space' which coincide with, rather than challenge or contest, the status quo (Deleuze and Guattari, 2004, p. 524).

The tension between smooth and striated space can be further explored by examining coalition demonstrations occupation of striated city spaces.

According to English law,[1] activists must inform the police of their intent to protest within at least six days of the proposed event. However, before the attack on the World Trade Center, the police seldom enforced these laws and invariably did their utmost to facilitate the organisation of mass demonstrations. This is partly because the police were (and still are) keen to maintain their reputation as fair and even-handed managers of legitimate protest. However, it also enables the police to 'enhance [their] control' of dissent, and by implication political disorder, by institutionalising these forms of public protest (Waddington, 1998, p. 130).

An examination of the negotiated routes for most London-based marches illustrates the institutionalisation of protest. Demonstrations in central London usually move between Hyde Park and Trafalgar Square. These locations allow protesters the space to assemble in large numbers, listen to speeches and then disperse within easy reach of the city's major transport links. However, there are two possible routes between Hyde Park and Trafalgar Square. The police invariably 'help' protesters choose a route that takes them along Park Lane and Piccadilly.

The Park Lane/Piccadilly route keeps protesters away from the more heavily populated pavements and therefore severely limits the impact protesters can make upon the mainstream's political consciousness. Moreover marches tend to be scheduled in such a way as to avoid peak periods in the day such as rush hour. Thus one can argue that by utilising the quietest roads and hours traditionally organised demonstrations purposefully keep protesters out of the public eye, ensuring that the articulation of dissent can be woven seamlessly into the pre-existing striations of the city. Thus the 'unofficial "standard route"' (Waddington, 1998, p. 120) enables the police to keep 'the march contained within a "'neat and tidy" boundary' (p. 122). In this way the police ensure that demonstrations are modulated evenly and predictably across both time and space.

However there is an alternative route, which would take protesters right through the heart of the consumerist city and allow protesters to engage the full attention of both motorists and pedestrians along Oxford Street and Regent Street. The fact that this maximum-impact approach is seldom utilised, lends credibility to activists' belief that protest is

---

1. The law states that protesters must notify the police of their intent to demonstrate. Notification is interpreted very differently by protesters and the police and continues to be the subject of much debate.

permitted, sometimes even encouraged, but only on the proviso that it is entirely ineffective (Reiner, 1998, p. 47). Protesters' sense of being, at best, managed within and, at worst, excluded from mainstream public arenas, led anti-globalisation activists to challenge many of the structures which shape public demonstrations. For example, while Reclaim the Streets were obliged by law to inform the police of their intent to demonstrate, they refused to enter into any of the usual pre-demonstration consultations. They justified this position by claiming that their rejection of hierarchies and bureaucracies rendered them organisationally incapable of engaging with the police and therefore maintained that they were unable to elect a leader/spokesperson/liaison officer to conduct negotiations on their behalf. They went on to argue that their horizontal power structures made such negotiation pointless as no single person or group would have the authority to direct protesters during the demonstration (unnamed protester, J18 1999).

This had a significant impact on how subsequent anti-globalisation protests such as J18 and the international summit demonstrations, produced themselves on the ground. Conventionally organised demonstrations offer onlookers a solar-eye view of an unfolding, but predetermined political narrative. However rhizomatically organised demonstrations (like the rhizomatically organised editorial spaces discussed in the previous chapter) refuse to rank or prioritise the political positions available. Consequently the familiar givens of a traditionally organised march are replaced by a sprawling ebb and flow of protest clusters, which emerge and dissolve, repeatedly and at random, throughout the day and across the city. This creates a demonstrative space in which participants, spectators and the police are all immersed in the muddled in-between spaces of everyday political struggle.

These demonstrative spaces deny protesters the sense of security and direction offered by arborescent organisations. They exist at 'ground level' and are composed by a myriad of 'footsteps' which 'cannot be counted because each unit has a qualitative character: a style of tactile apprehension and kinaesthetic appropriation' (De Certeau, 1984, p. 97). This type of space requires individual protesters to produce their own political position, via the links and connections they make with the people/materials around them. Thus rather than consuming the city from above, anti-globalisation protesters weave through the city streets creating the 'thicks and thins of an urban "text" they write without being able to read' (p. 93).

Of course the 'gleeful delight' taken by anti-globalisation protesters in the wilful 'scrambling of conventional categories' (Graeber, 2004, p. 209) is problematic for those charged with the maintenance of public order. Protesters' refusal to enter into pre-demonstration negotiations with the police has the effect of removing the usual temporal and spatial boundaries which normally constrain the articulation of public dissent. They refuse to be read by the 'totalising eye' of the state (De Certeau, 1984, p. 97). In this way Reclaim the Streets' rhizomatic organisational structures and systems clashed with the arborescent systems imposed by the police and other state powers. As a result the city streets became a site of contest between smooth and striated spaces, rhizomatic and arborescent systems, protesters and the police.

This deliberately unsettled position also impacts on the wider public interactions with both protesters and the police. While there are positive aspects of being forced to engage and encouraged to err, it can also create very real problems for the representations of rhizomatically organised protest coalition movements. The loss of orientation experienced by media organisations, accustomed to occupying a comfortable (but mistaken) solar eye position can trigger a reaction of panic. Consequently the mainstream media tend to frame polyvocal organisations as constituting an incoherent, uncontrollable and therefore potentially dangerous threat to civil society (Donson, 2004: Stein, 2001).

In summary, traditionally organised demonstrations are characterised by an ordered and segmented flow which allows them to coincide with the equally administered city spaces which surround them. In contrast Reclaim the Streets' rejection of hierarchical top-down organisational structures in favour of more flexible, horizontal communication systems, creates demonstrative spaces which are in a perpetual state of flux. This creates a dynamic in which the city streets can be represented as a site of contest between differently organised protest groupings as well as between protesters and police. This dynamic in actual space is replicated within the textual spaces constructed by mainstream news narratives. In this way the border between the two is characterised by the 'potential for unexpected encounters to flower between one site and another' (Routledge, 1996, p. 407). In the following section, I suggest that demonstrators' commitment to maintaining solidarity across different protest tactics may offer coalition protest movements a way of contesting dominant narratives in both material and symbolic space.

Militant Masses

> Consensus is no doubt necessary but it must be accompanied by dissent.
>
> Mouffe, 2005, p. 31

According to Habermas, the public sphere is brought into being every time private individuals gather publicly to 'confer in an unrestricted fashion . . . about matters of general interest' (Habermas, 1974, p. 49). However, the liberal bourgeois model's emphasis on the role of the individual in achieving consensus can be problematic. Thus, while Habermas refers positively to the ways in which newspapers and magazines, radio and television create a dispersed 'public body' capable of articulating public opinion, he remains ambivalent about the gathering together of actual public bodies in the form of mass demonstrations. This distrust is rooted in the perceived unreasonableness of the mass and the knowledge that the politically productive enthusiasm of 'the crowd' (Mouffe, 2005, p. 24) can metamorphose into the physically destructive hysteria of the mob.

Despite these theoretical tensions, protest organisations continue to rely on mass demonstrations to show the strength of their commitment, draw attention to their cause and recruit fresh support. Moreover, the size of the turnout is generally seen as an indicator of the success of a campaign. This is because there is a 'moral authority in numbers' (Neale, 2002, p. 148) which most democratic governments cannot be seen to ignore. Consequently one could argue that while mass demonstrations may not constitute a fully functioning public sphere in themselves, they do precipitate the creation of political spaces in which movement leaders can engage governmental leaders in reasoned debate and resolve conflict through consensus. Thus, for example, the Zapatistas' rally in the Zocalo eventually led to negotiations between the movement leaders and the newly elected president of Mexico, Vincente Fox.

However, as Fraser discusses in 'Transnationalizing the Public Sphere', the 'political efficacy' of public opinion has been complicated by the effects of globalisation (2007, p. 7). Consequently the public's ability to exert influence over the political processes of the nation state appears to be waning. Transnational organisations such as the World Bank and the International Monetary Fund occupy spaces constitutionally beyond the criticism and control of the citizenry and are therefore immune to public opinion. For example when the Mexican government 'chose' to amend its constitution in order to receive a $300 million loan from the World Bank, the Mexican people were entirely without democratic recourse.

The growing sense that the relationship between public opinion and governmental legislation is becoming increasingly tenuous has been further compounded by the failure of the United Nations to prevent the American led invasion of Iraq. The 2003 Stop the War demonstration in London was part of a worldwide weekend of protest and was attended by a record-breaking 750,000 people.[2] Despite the well organised demonstration, the government refused to recognise (and therefore legitimise) clearly articulated arguments concerning the relationship between military intervention in Iraq and acts of terror in America, Britain and Spain. As a result of the ease with which governments ignore public opinion, coalition protest movements have increasingly combined their organisationally specific political concerns with an overarching interest in 'protecting and building democracy' in the industrialised world (Bruno, *CorpWatch*, 25 June 2001). This is a concern which can also be identified in anti-austerity movements such as Occupy.

This sense of political distance and exclusion from below is accompanied by a contradictory rhetoric of inclusion from above, as global and national authorities are including more and more oppositional voices to demonstrate their legitimacy. Thus the authorities regularly call on non-governmental organisations, such as the International Red Cross, Save the Children and Oxfam, to report and advise (but not decide) upon matters which fall within the areas of their expertise. Similarly, popular cultural figures reputed to be highly critical of the establishment, such as Bob Geldof, Bono and Angelina Jolie are now routinely coopted by the state and offered a seat at the table of international summit negotiations. In this way, voices which were once part of a dissenting 'them' are redefined and repositioned as part of a consensus building 'us'.

However, Mouffe suggests that spaces which appear to be politically inclusive fail to recognise both the necessity of, and the potential in, partisan politics. She argues that the desire to establish a post-political realm beyond a partisan us/them relationship 'reveals a complete lack of what is at stake in democratic politics' (2005, p. 2). She goes on to claim

---

2. Organisers estimated attendance at closer to two million people. The regular discrepancies between the police's estimates and activists' estimates illustrate the ongoing importance of mass in the battle to secure political legitimacy for alternative ideas.

that a sense of political belonging, defined in an agonistic relation to other political groupings, is central to a well-functioning democracy. She maintains that, 'A well functioning democracy calls for a clash of legitimate democratic political positions . . . such confrontations should provide collective forms of identification strong enough to mobilise political passions. If this adversarial configuration is missing, passions cannot be given a democratic outlet and the antagonistic dynamics of pluralism are hindered' (2005, p. 30).

According to this view, an agonistic us/them dynamic creates a sense of political enthusiasm and precipitates participation in the democratic process, whilst the erasure of political boundaries (via the exclusion of democratically expressed public opinion and/or the recuperative inclusion of dissenting voices) is understood as being deeply harmful to democracy.

It is important to stress that Mouffe is not advocating a return to the class divides which have traditionally structured radical politics. Indeed she explicitly rejects the notion of any single binary divide. Instead she envisages a multi-polar world in which a plethora of political identities compete and intertwine. This is an understanding of the public sphere which foregrounds an uncomfortable and complex in-the-middle position and requires one to come 'to terms with the lack of a final ground' and to acknowledge the 'dimension of undecidability which pervades every order' (Mouffe, 2005, p. 17).

Mouffe goes on to claim that the move towards (an illusionary) post-political world pivots around a change in register from the political to the moral, arguing that politically productive agonistic boundaries are increasingly being replaced and re-articulated in fundamentally antagonistic terms: 'When instead of being formulated as a political confrontation between "adversaries", the we/they confrontation is visualised as a moral one between good and evil, the opponent can only be perceived as an enemy to be destroyed . . .' (2005, p. 5).

The political implications of this shift were evident in the aftermath of the 2001 attack on the World Trade Center. The Bush administration framed its response in terms of the War on Terror and, as Gilroy points out, this rhetorical device disallows dissent and makes the articulation of resistance a 'minor form of treason' (Gilroy, 2004, p. 65). Consequently political opponents become 'enemy combatants' who can be legitimately denied the rights and privileges commonly enjoyed by the citizen.

As Mouffe points out, an antagonistic us/them distinction forecloses and frustrates political debate which can lead to a situation in which protest organisations turn to alternative 'modes of civic resistance, both peaceful and violent' (Mouffe, 2005, p. 81). The Bush administration's use of epideictic[3] (rather than deliberative) rhetoric (Bostdorff, 1994), combined with the anti-globalisation search for alternative means of articulating dissent, created a situation in which the metaphorical boundary between the 'us' and the 'them' was extended and fortified by players on both sides of the divide.

The following section examines two aspects of the ways in which anti-globalisation protest coalitions negotiate the boundaries between agonistic and antagonistic us/them distinctions in their attempts to accommodate difference. Firstly it will analyse international summit demonstrations and explore the ways in which they offer a useful metaphor through which the theoretical us/them distinctions can be further explored. Secondly it will explore the ways in which those involved in the anti-globalisation movement have negotiated the us/them distinction in order to prevent themselves being categorised as an antagonistic 'them' and forfeiting their place within the mainstream public sphere.

In his book *One No, Many Yeses*, Paul Kingsnorth describes Seattle as the first 'post-modern street protest' (2003, p. 62). The demonstrations which took place in Seattle in 1999 were significant in that they included a huge range of protest repertoires, many of which were explicitly confrontational in their nature. As discussed above, these demonstrations were heavily influenced by the Zapatista uprising, but they were also shaped by the way in which international summit meetings occupied city spaces. International summits are unusual in that they require a geographically dispersed group of global players to congregate publicly, in the same place and at the same time. Consequently during summit meetings the intangible political and economic might of global organisations such as the World Trade Organisation or the International Monetary Fund, appears to materialise before our very eyes.

Summit spaces do not integrate into the urban spaces which surround them. Instead they occupy a position beyond the reach of citizens, encircled by a protective wall of concrete blocks and chain link fences. These barriers make the 'usually invisible wall of exclusion starkly visible' (Klein, *Guardian*, 23 March 2001) and in doing so actualise the metaphorical boundaries between the 'them' and the 'us'. As a result, the anti-globalisa-

---

3. Epideictic oratory is one of three branches of classical rhetoric. It is devoted to publicly apportioning praise or blame.

tion protest of the late 1990s tended to focus on breaching the barricades, which literally and metaphorically excluded citizens and activists from the democratic process. The emphasis inevitably led to conflict between activists and the police which protesters attempted to articulate as a 'clash' between legitimate political positions (Mouffe, 2005, p. 30).

The success of protest movements such as the civil rights movement in America in the late 1950s and 1960s was rooted, in part, in their use of non-violent protest. The protest repertoires employed by civil rights demonstrators, such as lunch-counter sit-ins and freedom rides, emphasised what could be described as the enlightenment end of 'value vectors': reason, freedom and sacrifice (Garnham, 2000, p. 274). As Waddington points out, it was in part, the 'dignity', 'eloquence' and 'high ideals' of civil rights leaders such as Martin Luther King which made 'the espousal of white supremacist views increasingly disreputable' (1999, p. 76).

However, the wider public's lack of enthusiasm for political matters, combined with the intensification of commercial pressures, has made it increasingly problematic for activists to access the media and influence the formation of public opinion. The difficulties inherent in accessing a neo-liberal public sphere have led some elements of the anti-globalisation movement to try to create protest positions which can accommodate grittier emotions and even the possibility of physical confrontation. While this understanding is clearly incompatible with Habermas's model of the liberal public sphere, it is one which can be accommodated by Mouffe's more radical interpretation of politics and the political.

Protesters have always felt strongly about their cause – indeed, political passion is almost a prerequisite for political action. Likewise as journalist and land reform activist Monbiot points out, conflict has always been 'an essential prerequisite for change' (Monbiot, 2001). However anti-global-isation protests were novel in that the physicality of a small number of particularly committed protesters was accepted as purposeful by the far larger number of protesters who chose not to engage in confrontational protest acts. In this way these developments were accompanied by a growing, 'painful and reluctant' realisation that 'the G8 leaders, the press and the millions of people for whom these issues were meaningless just a few years ago, are now discussing them only *because* of the fighting in the streets' (Monbiot, 2001, my italics).

However, whereas in the past property destruction and violent arrests were understood as politics gone wrong, they are increasingly being understood (by some elements of coalition movements) as an inevitable and in some ways mundane tool in the wider battle for democracy. Such a position moves away from the notion of confrontation as an almost personal act (often a sacrifice) made for the greater good and requires the legitimisation of the less virtuous ends of the binary pairings outlined above, i.e. passion, power and aggression. This has led many within the anti-globalisation movement to try to formulate an understanding of the relationship between impassioned protest and traditional reason-based democracy.

In Seattle, protesters realised that the 'threat of implied violence' from a minority of protesters inevitably increased the demonstrative potential and potency of the non-violent majority (an unnamed Earth First! protester, *Do or Die*, issue 9, pp. 12–14). As a result, certain elements within the anti-globalisation movement experimented with demonstrative tactics which attempted 'to make the idea of conflict legitimate again' (Tute Bianche spokesperson, Interview with Luca Casarini, 2001). This creates a particularly complex relationship between reason, political enthusiasm and physical confrontation within the public sphere and raises important questions for civil societies in a globalised era.

Physical confrontation has been viewed as the enemy of democracy, with advocates of Habermas's understanding of the public sphere arguing that violence at best distracts private individuals from the reasoned resolution of conflict and at worst coerces them into accepting resolutions which do not promote the greater good. In mature western democracies confrontational politics is therefore frowned upon and physical strength has been replaced, in principle at least, by the force of reason. Thus confrontational violence and hostility is perceived as 'an archaic phenomenon' (Mouffe, 2005, p. 3) in the process of being eradicated by the introduction of political systems which foreground transparency and reason-based communication processes.

Proponents of the liberal bourgeois models make a clear distinction between consensual political discourse and potentially criminal confrontational action. Indeed in many ways traditional protests are expected to be 'merely symbolic' and ensure that 'those whom protesters oppose will not be attacked' (Waddington, 1998, p. 130). So that confrontations which take place during public protests tend to be interpreted as a breakdown in the proper articulation of politics, rather than as a legitimate political expression. However, as discussed in Chapter 2, in a heavily mediated world, the boundary between demonstrative acts of violence and actual acts of violence is increasingly difficult to distinguish.

The anti-globalisation movement's capacity to function on many levels means that its demonstrations invariably go beyond merely symbolic forms of protest. Symbolic challenges, such as creating political tableaux in the heart of the city are accompanied by more disruptive actions, such as blockading buildings, as well as by actual challenges, such as smashing the windows of prominent banks. The fear, real or imagined, that demonstrators pose an actual physical threat to 'our' shops, banks and fast-food outlets creates an atmosphere that teeters on the brink of the revolutionary and complicates the agonistic/antagonistic divide.

The divides which underpin liberal bourgeois models of the public sphere are further complicated by the rise of identity politics which foreground the private by making it public. As Mouffe points out, according to classical models, in order to engage meaningfully in political debate, the individual must leave the private realm and enter the more dispassionate reason-based public realm. However, the postmodern tendency to blur boundaries complicates these neat divisions between public and private, reason and feeling (Simons, 2003, Van Zoonen, 2004). Thus, protest gestures from contemporary protest coalitions tend to be 'both intensely personal and intensely public' (Szerszynski, 2003, p. 197).

It is no longer enough to make (and mean) a political declaration in public – one must also live out the consequences of that declaration within the private sphere. For example, a public commitment to preserving the environment must be accompanied by personal willingness to consume less, recycle more and eschew unnecessary air travel. In this way the anti-globalisation movement's focus on authenticity rather than sincerity erases the traditional distinction between private feelings and public expressions, creating a route through which political passion can move from the private to the public realm. In doing so it creates a space in which the confrontational articulation of dissent can potentially be legitimised.

A key element of this debate focuses on a critical re-evaluation of the '"moves" permitted' by Habermas in the 'language games' which constitute a reasonable and well-functioning public sphere (Villa, 1992, p. 716). Dana Villa builds upon the radical democratic notion of a public sphere characterised by conflict rather than consensus. He discusses Lyotard's attempts to rescue 'the political by unmasking the ideal of consensus' and argues that the assumptions underpinning Habermas's classical model do 'violence' to both the heterogeneity of language games and the plurality of players. He goes on to suggest that Habermas's 'regime of discursive practices' represses the 'spontaneity, initiation and difference' which characterise 'agonistic speech' and therefore 'flattens' the democratic potential of a postmodern public sphere (Villa, 1992, p. 716).

This understanding of the public sphere attempts to conceptualise a space which can begin to accommodate the chaotic complexity and multiplicity of protest coalition movements. It also celebrates both the diversity and, perhaps more controversially, the volatility of the anti-globalisation movement and its 'pagan' style politics. According to Villa, the 'emergence of discordant language games' frees political practice from the 'tyranny of science' and opens up new and alternatively structured political spaces (1992, p. 716). I would suggest that these spaces are more able to accommodate rhizomatically structured elements of coalition protest movements which refuse to order or prioritise their articulations of dissent. This creates smooth political spaces in which a heterogeneous collection of protest pitches, tempos and intensities can flourish.

The unusually impassioned nature of anti-globalisation demonstrations calls into question the ways in which the numbers on a demonstration and the militancy of a demonstration must be calibrated in order to challenge the status quo whilst also maintaining public support for the values and ideals they espouse. The need to balance these two imperatives foregrounds two aspects of political communication which are of particular significance. The first concerns the ways in which different elements of coalitions distinguish their protest positions from those around them. The second focuses on the ways in which those different elements of coalitions maintain movement solidarity across difference.

Calibrating Militancy

> When instead of being formulated as a political confrontation between 'adversaries', the we/they confrontation is visualised as a moral one between good and evil, the opponent can only be perceived as an enemy to be destroyed . . .
>
> Mouffe, 2005, p. 5

The need to reconcile the 'varying goals and multiple identities' of protest coalitions with their 'commitment to respecting and protecting difference and diversity' (Bartholomew and Mayer, 1992, p. 144) has led to some protesters attempting to rethink the notion of political confrontation. In an article which has been reproduced and discussed extensively in alternative and activist forums, George Monbiot turns to the work of Islamic activist Hamza Yusef Hanson.[4] Hanson makes a distinction between *hamoq* which is defined as 'uncontrolled' or 'stupid anger' and *hamas* which is 'enthusiastic but intelligent anger' (Monbiot, 2001). Thus, according to Monbiot, *hamas* is an act of mindful violence which can be comprehended as both a 'protest and an exposition of the reasons for that protest' (www. guardian.co.uk). On the other hand acts of *hamoq* are gratuitously violent and contribute nothing to, but distract from, the wider public debates. This distinction is a particularly useful way of distinguishing between the many differing protest strategies of the anti-globalisation movement as it attempts to integrate confrontation into a traditional reason-based understanding of the public sphere.

One of the ways in which the anti-globalisation movement has attempted to calibrate militancy is through the use of affinity groupings. Affinity groups are a small collection of like-minded individuals and could be described as the smallest organisational unit in the network of organisations that make up the anti-globalisation movement. They were first developed during the 1996 International Encounter for Humanity and against Neoliberalism in Chiapas. However their ideological and structural roots seem to stem from an anarchist notion of autonomy and community rather than being explicitly anti-neoliberalist. Thus like anarchist cells, affinity groups claim to be 'voluntary, functional, temporary and small' and are designed to 'ebb and flow, group and regroup according to the task in hand' (Ward, 1972, pp. 137 and 138).

This combination of flexibility and mutual supportiveness is particularly relevant to anti-globalisation protesters. As a consequence of the lack of a centralised leadership structure, preparations for summit demonstrations are invariably chaotic and confusing. However these protest spaces are not without structure. In this way affinity groups are designed to streamline the decision-making process whilst also adhering to the principles of a fully participatory democracy. When faced with pre-demonstration decisions, each affinity group establishes a consensus and despatches a spokesperson to liaise with the wider anti-globalisation community. This

---

4. Hamza Yusuf Hanson is a western-born Muslim who has established an institute of Islam in America and teaches in Morocco's oldest and most prestigious University, the Karaouine in Fez.

process is, in principle, repeated and repeated until a unanimous consensus is established. This is, of course, an enormously time-consuming and frequently deeply frustrating process.

Affinity groups enabled protesters from all over the world to situate themselves both within the wider movement and within an unfamiliar urban landscape. They were also an attempt to support activists who have to contend with the fear engendered by such heavily policed demonstrative events. During the demonstration, affinity groups stopped being a deliberative arena and became a social support unit designed to protect members from the twin protest hazards of wrongful arrest and police violence. This unusual combination of fluidity and commitment is summed up by a protester in Genoa with the words 'with big hugs to my people I said goodbye. I acquired a new affinity group' (Kalpana cited in Neale, 2002, p. 147).

Affinity groups are characterised by a particular political focus and are colour coded accordingly. In this way activists can become a part of a 'red' communist-based affinity group or a 'green' ecologically-based affinity group. However these groupings go beyond straightforwardly political categorisations and also reflect activists' protest positions. The anarchist Black Bloc actively seeks conflict and confrontation while the White Bloc adheres to a strategy of strictly non-violent resistance. The appealing simplicity of the Red Bloc/Green Bloc, Black Bloc/White Bloc binary divide is consequently fractured by an almost infinite number of political/ protest style combinations. More militant environmental organisations such as Earth First! create 'green' affinity groups which are characterised by a very confrontational demonstrative style while many community-based anarchist groups eschew any forms of violence.

Yet, while anti-globalisation protest may look chaotically disorganised it is actually held together by a rather sophisticated and complex structuring system. I would argue that the networks of affinity groupings which constitute the anti-globalisation movement are inherently rhizomatic in their structures. The smooth spaces created by these rhizomatic groups are similar to those proposed by Deleuze and Guattari's analysis of patchwork. Thus, networks of affinity groups are constructed, 'piece-by-piece' in 'infinite, successive addition' to create 'an amorphous collection of juxtaposed fragments that can be joined together in an infinite number of ways' (Deleuze and Guttari, 2004, pp. 525 and 526).

Before going on to discuss the ways in which the anti-globalisation movement attempts to calibrate its many protesting voices, it may be helpful to pause and examine the three particularly illustrative affinity groupings in greater detail: the Pink and Silver Bloc, the *tute bianche* and the Black Bloc. Whilst these three affinity groupings do not represent the anti-globalisation movement in its kaleidoscopic entirety, their attempts to communicate with the mainstream best illustrate some of the problems experienced by anti-globalisation movements.

The Pink and Silver Bloc's demonstrative style plays on notions of carnival and rebellion. Activists often dress outlandishly in an attempt to emphasise the more pleasurable aspects of political protest. The *tute bianche* bloc is an off shoot of *ya basta*: a group of Italian anarchists who acted as a human shield for the Zapatistas in the early days of the Mexican uprising. They wear white padding in order to highlight the physical vulnerability of protesters in the face of frighteningly well-equipped state forces. Finally the Black Bloc are an anarchist-based grouping of protesters who utilise symbolic property destruction as an empowering means of courting the public's attention. These protesters are 'intentionally menacing'; they wear black clothing and masks in order to protect themselves from tear gas and governmental reprisals.

The way in which these groups function in relation to each other will be illustrated by examining the strategies used to coordinate the summit demonstrations in Prague and Genoa. On these occasions the streets surrounding the summit were divided up into 'pie slices' focusing in towards the red exclusion zone. Each slice was occupied by a particular affinity group utilising a particular tactic or means in order to converge on a shared goal or end. The Pink and Silver Bloc exploit the connections between carnival and rebellion. This protest position not only seeks to invert social order but attempts to do so with 'joyous abandon' (Carnival against capitalism, Quebec cited in Holmes, 2003, p. 346). These protesters follow Bakhtin in arguing that carnival is an inherently political act which creates a 'second world and a second life outside officialdom' (Bakhtin, 1941, p. 6). Moreover, by emphasising the more pleasurable aspects of protest, Pink and Silver activists are 'bringing in to question, subverting and overturning the hierarchical dualities that shape our thinking' (unnamed protester, Why we do it, Rhythms of Resistance). Thus I would suggest that the protest spaces they create, like the pages of *Circus Free*, can be understood as being rhizomatically structured and smooth in so far as they reject order, hierarchy, and stasis in favour of heterogeneity, flux and flow.

The Pink and Silver Bloc aim to create 'a zone through which a whole range of people, not just physically confident able-bodied adults, can act together in challenging the power of capitalism to order our existences'. Perhaps as a direct result of this emphasis on pleasure and inclusivity, the Pink and Silver Bloc has an unusually large female membership. This is particularly significant when one considers the almost inevitable violence of major summit demonstrations. As one protester from Quebec grimly stated 'No one has come here expecting a safe or peaceful struggle. Everyone who is here has overcome fear and must continue to do so moment by moment' (Starhawk, 2003, p. 340).

The Pink and Silver Bloc addresses the fear felt by women confronting all-male police lines, by exaggerating and exploiting the vulnerabilities traditionally associated with femininity. The photogenic contrast between the brightly coloured, fragile bodies of anti-globalisation protesters and the darkly helmeted, padded up bodies of the riot police also offers protection in that it inevitably attracts the media's attention. As one unnamed protester puts it 'no police department wants a reputation for beating a battalion of ballerinas' (Notes from Nowhere, 2003, p. 179). Thus the Tactical Frivolity dancers develop protest repertoires which 'place [. . .] the responsibility for the protesters' safety in the hands of the authorities' (Doherty, 2000, p. 71).

The creation of pleasurable political spaces also has important implications for the formation of activist/not-activist boundaries. The photogenic nature of Pink and Silver protesters tends to create an entertaining, and therefore implicitly less antagonistic 'them'. Moreover by challenging the authority 'of the policeman in our heads' as well as 'the policeman on the streets' (unnamed protester, Why we do it, Rhythms of Resistance) Pink and Silver activists challenge ordinary members of the public to 'expand their limits' (Notes from Nowhere, 2003, p. 175).

The frequent physical confrontations between protesters and police lead certain sections of the media to represent police as part of the mainstream 'us' and protesters, as an antagonistic 'them'. However, the Pink and Silver Bloc's use of carnivalesque protester repertoires enables them to unsettle these boundary distinctions and articulate alternative possibilities. They attempt to reach beyond the boundaries of the anti-globalisation movement as an alternative public sphere and communicate with a possibly sceptical but increasingly engaged mainstream. Consequently they entice the mainstream and attempt to politicise them by stealth.

The Pink and Silver Bloc occupy a celebratory position within the patchwork of political philosophies which make up the anti-globalisation movement. The inclusiveness of this ethos is articulated differently by other affinity groupings. Like the Pink and Silver, the *tute bianche* bloc aims to include as many people as possible. These groups accept that summit demonstrations will inevitably involve a degree of conflict but 'seek to minimise violence and aggression' wherever possible (Pink and Silver protester, Genoa: Pink and Silver on 'actions' day). This emphasis on inclusivity and participation is designed to encourage ordinary members of the public 'to step off the pavement and into the street' (unnamed protester, Why we do it, Rhythms of Resistance) and unsettles the mainstream notion of 'protester as elite expert' (Purkis, 1996, p. 205).

The Italian priest Don Vitaliano, who participates in the *tute bianche* bloc, maintains that 'in the face of the total control of the world, which the owners of money are exercising, we have only our bodies for protesting and rebelling against injustice' (Vitaliano, 2003, p. 175). It could therefore be argued that the *tute bianche* strategy shares the carnivalesque desire to bring 'the body back to public space' (Notes from Nowhere, 2003, p. 175). I would also suggest that this notion further develops Dana Villa's conceptualisation of a postmodern public sphere characterised by the 'agonistic dimensions' of emotion and the private self. A *tute bianche* protester describes the bloc's strategies as 'literally embodying our feelings – performing our politics with our whole bodies' (p. 202). Here the public sphere goes beyond being a discursive realm, characterised by reason and restraint and becomes a sphere of embodied and emotional conflicts.

The *tute bianche* also develop and extend the Pink and Silver Bloc's ability to deploy photogenic visual metaphors which differently articulate their position in relation to the police and the political mainstream. For example, the *tute bianche* attempt to focus the world's attention on the brutality of the state and to recast protesters as the political heroes of the day. However, whilst Pink and Silver activists self-consciously parody uniformed marching bands and military formations they ultimately aim to avoid, or at least minimise, violence. The *tute bianche*, in contrast, follow the protest tradition established by the civil rights movement and actively provoke state violence. They stand 'shoulder to shoulder' and repeatedly attempt to 'push into police lines with their shields' (Neale, 2002, p. 146). As a result of the inevitable violence provoked by the strategy, *tute bianche* volunteers 'wrap their fragile bodies with foam and padding' (Ryan, 2003, p. 357) in an attempt to 'shelter' themselves – and other less robust protesters, from the full force of the police's wrath.

In this way both Pink and Silver activists and the *tute bianche* attempt to unmask the violence of the state in much the same way as the advent of summit demonstrations has successfully unmasked the exclusivity of global institutions, such as the World Trade Organisation and the International Monetary Fund. The *hamas* of these activists can also be interpreted as an attempt to reframe or invert the way in which the mainstream media represents the relationship between protesters and the police. Protesters 'resist in a way that maximises their effectiveness but also exposes the contrast between the force used by the authorities and protesters' moral superiority' (Doherty, 2000, p. 70). Importantly, this interpretation of *hamas* and its role within the public sphere attempts to rehabilitate demonstrative violence whilst still condemning the gratuitous violence which alienates so many non-activist members of the public.

Despite the honourable intentions that underpin acts of *hamas*, many within and beyond the anti-globalisation movement remain unconvinced by the arguments of Pink and Silver or *tute bianche* protesters. For some this is a straightforward question of principle, whilst for others it is a more strategically complex issue. This is because, in the confusion and chaos of most summit demonstrations, the fine line between acts of *hamas* and *hamoq* can blend and blur into invisibility. Moreover even carefully thought out acts of *hamas* can quickly unravel into spontaneous acts of *hamoq*. These issues can best be illustrated by examining the role played by the Black Bloc during international summit demonstrations.

The Black Bloc are routinely criticised by both the alternative and the mainstream media. Their provocative demonstrative style has been condemned as at best ineffective and at worst dangerous. Thus the mindless violence of the Black Bloc is frequently thought to rob the anti-globalisation movement of the all-important moral high ground. The Black Bloc is also accused of distracting the media's attention from the anti-globalisation movement's political agenda. Perhaps most importantly it is thought that the antics of the Black Bloc minority give the state an excuse to 'crack down' on the far more peaceful majority and therefore deters ordinary members of the public from participating in future anti-globalisation demonstrations.

On first inspection, Black Bloc violence appears to be a straightforward case of *hamoq*. After all, how can 'the destruction of cars and amenities in the working class residential areas' (Genoa beyond the hype, Black Bloc protesters) of Genoa be interpreted as anything other than mindless violence? This understanding of the Black Bloc is accentuated by the mainstream media's 'perennial interest in novelty, spectacle' and, of course violence (Rootes, 2000, p. 38) which causes uncontextualised acts of violence to be photographed, magnified and sent around the world. As a result Kenny Bruno from CorpWatch argues that anti-globalisation 'demonstrations are in danger of losing their mass appeal as shattered glass, smashed ATMs and Molotov cocktail-wielding anarchists continue to be their most prominent feature' (Interview with Luca Casarini , 2001).

However, in his foreword to Deleuze and Guattari, Brian Massumi points out that 'A concept is a brick. It can be used to build the courthouse of reason. Or it can be thrown through the window' (Massumi, 2004, p. xiii). This duality of purpose complicates the rather neat and tidy categorisation of mindful and mindless violence. Where the mainstream and the more 'fluffier' end of the anti-globalisation movement see gratuitous violence, the more 'spiky' Black Bloc maintain that they are engaged in carefully controlled acts of 'symbolic physical damage to multi-national capitalism' (Black Bloc participant interview, 2000). According to this view, Black Bloc protesters are hurling concepts as well as bricks at the global authorities and are therefore engaged in a hostile, but legitimate, form of communication.

Black Bloc activists argue that their actions inspire rather than deter ordinary members of the public from participating in future demonstrations. Thus they suggest that 'people at the protest, and those at home watching on TV, can see that a little brick, in the hands of a motivated individual, can break down a symbolic wall' (Black, Letter from inside the Black Bloc). Some Black Bloc protesters even argue that 'finding joy in an act of militant protest' (Black Bloc protester, With love from a Black Bloc activist) which counteracts the crushing alienation of life under global capitalism is inherently empowering and 'beautiful' (Black Bloc protester, With love from the Black Bloc).

Finally, Black Bloc protesters also maintain that the Black Bloc's demonstrative style is as inclusive and protection-orientated as the Pink and Silver Bloc or the *tute bianche*. They argue that their 'intentionally menacing' clothes (Black, Letter from inside the Black Bloc) distort the truly inclusive nature of the Black Bloc's activist base. As Black points out 'the behaviour of Black Bloc protesters is not associated with women, so reporters often assume we are all guys'. In this way Black Bloc protesters suggest that their 'uniform' of black combat trousers and balaclavas puts 'the group before the individual' (Black, Letter from inside the Black Bloc) as well as protecting individual members from the pernicious gaze of the state.

Thus one could argue that the Black Bloc, like the Pink and Sliver Bloc and the *tute bianche*, use clothes to articulate their protest position, encourage participation and protect activists from state violence. If the juxtaposition of violence and positive emotion is unusual, the notion of protest as empowering and uplifting is common. According to these views one could argue that Black Bloc and Pink and Silver protesters are simply employing different methodological means of achieving the same ideological ends.

In this section I have argued that activists' occasionally violent attempts to enter the red zone can be seen as examples of *hamas* rather than *hamoq*. The Pink and Silvers and the *tute bianche* constitute inclusive utopic blocs intent on demonstrating the depressingly homogeneous nature of global capitalism. Similarly, the Black Bloc's attempts to force entry into the red zone confronts and challenges the authorities' ability to exclude them from the global decision making process. Thus the network of affinity groups which make up the anti-globalisation movement calibrates and literally embodies the determination of private citizens to be included in the global decisionmaking process. In doing so, affinity groupings expose the determination of the global authorities to exclude them from that process. In the following section I focus in more detail on the ways in which the inclusion/exclusion distinction is drawn.

An Entanglement of Voices

> An entanglement of many players who do their own thing while feeling a part of a greater whole.
>
> Notes from Nowhere, 2003, p. 178

As affinity groups are constructed around a personal commitment to shared political interests and protest strategies, it could be argued that well-functioning affinity groups constitute almost perfect classic public spheres. They are, after all, small consensus-based groups in which private individuals meet as equals in order to discuss the public issues of the day. However, while the 'norms of procedural rationality' (McLaughlin, 1993, p. 603) may be one method of achieving consensus within affinity groups, the anti-globalisation movement also privileges passionate and intensely personal discourses.

While affinity groups are apparently open and accessible to all, they are in actuality bounded by the exclusion of non-harmonising voices. However as Dahlberg points out

> All framing of meaning, including what it means to be rational, necessarily involves exclusion. A relation of inclusion/exclusion is part of the very logic of discourse, even democratic discourse (2007, p. 835).

Within protest organisations that plan to break the law and/or commit acts of violence, the inclusion/exclusion dynamic is frequently underpinned by an often justified sense of paranoia. As a result, those planning the logistics of J18 created a closed group in an (ultimately successful) attempt to thwart police surveillance and infiltration. This 'lack of transparency' creates a 'de facto "inner circle"' (unnamed protester, *J18 1999: Our resistance is as transnational as capital*, http://www.network23.nologic. org), which inevitably undermines the anti-globalisation movement's aim, to embody the open and horizontal democratic principles of a new and better order.

While Habermas's original conception of the public sphere cannot easily accommodate the existence of such us/them dynamics, the creation of an inner grouping is far less problematic for radical democratic models of the public sphere. Indeed it can be understood as a vital element in the 'clash of legitimate democratic positions' which constitute a well-functioning democracy (Mouffe, 2005, p. 30). The potential problem lies not in the formation of an us/them distinction but in the formation of us/them distinctions which are antagonistic in their nature. Consequently the challenge for protest coalitions is firstly to recognise the differences in their protest positions and then to legitimise those differences within the movement and the wider public sphere. This is something which anti-austerity coalition movement Occupy has done very successfully with the slogan 'we are the 99%'.

Anti-globalisation movements can be understood as individual elements of an 'overarching', egalitarian, multi-cultural public sphere (Fraser, 1990, p. 68). This interpretation allows affinity groups to be conceptualised as 'sites of direct or quasi-direct democracy' which enable individuals to take part in discussion designed to determine the protest strategies of both individual anti-globalisation movements and the anti-globalisation movement as a whole. Within this alternative sphere, coalition movements have developed a series of rhizomatic protest repertoires which foster difference 'in a form which does not deny political association' (Mouffe, 2005, p. 20). At the same time, the 'porousness, outer-directedness, and open-endedness' of such groups ensures that the inter-cultural communications between anti-globalisation movements are, on the whole, preserved (Fraser, 1990, pp. 68–69).

Kingsnorth maintains that the anti-globalisation movement is 'not really an organisation at all – it is rather a method' (2003, p. 73). I would argue that the anti-globalisation movement is actually a multiplicity of methods. The Notes from Nowhere collective revel in the pleasures of carnival while pragmatically noting that it 'is a tactic, nothing more' (2003, p. 179). Similarly, confrontational anarchists recognise the Black Bloc to be 'primarily a tactic and...a dress code' (K, 2001, p. 31). The anti-globalisation movement's decision to separate strategic means from ideological ends minimises internal conflicts. It also exploits weaknesses inherent in the authorities' use of rather traditional and very centralised communications systems. As a result there is a general consensus within the anti-globalisation movement that 'the key to the success' of summit demonstrations lies in a 'diversity of tactics, interrelating' and causing disruption in a way that is essentially 'unpoliceable' (unnamed protester, *Black Bloc Interview*, 2000).

The anti-globalisation movement differs from more conventionally organised radical left groups (such as the Socialist Worker's Party) in that it refuses to scapegoat its more militant members. To further reflect on the implications raised by the anti-globalisation movement's refusal to be divided (and ruled) by mainstream representations of protester violence it is necessary to return to my analysis of the summit demonstrations which took place in Genoa 2001. The ideological roots of the Black Bloc lie in autonomous anarchist movements. As a result Black Bloc activists place a great emphasis on genuineness in general and the realisation and expression of authentic private feelings in particular. The demonstrative actions of the Pink and Silvers and the *tute bianche* on the other hand are controlled and metaphorical and would be described by the Black Bloc as dubiously sincere, rather than truly authentic. The Black Bloc's distaste for the 'fake' or 'manufactured' vulnerabilities of the Pink and Silvers and the *tute bianche* is coupled with a willingness to place their own bodies 'directly in the cogs of the mega machine'. The body is transformed into a truly authentic 'weapon and statement of resistance' (Notes from Nowhere, 2003, p. 202).

Indeed many Black Bloc activists argue that their protest strategies are more honest and authentic than those proposed by less confrontational affinity groupings. Interestingly their criticism of *hamas*-based demonstrative strategies have much in common with reservations traditionally held by more conservative, if very different, cultural commentators, such as Jürgen Habermas and Daniel Boorstin. Thus an article provocatively entitled 'Beware of the white dressed cops' by self confessed 'Italian rioters' denounces actions by the *tute bianche* as 'fake'. Like Habermas and Boorstin, they maintain that these manipulated or manufactured protest scenarios inevitably pacify potentially active members of society. The Black Bloc argue angrily that the *tute bianche* merely aim 'to catch more and more potentially angry people, willing to practically attack Power and its meetings, and take them on a do-nothing-and-look-at-us fluffy aside' (*tute bianche* protester, Beware of white dressed cops).

This theory was taken to its limits in Genoa when the carabinieri shot and killed an anonymous and apparently threatening Black Bloc protester. The ensuing investigation revealed the protester as twenty-six year old Carlo Giuliani. An emotional and articulate internet posting entitled 'with love from the Black Bloc' resolutely maintains that 'if these summits take place to the sounds of helicopter blades amid burning barricades and tear gas it unmasks the real violence hidden by the slick corporate show' (Black Bloc protester, With love from the Black Bloc).

In the weeks after Genoa a cross-movement consensus emerged that argued that Carlo Giuliani's obvious vulnerability and his very public death shocked the global public into recognising the institutionalised violence of the state. The Black Bloc in Genoa provoked a situation in which the authentic vulnerability of protesters exposed the institutionalised violence of the state and therefore seriously 'undermined the legitimacy of the Italian government' (Black Bloc protester, *Genoa beyond the hype*, http://flag.blackened.net). As a result, one could argue that the violence of Black Bloc activists revealed the hidden vulnerabilities of democratic nation states.

Perhaps more surprisingly, and more importantly, echoes of this view-point emerged in the mainstream media. For example a 'bewildered' Monbiot, a life-long advocate of non-violent direct action, found himself arguing that 'it is simply not true to say that Carlo Giuliani died in vain' (*Guardian*, 24 July 2001). The alternative press too was surprisingly full of statements supporting the protest tactic of the Black Bloc. For example, *tute bianche* activist Wu Ming posted the following comment; 'we refuse to save our ass to the detriment of the Black Bloc, we regard them as fully legitimate part of the movement and refuse any distinction between "good protesters" and "bad protesters"' (Black Bloc protester, Non criminalizziamo il Black Bloc!).

Activists' refusal to be categorised by the mainstream press as either 'good' or 'bad' is the result of more than straightforward political solidarity. There is a growing belief that the anti-globalisation movement's 'extremely diverse' use of tactics is not a weakness but the source of its power (K, 2000). Many activists, such as George Monbiot describe the growing sense of political futility engendered by having lifetimes of 'polite representations' ignored by the mainstream press and the powers that be (Monbiot, *Guardian*, 24 March 2001). 'Mary Black' contrasts this depressingly familiar scenario with the shock and exhilaration she experienced the first time she 'saw someone break a window at a demonstration and suddenly we were all on the six o'clock news' (Black, Letter from inside the Black Bloc).

Violence clearly sells but, as most elements within the anti-globalisation movement recognise, it is not enough in itself. As Monbiot points out, Carlo Giuliani's *hamoq* 'forced a response because other people were practising *hamas*' (www.guardian.co.uk). Thus one could argue that while the violence of the Black Bloc is in many ways designed to 'court publicity' (Black, Letter from inside the Black Bloc), it is the demonstrative actions of the Pink and Silver Bloc and the *tute bianche* which add additional layers of meaning. In this way the Pink and Silver Bloc's butterfly wings and the *tute bianche*'s white padding provide an essential and photogenic media foil to the more confrontational actions of both other anti-globalisation protesters and the police authorities. Thus the anti-globalisation movement creates an 'entanglement of many players who do their own thing while feeling a part of a greater whole' (Notes from Nowhere, 2003, p. 178).

Anti-globalisation movements' successes in inter-cultural communications depend, in part, on their refusal to conflate strategic means with political ends. Whilst previous radical movements such as the Women's Liberation Movement tended to conflate means and ends in the belief that dubious methodologies could in some way contaminate the purity of an organisation's social and political goals, the anti-globalisation movement has purposefully separated means and ends. David Graeber argues that if the anti-globalisation movement had a motto it would be 'if you are willing to act like an anarchist now, your long-term vision is pretty much your own business' (2004, p. 214). This enables many disparate groups and organisations to avoid the factional conflicts which traditionally characterise left-of-centre politics and to coalesce into a single movement of many means and many ends or, as Subcomandante Marcos describes it, a movement of one no and many yeses (2001).

This is not to suggest that means and ends are entirely unconnected, but to argue that the anti-globalisation movement rejects a uniform or prescriptive attitude to political protest which enables them to deploy a complex combination of communicative strategies. This can range from the Pink and Silver's attempts to create a demonstrative style which seeks 'to minimise violence and aggression' but is also unashamedly 'confrontational' (Pink and silver protester, Genoa: Pink and Silver on 'actions' day – report) to the Black Bloc's more controversial commitment to the use of 'physical force against symbols of capitalism' (Black Bloc activist, *Genoa beyond the hype*, http://flag.blackened.net). Thus a Black Bloc activist movingly and intelligently describes the 'contamination' (Black Bloc protester, *A response to press misinformation*, http://ludd.net/retort/msg00200.html) between different affinity groups merging under police attack. S/he claims that this entanglement of tactics both 'gave the space life and refused to give it up' and therefore concludes by stating that 'the smashing and burning created by the Black Bloc is as important as the music and colour created by the carnival' (Pink and silver protester, Genoa: Pink and silver on 'actions' day – report).

Anti-globalisation protesters' rejection of the neat and tidy boundaries expected by the public and favoured by the police, is not a rejection of the notion of organisation per se. As American feminist Freeman points out 'there is no such thing as a structureless group – the only question is what kind of structure a group has' (cited by Landry et al., 1985 p. 10). Anti-globalisation organisations and spaces do have a structure – demonstrations as large and successful as the May Day marches, J18 and Seattle do not happen spontaneously! However, they are structured very differently from mainstream spaces and as such their demonstrational structure is often unrecognised. Just as we do not notice the 'severe distortion' (Rosello, 1994, p. 139) of space and time imposed by linearity so we fail to recognise the more rhizomatic systems which structure the smooth spaces produced by organisations such as the anti-globalisation movement.

This assertion can be best illustrated by briefly examining the role of marching bands. Bands have always played a key role in political and military campaigns. They attract the attention of spectators, provide an uplifting focal point of interest and boost the morale of flagging participants. Traditional marching bands (i.e. those with a 4/4 rhythm) have been rooted within working communities, enabling band members to meet up regularly, develop a suitable repertoire of numbers in a sociable and convivial atmosphere and creating a musical style that is cheerfully upbeat as well as carefully measured and disciplined. Anti-globalisation demonstrations have developed and extended this tradition by utilising a musical style based upon syncopated samba rhythms. These rhythms deliberately interrupt and unsettle the traditional one-two-three-four beat of a marching band. The introduction of samba also reflects how the traditional class-based binaries which underpin traditional protest is interrupted and unsettled by more complex, globalised identity positions.

The basic hiccupping samba rhythm lends itself to improvisation, which enables comparative strangers (many of whom may well have flown in from all corners of the world) to play together quickly and fluently. Samba blocs can be as 'flexible or fluid as you want' (Trice, interview, 15 June 2004) and are therefore uniquely equipped to respond to the chaotic ebb and flow of large-scale anti-globalisation protests. They require neither sheet music nor expensive instruments, which is particularly important in a protest environment which can quickly become confrontational. Moreover the porous nature of a samba bloc means individual players can fall behind, switch blocs, stop for a snack or get arrested, without jeopardising the continuation of the basic samba beat. In this way the samba band enables activists to coordinate their activities without forcing the individual to compromise their sense of self or their ability to move freely through differently organised demonstrative spaces.

The UK-based Rhythms of Resistance and the Seattle-inspired Infernal Noise Brigade are two of the most influential bands within the anti-globalisation movement. Rhythms of Resistance describe themselves as 'a subversive version, a circus parody of the uniformed military marching bands that accompany regiments into battle' (unnamed protester, Rhythms of Resistance, www.schnews.co.uk). In this way the increasing popularity of samba could be read as part of protesters' attempts to 'create a space of carnival, where all rules are broken and everything is possible' (Whitney, 2003, p. 216). This position attempts to combine the confrontational and the frivolous in a way that is particularly characteristic of the anti-globalisation movement.

This desire to subvert expectations and create new possibilities is echoed by the Infernal Noise Brigade who are explicit in their aim to go beyond the traditional marching band's role of inspiring joy and boosting morale. The Infernal Noise Brigade describes itself as a 'tactical mobile rhythmic unit' dedicated to the strategic movement of large crowds and the 'propaganda of sound' (Whitney, 2003, pp. 218–20). In this way samba bands are increasingly being used by coalition protest movements to coordinate the strategic movement of large, 'leaderless' crowds (p. 220). Thus the Infernal Noise Brigade not only subverts traditional protest repertoires, it also attempts to construct new ones.

The effectiveness of samba as an organisational tool was illustrated in an anti-globalisation demonstration which took place in Barcelona in 2001. The demonstration was 'tired' and on the verge of dispersing when rumours began to circulate that protesters had been arrested and were being detained without access to legal representation on the other side of the city. Rhythms of Resistance upped the tempo and led the demonstration across Barcelona to the police station where the activists were being held. Consequently protesters and their attendant camera crews were able to bear witness to the illegal activities of the state and so contributed to the eventual release of the activists.

Rhythms of Resistance, like the Infernal Noise Brigade, are a reaction against the 'bleated slogans and carried signs' of traditional demonstrations. This desire to interrupt and disorder the usual sequences of political time and space with 'disorienting rhythmic patterns', as the Infernal Noise Brigade themselves point out, is, 'entirely post-textual' (Whitney, 2003, p. 20). Samba bands bring an element of cohesion to an otherwise wild and uncontrolled form of protest. In doing so they illustrate that the anti-globalisation movement's refusal to cooperate with the authorities is not a sign of political weakness or a rejection of organisation per se, but an attempt to create alternative rhizomatic organisational structures which reflect the ideological positions of the activists involved.

While this structuring quality can be viewed as a strength – in that it offers anti-globalisation demonstrations a focal point in an otherwise undefined space – it can also be viewed as a weakness in so far as it creates opportunities for the re-striation of previously smooth spaces. This can best be illustrated by examining a demonstration which took place in London in 2001. For much of the day the rhizomatically organised demonstration had been spread unevenly (and uncertainly) across the city. However, in the afternoon a samba band began to draw the crowd, which had the unanticipated effect of creating an impromptu and very traditionally structured demonstration. This enabled the police to regain control of the city by corralling the massed demonstrators between two junctions, thus re-imposing the arborescent boundaries that constitute striated spaces.

5
Unsettling Spaces

However limited a public sphere may be in its empirical manifestation at any given time, its members understand themselves as part of a potentially wider public.

Fraser, 1990, p. 67

The escalation in violence which characterised many of the demonstrations called by the anti-globalisation movement in the late 1990s was abruptly halted by the attack on the World Trade Center in 2001. Governments hosting international summits citing the threat of terrorism, began to hold meetings in geographically inaccessible locations. For example, when Britain hosted the G8 summit in 2005 they chose an isolated hotel in Scotland. The removal of summit meetings from metropolitan centres effectively re-concealed the briefly-made-visible boundary between the politically included and the politically excluded. As a result, the radical left has begun to explore alternative means of accessing mainstream public arenas.

The development of alternative protest strategies was complicated by the introduction of the Patriot Act (2001) in America and the Anti-Terrorism, Crime and Security Act (2001) in the United Kingdom. Both these acts were hastily introduced in the aftermath of the attack of the World Trade Center and make it far easier for the authorities to pre-empt and/or control the articulation of dissent. Despite the frequently hostile reception, activists continue to promote alternative ways of thinking. However much of the time and attention which activists invested in challenging the political and social implications raised by the growth of neo-liberal policies has been re-channelled into attempts to coordinate a global response to the invasion and continued occupation of Afghanistan and Iraq. Despite this shift in focus, the anti-war movement continues to utilise and develop protest strategies introduced by the anti-globalisation movement.

In previous chapters I examined some of the ways in which rhizomatic organisational systems and structures contribute to the creation of smooth, potentially empowering political spaces. Chapter 3 focused on the relationship between organisational, technological and alternative media spaces while Chapter 4 explored the relationship between grassroots political movements and the organisation of protest spaces. As these chapters show, there are many organisational and ideological advantages to be derived from communications systems and structures that foster inclusive upward-flowing communicative networks. However, there are also more problematic consequences which can arise from the utilisation of such systems and structures.

This chapter examines the uneven frontier between the chaotic 'rhizomatic' structures of the anti-war movement and the more regimented or 'arborescent' structures of the mainstream. It will argue that the internet and demonstrative events can create spaces in which the mainstream's need for narrative order and protesters' preference for creative flux, temporarily overlap, circumventing some of the organisational differences which have traditionally underpinned the protester/non-protester relationship. Moreover, it will suggest that these shared spaces can contribute to the renegotiation of the boundaries which both separate and connect the political margins to the mainstream and therefore contribute positively to the formation of an invigorated and agonistically inclusive public sphere. These arguments are illustrated by an analysis of Brighton and Hove's anti-war movement in general and two of its protest groups in particular: Smash EDO and Save Omar.

Historically the town of Brighton has always existed on the physical and symbolic margins of the country. It grew in reaction to the 'ordered, confined, corporatist life' of spa towns such as Bristol and Bath and as such has always been 'associated with pleasure, with the liminal, and with the carnivalesque' (Shields, 1992, p. 73). Brighton and Hove is a city that enjoys pushing social boundaries and I would suggest that these qualities also characterise its political life. Brighton is home to many well-established and vibrant activist networks such as Schnews, Rough Music and Brightonactivist.net.[1] There are also a number of more globally orientated groupings that attempt to highlight issues raised by the on-going conflicts in the Middle East. These would include organisations such as the Brighton and Hove Palestine Solidarity Campaign, Sussex Action for Peace, Smash EDO and Save Omar.[2]

---

1. More information about these newssheets can be found at www.schnews.org.uk/index.php, www.roughmusic.org.uk/index.html and www.brightonactivist.net.

2. More information about these campaigns can be found at www.brightonpalestinecampaign.org, www.safp.info, www.smashedo.org.uk, www.save-omar.org.uk.

Sussex Action for Peace was set up in 2003 'to campaign against the occupation of Afghanistan and Iraq and US and UK foreign policy' (http://safp.info/). It used to meet fortnightly and has organised a number of events designed to express public dissatisfaction with the foreign policy decisions made by the New Labour government. For example, it commemorated the death of the 100th British soldier in Iraq by reading the names of those killed in the conflict at a candlelit vigil in Brighton city centre and organised a public demonstration in response to the continued bombing of Iraq, Afghanistan, Palestine and Lebanon in 2006.

Smash EDO is an anarchist/autonomous pressure group which campaigns to close down the British arm of a US-based arms multinational, EDO MBM Technology Ltd. EDO has a factory on the outskirts of Brighton which produces the release mechanisms of the Paveway bomb system. The campaign's activities were initially directed entirely towards the workers and management of EDO, with protesters engaging in a series of on-site direct actions. These included largely symbolic actions such as the weekly noise demos, during which activists attempt to disrupt the working day by banging drums, ringing bells and blowing whistles. These demos were supplemented by more elaborate demonstrative events. For example at Halloween, protesters were invited to attend a masked 'Ghosts, Goblins and Ghouls' party (email received 30 October 2006), while the bombing of Gaza and Lebanon was marked by a Horrors of War Exhibition 'for the staff of the death factory' (email received 18 July 2006).

Smash EDO has also engaged in far more forceful direct actions designed to impede the production of trigger mechanisms. The EDO site can only be accessed by a slip road. As a result activists have invested a considerable amount of time and energy in separating the factory from the rest of the city. For example a metal cage has been used to block the slip road, concrete and manure have been dumped at the gates, and the doors have been glued shut. Activists have also attempted to infiltrate the factory. They have organised telephone blockades, painted slogans on the walls and hung banners from the roof. Finally, unknown protesters have interrupted the manufacturing process by 'decommissioning' office equipment. As a result of these more confrontational actions, protesters' relations with EDO and the police became increasingly strained.

As the campaign progressed, arrests during on-site demos became more frequent. Protesters believed that the police were deliberately arresting and re-arresting individuals in an attempt to incapacitate the organisation and provide material which might justify the injunction brought against activists by EDO. In an effort to protect themselves from what they saw as police brutality, Smash EDO took the decision to move the focus of their campaign from the factory site on the fringes of the city into the heart of the city centre. This position was articulated by the campaign's spokesman, Andrew Becket, who told the Brighton and Hove *Argus* that 'part of the reason for holding demonstrations in the centre of town is so there are lots of people watching who can see how the police behave' (Anti-war protesters converge on city, 11 June 2007). Thus it was hoped that the state activities would be subject to 'critical scrutiny and the force of public opinion' (Fraser, 1990, p. 58).

Save Omar is a very different type of campaign. It is a civil liberties orientated organisation which campaigned for the release of a Brighton resident Omar Deghayes from Guantanamo Bay. Deghayes was born in Libya but fled with his mother and siblings following the assassination of his father in 1987. The family were granted exceptional leave to remain in Britain and settled down in Saltdean. In 2001 Deghayes went travelling and attempted to return to Britain following the attack on the World Trade Center. However, he was captured by bounty hunters in Pakistan who mistook him for a Chechen rebel and returned him to Afghanistan. He was held in Bagram airbase before being transferred to Guantanamo Bay, some time in 2002. His arrest, transportation, internment and torture were all breaches of his human rights as laid out by articles 5, 9 and 11 of the Universal Declaration of Human Rights. Having been detained illegally for five years, Deghayes was finally released without charge and returned to Britain in December 2007.

Save Omar activists engaged in tried and tested protest repertoires, such as gathering petitions, organising public meetings and lobbying key political figures. However the campaign also attempted to instigate change by embarking upon a series of public relations initiatives designed to win over public opinion and strengthen its negotiating position. Activists invested a considerable amount of time and energy in creating and promoting (through their increasingly close relationship with the local paper, the *Argus*) a series of eye-catching demonstrative events. Examples of such events would include creating political tableaux, orchestrating 'die ins' and performing *Air Guantanamo* in front of key mainstream and alternative venues in Brighton and Hove. Since Omar's release the group has changed its name to Brighton Against Guantanamo and campaigns for the release of the remaining 'enemy combatants' from detention and is particularly concerned with securing the release of Shaker Aamer, a detainee from Bournemouth.

Brighton and Hove's anti-war movement can be read as a rhizomatically organised protest coalition movement. The political aims and objectives of Sussex Action for Peace, Smash EDO and Save Omar frequently overlap. A small group of dedicated activists tends to be found splitting their time and attention between various meetings and events. The flux and flow of ideas and activists which characterises the inter-organisational linkages within the wider anti-war movement is replicated within Save Omar and Smash EDO's internal structures, which have expanded and contracted 'organically' over a period of years (Smash EDO activist, 2005). Notwithstanding the sense of inter-organisational flow which characterises Brighton and Hove's anti-war movement, the coalition is not a homogeneous grouping; it is perpetually shifting, textured and uneven.

Bailey et al. maintain that rhizomatic (media) organisations are elementally defined by 'elusiveness and contingency' (2008, p. 27) and argue that these qualities enable them to destabilise the 'rigidities and certainties' of both market and state whilst also protecting them from the mainstream's dominating force (p. 29). However despite this sense of optimism, Bailey et al. are forced to acknowledge that the 'lack of a clear "common ground"' (p. 30) between differently constituted organisations has the potential to create a whole new series of problems. For example, the lack of a 'unifying structure' identified by Bailey et al. (p. 30) almost inevitably creates a communications gap between rhizomatically structured protest coalitions and more arborescent mainstream organisations.

Such a gap is particularly problematic in mature western democracies, where political change is predicated on the increasing support of the electorate. In these circumstances the need to communicate effectively with the wider public becomes paramount. The mismatch between rhizomatic and arborescent communication systems can impede the flow of information from the political margins to the mainstream. This clash is experienced particularly acutely by those who are accustomed to working within more bureaucratic or arborescent systems. Journalists, for example, who are accustomed to working within the tree-like command structures of subject desks frequently find themselves at a loss when attempting to access organisations which have chosen not to develop similarly 'hierarchical modes of communication and pre-established paths' (Deleuze and Guattari, 2004, p. 23).

Acknowledging the need to bridge the gap between their own marginalised political spaces and the wider mainstream, many resource-poor organisations began to use internet press rooms to promote their concerns. Organisations such as Save Omar and, to a lesser extent, Smash EDO, also use demonstrative events in their efforts to create durable and positive frames around complex global issues. These protest strategies construct spaces in which the needs of coalition activists and professional journalists temporarily overlap, creating a route through which information can travel from the political margins to the mainstream.

Changes in the media environment make such spaces particularly attractive to mainstream media providers. As a direct result of economic pressures, corporate news organisations are moving away from the expensive and time-consuming strategies of investigative journalism. Instead, they are moving towards more reactive forms of journalism that rely on a 'routine source supply' (Curran, 2000, p. 35). As Brighton and Hove *Argus* journalist Andy Dickenson points out, many news stories reach journalists through their inboxes (in interview, 2007). Thus, while protest organisations remain at a considerable disadvantage in that they must enter mainstream arenas without the economic resources *and* professional expertise enjoyed by their establishment opposition, this type of information management can redress some of the power imbalances traditionally experienced by resource-poor organisations.

Demonstrative events in fact offer protest organisations an advantage over their more arborescently organised corporate counterparts in that they tend to be 'colourful, fun, outlandish and outrageous' and more likely to capture the jaded eyes of professional journalists (Monbiot, n.d.). Of course 'passive news gathering' (Aldridge, 2007, p. 46) is viewed by some as 'a deadly serious dependency' which both demeans and undermines public trust (Dinan and Miller, 2007, p. 3). This is a view which has been explored thoroughly by academics such as Franklin (1994), Howard Tumber, (2000) and Dinan and Miller (2007) and is shared by many anti-war activists in general and Smash EDO activists in particular. As a result the push towards engagement with the wider public is complicated by a simultaneous desire to maintain a critical distance from mainstream organisations, such as the media and, less surprisingly, the police.

Preserving the Gaps

Policeman: 'I believe that you are an organiser of this procession. I notify you that . . .'
Protester: 'I'd like to notify this officer that there are no organisers on this procession . . .'

Anti-arms trade protest 2005

As an anarchist/autonomous organisation, Smash EDO foregrounds the rejection of fixed roles and bureaucratic hierarchies of traditional organisational systems in favour of horizontal communications flows and collective decision-making. The absence of formalised communication structures combined with activists' reluctance to adopt potentially incriminating roles such as 'leader' or 'organiser', means that such organisations seem to find communicating with a hierarchical 'mainstream' particularly problematic. This situation is further exacerbated by the fact that mainstream organisations frequently interpret the reluctance to adopt social roles as wilfully abstruse at best and downright hostile at worst.

These issues can be further explored by examining the online and offline debates prompted by Smash EDO's strategy of non-engagement with the police. Smash EDO is part of a DiY protest tradition which tends to be a 'youth-centred and directed cluster of interests and practices' (McKay, 1998, p. 2). These counter-cultural clusters frequently define themselves in direct opposition to the interests and practices of the mainstream and foreground lifestyle issues which 'have left the realm of the intimate and the private and become politicised' (Mouffe, 2005, p. 40). Consequently George McKay has described the attitude of many anarchist/autonomous protest groups as 'cagey' (1998, p. 9). This is unsurprising given the borderline legality of many direct actions.

Indeed, in many ways protesters are quite right to feel suspicious of 'outsiders'. An inquiry found that following the attack on the World Trade Center, the online and offline activities of anti-globalisation protesters was routinely monitored by American intelligence services ('NY police spied on anti Bush protesters', *Guardian*, 6 March 2007). It has also been revealed that the police authorities regularly recruit 'informants' from within the activist community ('Police paid informants £750 000 in four years', *Guardian*, 8 May 2009; 'Police caught on tape trying to recruit Plane Stupid protester as spy', *Guardian*, 21 April 2009). Legal action is currently being brought against the police by ten women who were 'duped' into forming long-term relationships with undercover officers who had infiltrated their protest groups (Evans and Lewis, 2013).

Smash EDO's decision to define itself in opposition to the mainstream creates clearly demarcated spatial, political and cultural spaces between activists and non-activists in which pre-existing subcultural tensions are exacerbated by activists' more recent occupation of internet-based subaltern spheres. Some academics argue that the internet allows 'global activists' to 'communicate with each other under the mass media radar' as well as enabling them to 'get their message into mass media channels' (Bennett 2003, p. 18). Proponents of this view suggest that the internet can fulfil the dual functions assigned to subaltern public spheres by Fraser, whereby 'on the one hand, they function as spaces for withdrawal and regroupment, on the other hand they function as bases and training grounds for agitational activities directed towards wider publics' (Fraser, 1990, p. 68). However, this position fails fully to recognise the important and contradictory tension which exists between these two functions.

In analysing this contradictory dynamic, Sarah Thornton's work on rave culture is helpful. Thornton maintains that the movement of 'previously subversive signs' (1994, p. 180) from the sub-cultural margins to the mediated mainstream is frequently perceived as a form of cultural betrayal. According to this view, the cardinal cultural sin of 'selling out' actually means '*selling to outsiders*' (Thornton, 1994, p. 180). This dynamic is particularly problematic when the sub-culture in question has an explicitly political dimension. In these circumstances the need to communicate with the wider public is complicated by a desire to maintain the boundaries which separate them from what they perceive to be a commercially mediated and essentially inauthentic mainstream.

Unsettling Space

There was a distinctly 'cagey' quality to communications leading up to direct actions which took place in the build up to the 'Blix bloc inspection'. In order to commemorate the 2003 invasion of Iraq, Smash EDO activists performed a 'citizens' weapons inspection' of the factory site (Blix bloc in Brighton, 11 August 2005). Protesters wearing white boiler suits and dust masks marched up to the gates of the EDO factory and demanded the right to inspect the property for weapons of mass destruction. As a result the police, citing the threat of intimidations and coercion, restricted the demonstration to an hour under section 14 of the Public Order Act (1986). When some activists refused to disperse within the allotted time, several arrests were made.

The organisation of the Blix bloc inspection took place in face-to-face meetings between activists in traditionally alternative venues. Smash EDO's preference for this type of meeting stems from a long anarchist tradition designed to foster an atmosphere of 'trust and mutual support' (Hollingsworth, 1986, 295). Such exclusive face-to-face meetings are particularly important to direct action organisations as they enable activists to accept newcomers into the activist community, whilst controlling the outward flow of potentially incriminating information. In this way, geographically bounded subaltern spheres enable activists to 'undertake communicative processes that were not, as it were, under the supervision of dominant groups' (Fraser, 1990, p. 66).

Despite the implementation of these protective organisational strategies 'the impossibility of a fully inclusive "rational consensus"' (Mouffe, 2005, p11) was revealed by the discursive aftermath of the Blix bloc inspection. Following the arrest and eventual release of the arrested Blix bloc inspectors, it became clear that divisions existed within Smash EDO regarding the strategies which had been employed during the demonstration. These divisions were articulated on the Indymedia South Coast website and illustrate how the loss of the reassurance offered by traditional face-to-face communications contributes to a situation in which the friend/opponent distinction can tip over into a far more antago- nistically orientated friend/enemy distinction.

Interestingly, the arrested activists' ire was directed not at the police who arrested them, nor at the journalists who later misrepresented them, but at the distinctly un-cagey activists who had chatted to the police during the demonstration. Thus, despite articulating a strategically reasonable argument in favour of engagement with the police (based on the idea that if everyone was arrested and constrained by bail conditions then the day-to-day running of the campaign and the weekly noise demo would become unviable), these activists were perceived as being somehow less 'committed' to the cause and subjected to very high levels of counter- cultural disapproval for infringing the unofficial embargo on inter-sphere communications.

The online discussion began with one of the arrested activists forcefully maintaining that 'on good demonstrations, the police are made to feel unwelcome and are made to go and stand away from protesters' (Jaya, 2005).[3] When another activist questions the validity of this strategy s/he is quickly turned upon by other members of the group who suggest that s/he 'examine some of the secrets of your soul and see where that leads you' (Taff, 2005). These comments suggest that subaltern spheres are as effectively policed from the inside as they are from the outside and that the borders of alternative or subaltern spheres, like the borders of the mainstream, are in a state of perpetual re-negotiation.

3. Jaya, Taff and Baa-Baa Black Sheep's comments can all be read at 'Blix bloc in Brighton' www.indymedia.org.uk, 11/08/05).

The hostility directed towards activists who interacted with the police can be read within the context of the 'advent of sub-politics' (Mouffe, 2005, p. 32). In her work on direct actions within the environmental movement, Szersznski argues that the demonstrative actions of protesters invite us 'to understand their signs, gestures, as in some way extensions of their personal beings' (1999, p. 193). According to this view, a willingness to be arrested demonstrates the 'authenticity...commitment... [the] rooted realness of action' upon which protest culture is predicated (McKay, 1998, p. 32) so that individual transgression of these values can be read as a dubious, inauthentic and a potentially contaminating weakness which devalues the 'sub-cultural credibility' of the group as a whole (Doherty, 2000, p. 71).

As Mouffe points out, 'in the field of collective identities we are always dealing with a "we" which can only exist by a demarcation of a "they"' (2005 p. 15). This is a view shared by Dahlberg who argues that a 'relation of inclusion/exclusion is part of the very logic of discourse, even democratic discourse, (2007, p. 835). In this instance I would suggest that the more committed or 'spikey' activists felt that the more conciliatory or 'fluffy' activists were 'putting into question the identity of the "we"' (Mouffe, 2005, p. 15). Moreover the antagonistic us/them distinction involved securing the 'goodness' of activists willing to provoke arrest through the 'condemnation of the evil' in those activists who were reluctant to do the same (Mouffe, 2005, 74). This 'move' served to justify the exclusion of voices that were perceived to be 'bad' from public debate.

Jaya's comments were quickly followed by a discussion as to whether the site is a 'safe' place to have a 'private' discussion. Thus 'Baa-baa Black Sheep' maintained that 'a public forum like this, accessible to all is not the place to do it...publishing this kind of internal conflict only strengthens the enemy and also gives them information they can use against us' (Baa-baa Black Sheep, 2005). This comment presumes that the site is being monitored by hostile forces and illustrates how even dialogic encounters between 'friends' and 'opponents' can be haunted by the ever present possibility of 'enemies'.

An incident which took place on the Indymedia website in December 2005 illustrates this more negative conceptualisation of the public sphere. A Smash EDO activist posted an e-mail she had received from community police officer Sean McDonald, addressing the group's refusal to discuss possible demonstration routes. It was widely ridiculed as 'bizarre' and 'unrealistic' by activists (Police try to 'negotiate' EDO march, 2 December 2005, and Additions; march summary). However, humour quickly turned to anger when PC McDonald confirmed activists' fears that the site was being monitored by attempting to engage them in the debate. PC McDonald was promptly and vigorously flamed off the site. This leads one to conclude that the virtual subaltern sphere, like the actual official sphere, employ ridicule and vilification to police its own 'private dinner party' boundaries (Hollingsworth, 1986, 288).

The fear of surveillance means that despite its many logistical advantages, virtual subaltern spheres are frequently perceived by activists to be essentially unknowable and therefore un-trustable places. Thus, while in the early days of the anti-globalisation movement activists benefited from the police's general lack of internet awareness, the anti-war movement now functions in the knowledge that its activities are almost certainly being monitored by state authorities. This realisation inevitably challenges the notion of the internet as offering secure and inclusive sites for political communication. The Habermasian vision of a transparent, sincere and universally accessible public space has been replaced by a Foucauldian nightmare in which individuals communicate under the silently disciplining gaze of dominant groups.

While the classical liberal model's emphasis on the universal accessibility of the public sphere inevitably renders such interactions problematic, radical democratic models are more able to accommodate such frictions and fractures. Provided one accepts the radical democratic notion of a multiplicity of themed spheres which stand in a sometimes contestatory relationship with one another, exclusion does not necessarily constitute a threat to a well functioning democracy. Indeed, as Mouffe points out, a radical democratic approach strives *not* to overcome the we/they distinction. Instead it struggles to 'envisage forms of construction of we/they compatible with a pluralistic order, (2005, p. 115). In this way, radical democratic models strive to foreground, rather than deny, the boundaries which necessarily formulate the construction of the public sphere. A clearer understanding of the inclusion/exclusion distinction is of particular relevance to the understanding of coalition protest movements which must constantly negotiate the boundaries between different coalition elements. Moreover coalition protest movements must grapple with issues whilst simultaneously managing the boundaries which exist between themselves and the mainstream.

A Shared Here?

Despite the tendency to occasionally preclude spaces in which smooth and striated ways of thinking can overlap, the internet does offer more open transitional spaces in which newcomers can gather information. For example the pressure group websites, which tend to be used as holding spaces for protest information, rather than as discussion forums, have the potential to bridge the gap between smooth subaltern spheres and their more striated and official counterparts. Thus while internet archives create an, albeit problematic, entry point into previously inaccessible political spaces, internet press rooms can afford a more controllable route through which previously unheard arguments can travel towards the mainstream. Virtual press rooms are particularly significant to anarchist protest groups in that they enable protesters to bypass the mainstream's striated and vertical forms of communication and replace them with smoother, more empowering 'horizontal linkages' (Downing, 1995, p. 241).

Smash EDO's website occupied by two virtual spokespeople called Andrew Becket and Michelle Tester, demonstrated this dynamic. The presence of electronic virtual spokespeople enables Smash EDO activists to remain loyal to key anarchist tenets such as collectivity and anonymity, whilst also meeting the communicational requirements of striated mainstream organisations such as the *Argus*. For example, when 'outsiders' such as journalists contact Smash EDO, potential responses are discussed in a face-to-face environment until a satisfactory collective response has been formulated. This response is then passed on to via email and consequently enters the 'official' public sphere (Smash EDO activist, personal interview, 2006).

The ability to communicate anonymously and collectively in this way is particularly significant given EDO's repeated attempts to bring court actions against the 'leaders' and 'organisers' of Smash EDO. Virtual spokespeople are purposely unaccountable figures. In this way Becket and Tester continue a long and respected tradition established by semi-folkloric figures such as Captain Ned Ludd or Captain Swing. However electronic spokespeople are more than mere mouthpieces: they act as a mechanism which enables an organisationally smooth space to be constantly 'translated and traversed into striated space' and striated spaces to be constantly 'reversed and returned into smooth space' (Deleuze and Guattari, 2005, p. 524). Thus the Smash EDO website theoretically enables outsiders to access an otherwise complex and inaccessible sub-cultural milieu, whilst also enabling protesters to assert and maintain some level of control over both their organisational structure and their representation in the mainstream.

Journalists from the *Argus* seem to be unaware of Becket and Tester's un-embodied existence. Letters from 'Andrew Beckett' and 'Michelle Tester' appear regularly in the letter pages and their views are routinely included in articles relating to Brighton's anti-war movement. Internet-mediated communications therefore seem to enable protesters to bypass the mainstream's striated and vertical forms of communication. Consequently, it would appear that virtual press rooms can accommodate the strategic needs of both activists and journalists, enabling activists to act autonomously while also providing journalists with a single, quickly verifiable and economically viable source of information.

This is not to maintain that such spaces solve all or any of the problems commonly associated with the radical left's attempts to communicate with the mainstream media, but to suggest that these spaces temporarily unfix the meanings usually ascribed to them, thus enabling 'each interested party' to attempt 'to place their discourse onto it' (Purkis, 2000, 216). This understanding of the relationship between alternative and mainstream spheres 'requires coming to terms with the lack of a final ground and acknowledging the dimension of undecidability which pervades every order' (Mouffe, 2005, p. 17). While this approach refuses the stability of a permanent order, it is useful in that it can accommodate the complexities and contradictions of organisations which are predominantly, but never entirely, smooth.

Bridging the Gap

> Like rhizomes, alternative media tend to cut across borders and build linkages between existing gaps.
>
> (Bailey et al., 2008, p. 28)

From online pressrooms as spaces in which the rhizomatic activities of protesters and the more arborescent practices of professional journalists temporarily overlap I now turn to similarly overlapping spaces in offline environments. Activists from the Save Omar campaign appear to have circumvented many of the problems experienced by grassroots activists attempting to attract and maintain the wider public's attention, by organising an ongoing series of interlinked demonstrative events which are 'colourful' and 'fun' (Monbiot, n.d.). Such events add flavour to a campaign characterised by an otherwise dull and inaccessible series of consultation papers, legal discussions and governmental committee meetings.

The demonstrative events utilised by the Save Omar campaign were always framed locally. In 2005 anti-war activists produced a picture postcard which plays upon Brighton's traditional seaside image. The familiar pebble beach fills the foreground while the sea, sky and pier stretches away in the distance. The curly script, expresses the familiarity and warmth usually associated with postcard writing and cheerily reads 'Wish you were here!' However, this familiar and formulaic scenario is made stark and strange by the postcard's fourth element: an orange jump-suited figure kneeling, bound and hooded on the shingle. The blocked letters to the right of the figure read 'Brighton: Home of Guantanamo Detainee Omar Deghayes'. The colour orange gathers and foregrounds the phrase 'Wish you were here', the jump-suited figure and the word 'Brighton' and suggests – without offering any explanation – that these three elements are in some way meaningfully interlinked.

The juxtaposition of contradictory elements deliberately unsettles our understanding of the seaside postcard as a genre. In doing so it throws up a number of unexpected questions which must be addressed and evaluated before they can be fully understood. 'Why would a Guantanamo detainee be on Brighton beach?' 'Why would we wish him to be in Brighton rather than in Guantanamo?' 'Where is here?' The text on the back of the postcard further develops this visual conundrum. It reads

Dear Margaret Beckett,
We ask you to make representations to the US government about the illegal detention of Omar Deghayes. If you need to know more about his case please visit www.save-omar.org.uk or come and talk to us in Brighton.

                                                            Yours sincerely

Thus while the image on the front of the postcard addresses the spectator, the message on back addresses the government. As Billig points out, 'national topography is routinely achieved through little banal words' (1995, p. 96). In this instance the words '*we* ask *you*', and 'talk to *us*' (my italics) creates a liberal, civil rights based dexis of home and community. Moreover by requesting the government to engage in transnational talks with the US government it invites 'them' to reposition themselves and become part of a localised 'us'. In this way the postcard attempts to highlight and disrupt the local, national and global identity formations which define, and to a certain extent constitute, the debates around the War on Terror

The website address signposted on the back of the postcard leads to the Save Omar Campaign's homepage which gives a comprehensive account of the circumstances surrounding the detention of Deghayes. Whilst material produced by the Save Omar Campaign's website clearly asserts a belief in Omar's innocence it did not demand his unqualified release. Instead it emphasised the human rights abuses suffered by Deghayes and called for his right to a free and fair trial under the rules of the Geneva Convention. In doing so it attempts to challenge the discourse around his detention and question the friend/enemy distinction which positions detainees as enemies 'whose demands are not recognised as legitimate and who must be excluded from the democratic debate' (Mouffe, 2005, p. 5).

The uncompromising 'with-us-or-against-us' rhetoric of US foreign policy makes maintaining a nuanced position within the public sphere particularly difficult (Bush, *CNN*, 6 November 2001). In line with this rhetoric, mediated public debates surrounding the war on terror tend to foreground religious, political and cultural differences. For example, public discourses on Muslim women's role in the western workplace centred on the notion of the veil as a 'barrier' or 'mark of separation' (Veil should not be warn says Muslim peer, *Guardian,* 20 February 2007) . These antagonistic divisions make it particularly difficult for groups like the Save Omar Campaign to overcome the 'friend/enemy distinction' (Mouffe, 2005, p. 15) and articulate a coherent and cohesive public response to the detention of 'enemy combatants' in Guantanamo Bay.

In order to move away from a view of demonstrative events and visual metaphors as somehow inherently hollow, and towards an understanding of political imagery as potentially beneficial, it is necessary to focus in more detail on the nature of the visual. Stafford points out that there is a long and sophisticated line of thought which differentiates between 'imagery used as equivalents to discourse (or as illustration)' and imagery used as 'an untranslatable constructive form of cognition (as an expression)' (1996, p. 27). According to this second definition, images should be understood not as empty displays of visual rhetoric but as meaningful acts in themselves.

Crucially, according to traditionalist critiques, the manipulation of the masses by the media in general and the public relations industry in particular, takes place '*without* public awareness of its activities' (McChesney, 1997, p15, my italics). However activists' deliberate use of artifice, like their use of masks, enables protesters to foreground (rather than disguise) the persuasive nature of their appeal and thus side-step the 'sense of deceitfulness' which Corner identifies as being at the core of both propaganda and spin (2007, p. 673). In this way their symbolic forms of protest allow them to distinguish themselves from the 'self-interested strategizing . . . and vapid slogans that are customarily imputed to candidates for governmental office' (Feher, 2007, p. 13). Similarly, the Save Omar Campaign's use of explicitly constructed images enables them to maintain an elevated degree of authenticity and avoid both external and internal accusations of spin.

Unsettling Spaces

Activists' use of artificially constructed visual metaphors to produce real change in political circumstances and create new ways of thinking within the community is evident in their mobilisation of demonstrative events. In the summer of 2006, Save Omar activists learned that Starbucks was selling coffee to American service personnel stationed in Guantanamo Bay. They e-mailed the company asking them to clarify their role in operations at the camp and received a reply stating that as an international company Starbucks was obliged to 'refrain from taking a position on the legality of the detention centre at Guantanamo Bay' (e-mail received, 26 May 2006). The company went on to deny having a Starbucks outlet on the island whilst simultaneously acknowledging that they did provide coffee to US service personnel based at the camp. The exchanges between Starbucks' executive liaison officer and various anti-war activists were circulated widely along the protest networks of the web (www.business-humanrights.org/Links/Repository/587011; www.reports-and-materials.org/Further-exchange-between-Starbucks-Quilty-about-Guantanamo-May-2006.doc).

In an attempt to inform a wider non-activist, non-internet based public of this contradictory position and capitalise on another campaigning opportunity, Save Omar campaigners orchestrated a demonstrative event which took place in two Brighton Starbucks outlets. On June 3 2006, 25 activists entered Starbucks on Western Road and North Road. Each group of activists included two members dressed in the iconic orange jumpsuits and black hoods that have come to signify civil rights abuses in Guantanamo Bay. These activists stood or crouched in silence while another member of the group read out a brief statement asking customers to reflect upon the circumstances surrounding Deghayes' illegal detention and Starbucks' role in operations at Guantanamo Bay *while* they drank their coffee. They also distributed leaflets which gave a fuller account of Starbucks' relationship with the US military and appealed directly to the 'people of Brighton' to differentiate themselves from the global brand by 'not . . . refrain[ing] from taking a position' (personal e-mail, 26 May 2006).

The Save Omar Campaign's strategy follows in the methodological footprints of previous grassroots campaigns against international companies such as Starbucks, Nike and Gap. These campaigns attempt to tag global brands with negative connotations in order to provoke political, social or cultural change. In his analysis of the North American Fair Trade coffee network, Bennett argues that the organisation successfully attached its political message to the Starbucks' coffee drinking experience, thereby persuading 'one of the chief corporate purveyors of that experience' (2003, p. 30) to fundamentally alter their business practices. Whilst Nike and Gap have been somewhat recalcitrant in accepting the criticisms of anti-globalisation protesters, Starbucks have positively embraced an apparently ethical, humanitarian business ethos. In this way what was once a source of shame and embarrassment for Starbucks has become one of its most potent selling points.

Starbucks remains acutely aware of the impact that an orchestrated and sustained campaign can have upon its economic bottom line. Indeed, the brand is still frequently associated with negative economic and cultural trends such as global homogenisation and corporate domination. The week before the Save Omar Campaign's occupation of Starbucks, just such an article had appeared in the *Argus* ('Coffee chain bid scares traders', 26 May 2006). While campaigners were clearly attempting to mobilise a stakeholder boycott of Starbucks, I would argue that this was not necessarily their sole concern. The occupation of Starbucks, like the postcard discussed at the start of this section, is explicitly dual in its address and Save Omar campaigners were also attempting to access and then re-articulate what the company's customer care specialist describes as 'the very personal connection customers have with Starbucks' (Online emails between activists and Starbucks, May 2006). In this way campaigners hoped to provoke a re-evaluation of public opinion in relation to Guantanamo Bay in general and Omar Deghayes in particular.

In order to make this connection, Save Omar activists employed a spatial metaphor. In their article 'Grounding Metaphor: Towards a Spatialised

Politics', Smith and Katz argue that 'Metaphors work by invoking one meaning system to explain or clarify another. The first [source domain] meaning system is apparently concrete, well understood, unproblematic, and evokes the familiar . . . The second 'target domain' is elusive, opaque, seemingly unfathomable, without meaning donated from the source domain (Smith and Katz, 1993, p. 69). Smith and Katz maintain that 'it is precisely the apparent familiarity of space, the givenness of space, its fixity and inertness that makes a spatial grammar so fertile for appropriation' (1993, p. 69).

The ways in which this dialectic between source and target domains can be opened out to create a plethora of resisting domains can be illustrated by examining the metaphorical implications raised by the Starbucks action in more detail. According to Bennett 'entering a Starbucks puts one in a quiet world with quality product, surrounded by quality people, soothed by demographically chosen music . . . and tempted by kitchen coffee gadgets . . .' (2003, p. 29). Starbucks can be seen as offering the individual 'cultural materials to fashion an identity' (Barry et al., 2000, p. 122) in an environment designed to 'put people at ease for the purpose of spending time and money' (Purkis, 1996, p. 215).

Moreover the outlets chosen by Save Omar activists constitute a particularly potent source domain because they are both situated in newly regenerated parts of Brighton which have come to symbolise the move away from the city's traditionally slightly seedy seafront appeal and towards a far more urban and aspirational cultural ethos. Thus, for example, the hundred-metre stretch of road which brackets the North Road outlet is occupied by an award-winning environmentally friendly library, a Brazilian cocktail bar, a Japanese noodle bar and the quality food emporium Carluccio's. In this way the Starbucks on North Road exists within an architectural context designed to articulate to those both within and beyond the community that Brighton is a cool, cultured and cosmopolitan place to live.

George Ritzer maintains that '*Starbuck's major innovation has been in the realm of theatrics*' (his italics) and goes on to argue that customers take 'pleasure in witnessing the ongoing show taking place in their local Starbucks' (2007, p. 9). However, this careful cultural construction is immediately and deliberately complicated by the activists' articulation of the metaphor's target domain, i.e. the bound and hooded faux detainee. Activists' entry into Starbucks immediately crystallises two contrasting forms of public discourse into a single 'ideologically loaded' image (Ruiz,

2005, p. 201). The normally unobjectionable activity of consuming coffee is juxtaposed with the appalling human rights abuses suffered by 'enemy combatants' in Guantanamo Bay. In this way protesters' actions create a situation in which not only 'the strange is rendered familiar, but the apparently familiar is made equally strange' (Smith and Katz, 1993, p. 71). As with the postcard, this demonstrative action requires viewers to confront this clash of contradictory elements and cognitively evaluate a number of unexpected issues before being able to resolve the visual conundrum.

Smith and Katz maintain that modernist critics have neutralised space rendering it politically and analytically blank in order to provide a 'semblance of order in an otherwise floating world of ideas' (Smith and Katz, 1993, p. 80). However, more contemporary commentators (Fournier, 2002; Cupers, 2005) have questioned this understanding, arguing that small-scale grassroots movements are particularly adept at creating politically challenging conceptual spaces. For example Szerszynski maintains that visual metaphors create a political semiotic field without 'a zero degree', one in which there is 'no stable ground on which to stand, rather an ever-shifting surface of partial perspectives' (2003, p. 201).

Further, Purkis argues that such protest spaces are particularly potent when they are located in private places – such as coffee shops – which are 'normally conceived of as safe from political agitation' (1996, p. 215). '"Colonizing" private space' (1996, p. 215) in this way disrupts the status quo and creates a sense of 'estrangement' which makes perfectly 'normal' activities – such as drinking coffee – look suddenly 'strange, absurd, grotesque' (Fournier, 2002, p. 194). The unsettled nature of these spaces can temporarily 'unfix' the meanings usually ascribed to them, enabling 'each interested party' to attempt 'to place their discourse onto it' (Purkis, 2000, p. 216).

On these occasions, protesters create an 'ambivalent position between strangeness and familiarity' (Cupers, 2005, p. 12) which jolts spectators out of their usual state of distraction and encourages them to re-evaluate the discourses which surround them. Chatterton goes further and maintains that the construction of explicitly 'uncommon ground' between actors and spectators creates connections which can unsettle the essentialisms between 'activist and public, the committed and the caring' (2006, p. 272). Activists' use of visual metaphors open up 'a moment of hope' which 'undermines dominant understandings of what is possible and offers new conceptual spaces for imagining and practising possible futures' (Fournier, 2002 p. 184)

These spaces are particularly valuable to resource-poor protest groups as they enable them to call the dominant narrative into question. Moreover, their intrinsically photogenic nature means that such events are frequently reported in the mainstream press ensuring that they reach as wide an audience as possible. Despite Starbucks' customer care manager's reassuring emails, the issue was raised and discussed further, both within the alternative and the mainstream community (Starbucks action in Brighton, 3 March 2006; Can the coffee, *Argus*, 31 May 2006). Thus these metaphors create a space in which source and target domains temporarily overlap, forcing even reluctant participants to engage in an 'untranslatable constructive form of cognition' (Stafford, 1996, p. 27).

The activists' decision to deploy their 'prestigious right bearing bodies' (Gilroy, 2004, p. 89) in a key community space created an all-important 'sense of there being an elsewhere' and of that 'elsewhere being in some way relevant' (Silverstone, 2007, p. 10) to Brighton's collective sense of identity. Their sophisticated use of photogenic and ideologically potent visual images contributed to the wider dissemination of alternative understandings of Omar Deghayes as an 'enemy combatant' in particular and of Guantanamo Bay in general. Activists enabled the absent and silenced Deghayes to escape categorisation as part of a globally feared terrorist 'them' and become part of a locally identified 'us' instead. In addition as a result of such events the Save Omar campaign gradually acquired a reputation as a reliable and innovative news source able constantly and consistently to 'come up with a new thing' (Dickinson, 2007, in interview).

Another Shared Here?

From mid-2005 the *Argus* gave Save Omar extensive and favourable coverage, promoted its fundraising events and lent its weight to many of its campaigns. The increasingly warm relationship between activists and the *Argus* culminated in the newspaper's formal adoption of the issues raised by Save Omar in September 2005. While the paper's campaign ran under the title of 'Justice for Omar', in many ways, it simply piggybacked on the work being done by activists. For example, the postcard discussed in the section above was reproduced in the pages of the *Argus* alongside an invitation to readers to 'make your voice heard for justice' (10 July 2006).

While the paper's support of Save Omar undoubtedly amplified the campaign's concerns, it was not (sadly) an example of commercial media's conversion to a more altruistic, community-minded way of being. Indeed, their impetus for doing so had an important economic dimension. This point was underlined by the paper's most politically supportive journalist, who pointed out that regional papers will only publish what they believe the local community will buy. Thus while the *Argus'* support of the Save Omar campaign might have had a political dimension, it was also based on an understanding that the city's audience would, quite literally, buy into this particular campaign.

Nevertheless, once the decision had been taken, the interests of the campaign and the paper became inextricably intertwined. The overlapping nature of this space is evident in a series of articles mobilising public support for Omar Deghayes. These articles ran for the first year of the joint campaign under headlines such as 'Religious leaders back detainee' (5 September 2005), 'Union backs Guantanamo detainee' (6 January 2006), 'Famous faces back the fight to free Omar' (6 April 2006) before finally culminating shortly before Omar's release with 'Sussex MP campaigns for Omar' (7 May 2007). These articles were interspersed with wider appeals targeting the paper's general readership 'Sign up to support Omar' (18 October 2005), 'Badge of support for Omar' (27 October 2005) and 'Make your voices heard for justice' (10 July 2006).

As example of how the different interests and needs of the paper and the campaign overlapped, and which required very little in terms of journalistic resources, they were an economically efficient means of producing copy. The journalist covering the campaign simply rang around her list of community spokespeople and elicited the desired response. The same task would have been a huge strain on a resource poor organisation such as the Save Omar campaign. In this way both the newspaper and the campaign benefitted from articles offering new angles on a story which was always in danger of becoming old.

The inexorable decline of local newspapers has become the subject of widespread debate in the national media and the Houses of Parliament (Universities must fight for local papers, *Guardian Online*, 3 April 2009; BBC internet plans will kill off local newspapers, *Daily Telegraph*, 14 August 2008; MPs fearing decline of local news *BBC Online*, 19 March 2009). There is a widespread consensus that local public forums are in jeopardy and that this will have a detrimental effect on the workings of both local and national politics. Aldridge describes how many regional titles are attempting to protect what remains of their traditional market share by taking on an explicitly campaigning role. She maintains that this strategy allows regional papers to foreground the uniqueness of their selling position by promoting themselves as 'active and important players in local affairs' (2007, p. 66). In this way local papers distinguish themselves from the free, but more lightweight and disposable, news sources currently challenging their market share.

However as Aldridge points out, these campaigns tend to focus on relatively non-controversial subjects, such as combating preventable disease or reducing street crime, and therefore address the reader as a consumer of council services rather than as a citizen of the nation state. Consequently local papers frequently produce rather bland and politically innocuous 'campaigns'. The *Argus* has followed this trend by reporting on a number of localised campaigns. There are many reasons why local news editors choose not to cover overtly political campaigns such as Save Omar and Smash EDO. As a journalist for the *Argus* points out, distant war and allegations of terrorism are perceived as 'unglamorous' news subjects (interview, 2007). They tend to be slow-moving and politically complex stories populated by unpopular and un-photogenic characters such as politicians and lawyers. Moreover these narratives are invariably structured around interminable court cases which only very occasionally lead to incremental changes to the status quo. As a result neither campaign is particularly suited to the photo-led panels or nibs (news in brief) which make up a large part of the *Argus*.

Despite these drawbacks the *Argus* has been consistent and occasionally generous in its coverage of the local anti-war movement. While articles covering these stories clearly retain a local dimension, they are in many ways geographically distant and politically removed from the paper's traditional readership. However, as Wells points out, 'the *Argus* is projecting Brighton news onto the international stage and vice versa' (*New Statesman and Society*, 31 October 2005). The Justice for Omar campaign strives to make American foreign policy a constituency issue, collapsing the distinction between local and global. The paper's decision to cover the anti-war movement in general and to campaign for Omar Deghayes in particular has been described by Miriam Wells as 'a pretty radical departure for a local rag' (*New Statesman and Society*).

Articles such as those described above are hugely important to political movements. This is because a roll call of respected public figures legitimises their position and enables what was previously perceived as a fringe concern to move from the margins of the public's attention to the political mainstream. Indeed these articles renegotiated the parameters of the debates surrounding the 'War on Terror' by reaching out across a local community to create a swell of paper-buying public opinion.

By the end of 2007 it would have been hard to find a public figure who did not support the release of Omar Deghayes. As Francis Tonks, one of Brighton and Hove's Labour councillors, puts it in an internationally accessible YouTube address – Omar Deghayes is 'one of our residents . . . a local guy . . . part of our community' (Tonks, www.youtube.com). The paper's adoption of Deghayes inevitably boosted support for the campaign and enabled it to move from being a marginal issue to one being advocated by public figures in the heart of the community. In this way activists' explicit use of artifice has enabled them, in conjunction with the local paper, to bring 'human rights abuses and the disastrous nature of the war on terror to the doorsteps of Brighton residents' (Wells, *News Statesman and Society*, 31 October 2005). I now examine the way in which the campaigning activities of Smash EDO and the Save Omar combine in order to articulate a more nuanced and textured protest position.

Closing the Gap

> One task for critical theory is to render visible the ways in which societal inequality infects formally inclusive existing public spheres and taints discursive interactions within them.
>
> Nancy Fraser, 1990, p. 65

In many ways, Save Omar's unusually productive relationship with the *Argus* is rooted in journalists' relationships with particular protesters. Unlike the majority of ongoing stories in the *Argus*, the Save Omar campaign is covered by a dedicated journalist. Indeed this is a rare instance of an individual journalist requesting (and being granted) ownership of a particular story. Partly as a consequence of this allocation, the individual journalist and campaigners have been able to build personal relationships and therefore bypass many of the organisational barriers which frequently impede the communication process. In contrast, links between Smash EDO and the media are 'individual rather than organisational' (personal email from Andrew Beckett, 2006). The organisational gap between Smash EDO and mainstream media providers was least evident in the campaign's relationship with the national papers. I would suggest that this is because such interactions were undertaken on a one-off basis which enables both protesters and journalists to background their organisational differences.

However while such ad hoc linkages work well on an occasional basis, they become problematic when a rhizomatically structured group attempts to engage with more arborescent media organisations on a long-term basis. Andrew Beckett described The *Argus*' coverage of the Smash EDO as 'patchy and inaccurate' (email received 16 September 2006). The campaign's failure to secure the type of local media coverage enjoyed by the Save Omar campaign is rooted in Smash EDO's reluctance to foster a face-to-face relationship with journalists from the *Argus*, i.e. that the coverage of the Smash EDO campaign has depended on it being 'taken up by whoever's free or has found it' (interview, 2007). As a result of this somewhat arbitrary and uncoordinated allocation of journalistic attention, the demonstrative events organised by Smash EDO have not been covered particularly well by the *Argus*.

The lack of face-to-face interaction between journalists from the *Argus* and activists from Smash EDO created a narrative void which was quickly occupied by Brighton and Hove's police force. As Couldry points out, the media's tendency to construct reports from police briefings inevitably frames the representation of political protests (2000). Protest organisations have traditionally relied on public demonstrations to show the strength of their commitment, draw attention to their cause and recruit fresh support. Here I analyse three public demonstrations in Brighton and Hove which represent key moments in the development of mainstream narratives about Brighton and Hove's anti-war movement. These demonstrations also developed the anti-globalisation movement's 'policy' of non-engagement with mainstream authorities with activists refusing to take part in any pre-demonstration collaborations with the police.

The first demonstration was called by Smash EDO in the summer of 2005. Protesters refused to liaise with the authorities and marched from The Level to Brighton and Hove police station where they handed in a charge sheet accusing the directors of EDO MBM of complicity in war crimes ('Anti war protesters to descend on city', *Argus*, 10 June 2005). The second was also called by Smash EDO and took place a few months later. This demonstration took place in the city centre and was widely perceived to have been harshly policed. The third and final demonstration was called by Sussex Action for Peace and the Brighton and Hove Palestine Solidarity Campaign, which were acting as an umbrella organisation for Smash EDO,

Save Omar and other loosely affiliated organisations. This demonstration was also 'unauthorised' by the police but passed peacefully.

During the early stages of the Smash EDO campaign, the police and legal authorities downplayed the significance of the protests. For example EDO MBM's lawyers dismissed the protesters' argument that the right to protest would be curtailed by the imposition of an injunction as 'malarkey' ('Demo Plea by Weapons Firm', *Argus*, 14 April 2005). Similarly, when Smash EDO activists announced their intention to deliver evidence of EDO MBM's complicity in war crimes to the police station, Superintendent Kevin Moore described protesters as ridiculous. He told the *Argus* that his officers would 'not be investigating them [EDO MBM] for war crimes because that is nonsense' (Moore, 'Anti war protesters to descend on city', *Argus*, 10 June 2005).

However, as the Smash EDO campaign gained momentum, Brighton and Hove police altered their approach and began to establish a 'chaos and disorder' frame around the protests. In an article published immediately after the second Smash EDO demonstration, Superintendent Moore claimed that the march was not 'about lawful protest for their cause' but 'solely about bringing disruption and inconvenience to the city' ('80 year old arrested at protest', *Argus*, 15 August 2005). This article was followed a few months later by one in which Moore claimed that the Smash EDO demonstrations were not about 'beliefs' but 'about causing havoc and disorder to thousands of people in the city' ('Chaos fears over rally', *Argus*, 3 December 2005). In this way, the police deployed the 'Mohawk Valley Formula',[4] whereby those who articulate dissent are represented as 'disruptive, harmful to the public and against common interests' (Chomsky, 1997, p. 19).

The struggle between protesters and the police began, not on the streets of Brighton but in the pages of the *Argus*. Debates revolved around two interconnected issues. Firstly, there was disagreement about what constitutes 'notification'. Protesters maintain that the 1986 Public Order Act requires activists to do nothing more than give written notice of their intention to march. The police maintain that the act requires protesters to provide additional details such as the names of organisers, the route

---

4. The Mohawk Valley Formula was first used to break a steel strike in Johnstown in 1937 (Chomsky, 1997).

they intend to take and the numbers of marchers they expect to attend.[5] Secondly, there was some debate over how this information should be communicated to the police. While information about the march was freely available in subaltern media forms such as flyers, posters, graffiti, stickers and websites, the police maintained that there was no information available in the public domain ('80 year old arrested at protest', *Argus*, 15 August 2005; Protesters should have kept us informed, *Argus*, 19 August 2005). As a result of this 'absence', the police argued that protesters had failed to give due notice and thus classified the march as illegal.

As a consequence of these unresolved issues, Brighton and Hove police published a letter in the *Argus* appealing for leaders to come forward and negotiate an 'acceptable' route: 'We are happy for them to march as long as they go where we want them to go. If they move outside of that we will stop them' (Moore, 'Anti war protesters to converge on city', *Argus*, 10 June 2005).

However in laying out the boundaries of what the police authority deemed to be acceptable, Superintendent Moore inadvertently made the usually unnoticed constraints on public dissent visible. Moreover his comments drew attention to the preparedness of the state to impose 'order' upon the people and, in doing so, unmasked what Fraser has described as the 'back grounded and disguised' power dynamics of public discourse (1990, p. 65). The police offer to 'help' protesters organise a demonstration was revealed to be a means of controlling, rather than facilitating, the articulation of dissent in public spaces.

Chief Superintendent Moore's letter created a discursive opportunity for protesters in general, and Smash EDO's cyber spokespeople in particular, publicly to challenge the police's right to prescribe the boundaries of protest and classify protesters as criminal. Following this letter, a protester replied saying: 'We don't liaise with the police because they just use the information to stop us more effectively' ('80 year old arrested at protest', *Argus*, 15 August 2005).

Thus protesters were able publicly to justify a protest strategy which has always been susceptible to being framed as mere chaos and disorder. As a result of this public re-positioning in the papers, the confrontation between police and protesters which took place on the ground during the second demonstration could be more easily read by citizens of Brighton and Hove

5. Differing interpretations of the 1986 public order act are currently being reviewed by the courts.

as a mindful act; in other words as an act of *hamas* rather than *hamoq*. In this way 'assumptions that were previously exempt from contestation' (Fraser, 1990, p. 67) were forced into mainstream public arenas.

The boundaries which had been drawn by police and refused by protesters in front of the readers of the *Argus* became actual on the day of the second demonstration. At midday on 13 August 2005, protesters and police began to collect outside Brighton's main shopping centre. At this point the demonstration was a smooth space in so far as it was comprised of heterogeneous and loosely affiliated clusters of protest groups. There was no centralised organisation and the communicative systems were all horizontal. For example, rather than the crowd being addressed by speakers/leaders, there was an open-mic session in which anyone could address the crowd, on any issue and at any length. This rhizomatically organised system meant that the speeches, like the pages of *Circus Free* and *The Greenham Factor* were fluid, not prioritised, and were occasionally unruly. Finally, and after much milling about, the collective tipping point was reached and at about 12.30 p.m. the march set off, past the clock tower and down Western Road. Having failed to impose their boundaries in the pages of the *Argus*, the police set about asserting their control on the streets of Brighton and Hove. They did this by employing three interrelated policing techniques now known as 'kettling'.

Firstly, the police formed a line across North Street which halted the progress of the demonstration. At the same time a second police line drew up behind the march and compressed the demonstration into a 100-yard stretch of the road. These two police lines then pressed protesters off the carriageway and into Windsor Street which had already been blocked by a third police line. This had the effect of confining protesters within an area cordoned off by three lines of police. Each of these lines was two officers thick and supported by a number of police vans and other vehicles. In this way a march which had been rhizomatic was 'captured' and 'enveloped' by the police's imposition of rigid boundaries (Deleuze and Guattari, 2004, p. 524). The uneven fluidity of the march was contained and compressed.

Having imposed these boundaries on the demonstration the police then went on to create an unbridgeable gap between the spaces inside and outside the cordoned-off area. Protesters who attempted to breach the cordon, in order to talk to passers-by or hand out leaflets were 'aggressively prevented' from doing so and pushed back into the space allocated to them ('Bullying tactic won't keep us quiet', *Argus*, 13 December 2005). In addition, members of the public who became angered or distressed by the escalating violence were physically escorted from the scene. The police imposed a space of about five to ten feet between protesters and the public, making the two citizen groupings separated and discrete. This technique is particularly significant because, as Waddington points out, 'patrolling the boundary of inclusion and exclusion' involves bestowing (and withholding) citizenship on the people. This imposition of striated boundaries eradicated the possibility of an overlapping in-the-middle position and ensured that there could be no potentially contaminating movement or intermingling across the previously porous boundary. In this way the possibility of being a protester *and* a member of the public was disallowed.

The police went on to impose a second distinction between 'good' protesters and 'bad' protesters. They did this by appealing to different categories of people to leave the enclosed area. So, for example, the police offered to escort the elderly and people with small children beyond the striating police lines and into 'safe' public space. However, in keeping with the spirit of the anti-globalisation demonstrations discussed in the previous chapter, activists from very differently orientated protest groupings collectively decided to decline this offer. In this way, a coalition of protesters refused to be divided into separate groupings and chose instead to maintain solidarity across difference.

The removal of 'good' protesters would have altered the demographic dynamic of the demonstration. It would have created a homogenised space occupied only by protesters physically and emotionally strong enough to withstand the escalating tensions. This type of demonstration would almost inevitably have been dominated by the young and the physically able. Consequently it would have been particularly vulnerable to being delegitimized as an aggressive, antagonistic and borderline criminal 'them'. Such a demonstration would have justified the authorities' view of Smash EDO protesters as unreasonable individuals 'hell bent' on operating 'outside the law' ('The law is key to EDO harmony', *Argus*, 9 June 2005).

Having attended this demonstration in person I can testify to the levels of discomfort and determination that this sort of refusal requires of individuals who clearly consider themselves to be 'socially responsible', 'law abiding' members of their local community (Sometimes we have to stand up to the state, *Argus*, 6 September 2005; 'The way we are headed', *Argus*, 20 April 2005). The 'good' protesters' resolve to remain within the cordoned-off area, despite being 'shoved around, shouted at and generally overwhelmed by the police' ('Heavy handed policing threatens free speech', *Argus*, 13 December 2005), prevented the demonstration from being 'translated and traversed' back into a striated city space (Deleuze and Guattari, 2004, p. 524).

The demonstration's prolonged and disruptive occupation of the city centre meant that the police's behaviour had been witnessed by large numbers of the public. As a result of this conflict, the 'uncommon ground' between protesters and the police became an 'entry point for critical engagement' with the issues raised by protesters (Chatterton, 2006, p. 273). This impacted significantly upon the way in which street protests and Smash EDO demonstrations in particular were framed in subsequent coverage. In this way, rather than dissolving the frontier between protesters and the police, the alternative and the mainstream became stark and highly visible.

The march became the focus of an increasingly supportive public debate on the letters page of the *Argus*. Protesters involved in the demonstration wrote to the paper complaining about how they were 'hemmed in and made to feel like a criminal' ('Heavy handed policing threatens free speech', *Argus*, 13 December 2005). Shoppers who were delayed by the demonstrations and questioned by the *Argus* maintained that the march had not prevented them from 'enjoying their day'. Those whose shopping had been affected asserted that having 'the freedom to demonstrate is so much more important than a five minute delay to your journey' ('Scuffles and arguments as marchers take to city streets', *Argus*, 13 June 2005).

When a few months later a Save Omar activist wrote a letter to the *Argus* about the series of marches, it was published in full. The unusually long letter began: 'PC Sean McDonald's views of the two recent marches in Brighton would appear to suggest that a situation which could easily be resolved by demonstrators simply informing police of their intention . . .' and went on to outline the arguments against engagement with the police and concluded by suggesting that:

> . . . There is always a degree of unpredictability and tension on both sides at demonstrations, but a tolerant police approach without the assumption that those who choose to protest without approval are simply a criminal element might surprise us all. ('Sometimes we have to stand up to the state', *Argus,* 6 September 2005)

The public support of Save Omar was particularly significant in that, by the summer of 2005, the campaign had already garnered considerable mainstream support. Thus the campaign brought with it the implicit backing of important cultural arbiters such as the *Argus*, the city council and various MPs. Moreover the Save Omar campaign's successful renegotiation of previously antagonistic us/them distinctions within the pages of the *Argus* lent its position further credibility.

In this way letters published in the *Argus* after the first two demonstrations began to construct an alternative narrative frame which defended the protesters' right to protest and accused the police of being heavy handed. The police found themselves in a position where protesters' citizenship was retrospectively 'redefined' by the wider public and their policing of the demonstration was 'regarded as impermissible' (Waddington, 1999, p. 61). The textual consequences of their containment of the demonstration meant that the boundaries between alternative and mainstream spaces were drawn very differently in the press coverage leading up to the third demonstration.

Indeed public support for the protesters was such that by the spring of 2006 the coalition demonstration called by Sussex Action for Peace passed without incident. Once again protesters refused to liaise with police but on this occasion the demonstration marched peacefully through Brighton city centre without the consent or the 'guidance' of the police ('Marchers fight for their right to demonstrate', *Argus*, 19 March 2006). The march moved smoothly through the city and was characterised by much meandering, occasional 'rests' at major junctions and a sense of quiet euphoria.

Headlines such as 'Chaos Fears over Rally' (3 December 2005) and 'Factory Sparks Another March' (10 August 2005) which characterised the early days of the anti-war movement's activities in Brighton and Hove were gradually replaced by headlines which emphasised the authority's role in policing dissent such as 'Protesters Slam Over Policing' (2 March 2006) and 'Protesters Accused of Protest Overkill' (24 August 2006). By 2006, demonstrations called by anti-war protesters in Brighton and Hove were being attended by city councillors Francis Tonks and Joyce Edmond-Smith ('Police accused of overkill', *Argus*, 24 August 2006). Moreover, the narrative strand which had focused on the way in which protesters were 'deliberately evasive' ('Part of the local community not anti it', *Argus*, 7 December 2005) was replaced by one in which the police refused to answer councillors' questions about the cost of their policing strategy ('Anti-weapons march takes place peacefully', *Argus*, 12 December 2005 and 'Protesters Slam Over Policing', *Argus*, 2 March 2006).

During the demonstrations outlined above, the usually unnoticed frontier between smooth and striated, textual and actual spaces was made visible and publicly contested. Smash EDO's 'policy' of non-compliance and use of virtual spokespeople, together with Save Omar's carefully cultivated re-articulation of localised us/them dynamics, combined to create a nuanced, powerful and persuasive coalition voice. This mix of different systems and structures unsettled the boundaries of inclusion and exclusion and drew protesters, the police and the public into a series of complex structural interactions. This enabled coalition activists to alter the mainstream's narrative frame and articulate an alternative and less familiar truth.

6

Austerity Measures and National Narrative

In the kind of modern society that the idea of publics has enabled, the self-organisation of discourse publics has immense resonance from the point of view of individuals.

(Warner, 2002, p. 52)

Debates about the role of 'the public' in the processes of democracy, which I have outlined previously, have been further complicated by the continued rise of global capital. This is partly because the advent of unelected bodies such as the World Trade Organisation and the International Monetary Fund clearly transcend the authority of democratically elected governments (Fraser, 2007). Moreover, the 2008 financial crisis has dramatically highlighted politicians' inability to determine the economic fate and fortune of their countries without reference to the wider economic system. Consequently there is a new awareness of the ways in which apparently autonomous nation states are actually interconnected, which has further obscured the relationship between public opinion and the nation state.

The financial crisis, like the attack on the World Trade Center in 2001, has had a significant impact on both the articulation of dissent and its representation within mainstream media arenas. As Rantanen points out, in times of crisis there tends to be a retreat from the global and a re-entrenchment of the local (2005). While Rantanen discusses these dynamics in relation to the transformation of physical boundaries, such as those instigated by the formation and expansion of the European Union, I would argue that a similar re-orientation can be identified in relation to the economic boundaries that bind a nation state. Thus while anti-austerity protests clearly retain a transnational dimension which echoes that found in the anti-globalisation movement and the anti-war movement, they are also, and at the same time, curiously local in their organisation and outlook.

European governments have responded to the global financial crisis by turning inwards and cutting back on expenditure at a national level. In some instances, such as in Greece, Portugal and Spain, these cuts are a pre-requisite of the loan agreements offered by the EU, the IMF and the European Central Bank. In other instances, such as in the UK and France, cuts have been implemented by national governments mindful of the need to maintain their credit ratings within a financial market made nervous by global uncertainties. In both instances, while the financial crisis is unquestionably global in its nature, austerity measures are invariably implemented by governments, and experienced by people, on a national level.

As a result of these dynamics, protest is also being articulated on both a national and a transnational level. In this way, resistance to very specific governmental measures, such as the increases in the cost of public transport in Brazil or the commercial development of a public park in Turkey, increasingly precipitate an immediate response which then quickly escalates to far more volatile and amorphous outbursts of more generalised public unrest. While these demonstrations are clearly rooted in very specific human geographies and political contexts, they are also oddly and intimately connected with each other. Taken together, these demonstrations constitute an impassioned response to the consequences of globalised neo-liberalism which are unfolding beyond the reach and influence of national citizenries.

Since the start of the financial crisis it is clear that those challenging the neo-liberal hegemony and re-asserting a politics of redistribution have been gaining traction in many countries. However, this has not led to the return to the class-based politics that characterised previous generations of protest. Instead, politics has become individualised and is increasingly seen as 'an expression of personal hopes, lifestyles and grievances' (Bennett and Segerberg, 2012, p. 743). These fragmented but re-invigorated movements frequently take the form of a networked enterprise in which various clusters of distinct but loosely connected activists mobilise around a particular event or situation before dissipating back into wider culture and society. Consequently grassroots protest groups tend to emerge and then re-emerge in a series of ever shifting socio-political coalitions and networks (Diani, 2010).

Within this terrain, the shift from an industrial to an informational economy and the centrality of mediation has also impacted upon the construction of political action and collective identities (Castells, 2007; Cammaerts, 2012). The way in which contemporary understandings of political protest are changing can be briefly illustrated by looking at a cover of *Time* magazine. In 2011 *Time* recognised the transformative potential of protest by nominating 'the protester' as its person of the year. This edition of the magazine looked at protests from around the world and included interviews with various protesters, and first person accounts from journalists in the field. However rather than depicting a particular protest or protester on the cover, *Time* presented its readers with an imaginary protester.

The background of this cover depicts muted images of demonstrations from the era, in which 'protest was the natural continuation of politics by other means' (*Time*, December, 2011). Thus, the anonymous masses, suffused in a revolutionary red, can be seen collectively raising their faces up to the powers that be, their arms holding placards, their mouths calling for action. In contrast, the foreground is occupied by a single figure; a masked protester. This protester's identity is almost entirely concealed by a woollen hat and a cotton neckerchief. Consequently the usually identifying features of the human face are concealed, the individual's gender, race and age remain deliberately undetermined. The protester's eyes, which are brown, are the only distinguishing feature. They reach out through the fabric of the mask that covers the face and beyond the borders of the magazine that frames their face. They are calm and determined but also defiant. They interrogate, rather than invite, the reader's gaze. In this way 'the protesters' masked face speaks for all those who perceive themselves to have been excluded from the process of democracy' (Ruiz, 2013).

If, as Castells suggests, the media are the 'space where power is decided' (2007, p. 242) then the appearance of this potentially challenging image, in a mediated space as mainstream as *Time* magazine, signals a shift in the way in which protest is perceived by the wider public (Cottle, 2012). This image encapsulates a 'common understanding' of the practice of political activism and highlights changes in the way in which 'ordinary people' imagine the role of protest within the public sphere (Taylor, 2003, p. 23). Thus, it emphasises the individual over the collective, the anonymous over the known, the generic over the specific, and hints at the potential for material as well as symbolic confrontation.

However, the liberal bourgeois model's emphasis on the role of the individual in achieving consensus can be problematic. For while Habermas refers positively to the ways in which newspapers, magazines, radio and television create a dispersed 'public body' capable of articulating public opinion, he remains ambivalent about the gathering together of *actual* public bodies in the form of mass demonstrations. This distrust is rooted in the perceived unreasonableness of the mass and the belief that the politically productive enthusiasm of the crowd can easily metamorphose into the physically destructive hysteria of the mob (Calhoun, 1992; Mouffe, 2005).

As previously discussed, the anti-globalisation movement challenged this view by forcefully drawing attention to the ways in which transnational organisations such as the World Bank and the International Monetary Fund occupied spaces constitutionally beyond the criticism and control of the citizenry. In doing so, anti-globalisation protesters created a space within which many forms of protests, including more confrontational approaches, could flourish. Unfortunately, this emphasis on gaining physical access to trade talks meant that mainstream coverage invariably focused on demonstrations as sites of conflict. While this enabled activists to deploy spatial metaphors that embodied many of their arguments, it also limited the extent to which many of the more complex underlying issues could be discussed in public spaces.

In contrast, Occupy's simultaneous occupation of multiple city spaces brought the marginalised majority into the global mainstream and made them visible both on the streets and in news narratives. In this way protesters unsettled the boundary as it has traditionally been drawn between protesters and publics and positioned the previously excluded 99 per cent securely within the mainstream social spaces in which power is decided (Castells, 2007). Thus by consciously eschewing more confrontational protest repertoires, anti-austerity movements have moved beyond demanding the right to *access* democracy and begun a debate about the processes of democracy (Chomsky, 2012).

This, in conjunction with the global/local dynamics outline above, has inevitably shaped the construction of both protest, and the representation of protest, within the mainstream media. This can be seen in mainstream representations of mass demonstrations. When depicting civil unrest in distant countries, they are invariably framed as evidence of a legitimate political uprising. However, similar scenes of social disorder within the boundaries of the western nation state are more commonly framed as evidence of criminal activity. Thus, for example, youths responding to the death of 26-year-old Mohamed Bouazizi in Tunisia were described as 'casting off their fear' in acts of 'generalised protest' (Whitaker, 2010) while youths responding to the death of 29-year-old Mark Duggan are described as 'throwing missiles' in 'isolated pockets of criminality' (Moore, 2011).

Technology constitutes a second structuring trope within contemporary protest narratives. There is a tendency within both popular and academic narratives to see technology-enabled networks as constituting 'flexible organisations in themselves' (Bennett and Segerberg, 2012, p. 752). Moreover this trope is used with a similarly polarising effect. Thus, protesters' use of Facebook and Twitter is interpreted as a powerful new tool in the fight against authoritarian regimes in faraway locales, whereas at home it is read as a destabilising force that must be brought under control by governmental authorities. Both framings attribute an enormous amount of democratic potential to new communications technologies and are rooted in the work by scholars such as Castells and Benkler who both offer a vision of society in which new communications technologies successfully challenge the top-down power of traditional elites (Castells, 2007; Benkler, 2006). According to such understandings, new technologies are creating spaces in which alternative organisational and ideological systems can flourish. This view of new technologies dominates public debate surrounding contemporary protest despite the many studies that qualify and contextualise such claims (Morozov, 2011, Newburn, 2011).

This chapter examines protests that are organised via new communications technologies within the boundaries of the nation state by focusing on the demonstrations which took place against rises in student fees at the end of 2009 in the UK. It develops and then extends discussion introduced in Chapters 2, 4 and 5 by reflecting upon the ways in which anti-kettling applications such as Sukey offer protesters a solar-eye view of the demonstrations they constitute. As such it focuses on the potential of mobile technologies to challenge and renegotiate existing relationships between protesters, police and the public on the ground and in national news narratives. In doing so, I reflect upon the way in which the notion of 'alternative media', which has traditionally had both technological and political connotations, is being developed/altered by activists' use of 'commercial' or 'mainstream' virtual spaces.

The Cartographies of Protest

Polly put the kettle on . . .

> Sukey invites people taking part to share their experiences via social media and combines this with information from traditional news sources to hand it straight back to the crowd and let them see what is going on around them as it happens.
>
> (Sukey press release, 27 January 2011)

Kettling has been used during both local and national demonstrations for a considerable number of years in the UK. The police describe kettling as the tactic of 'progressively isolating problematic groups and individuals from peaceful protesters' (Policing Public Order, 2011, p. 7). However, it is perceived by activists as an attempt to repress citizens' right to protest. This view is exemplified by activists from Sukey.org who described kettling as 'brutal and undemocratic' in 2010 (www.sukey.org).[1] Anti-globalisation protesters have challenged the practice of kettling in the High Court, the Court of Appeal and the European Court of Human Rights, on the grounds that kettling contravened Article 5 of the European Convention of Human Rights, although these debates failed to gain much traction within wider public arenas.

For a number of years the police tactic of kettling has gone largely unchallenged within wider public arenas, however, the 'containment' of teenage schoolchildren during protests outside Whitehall on the 24 November 2009 brought the issues surrounding kettling to the forefront of public opinion. The classification of secondary school children, some as young as eleven, as 'problematic' and their subsequent containment without access to food and water for more than six hours has been widely read as an example of 'indiscriminate punishment' (Bowcott, 2011). As a result, the police have found themselves in a position where the tactic of kettling or containment is being retrospectively 'redefined' by a wider public as 'impermissible' (Waddington, 1999, p. 61).

This shift in the public perception of kettling may have been influenced by changes in the way in which the police themselves are represented

---

1.   Sukey's website was undergoing maintenance as this book was going to press. An archive of their pages can be found at http://web.archive.org/web/20130513134039/http:/www.opensukey.org/about/.

in the mainstream. As previously discussed, kettling depends upon the police's ability to draw a series of distinctions between the public and protesters, between 'good' protesters and 'bad' protesters, and between 'bad protesters' and criminals. Historically, the police's privileged position as a source of reliable information means that their interpretation of these distinctions has invariably been replicated in the press. Thus classic studies, such as those conducted by Halloran et al. in the 1970s and Gitlin in the 1980s, developed a nuanced account of the way in which media representations of protest contribute to the wider public's understanding of politics. More recently, scholars investigating the mainstream media's representation of anti-globalisation demonstrations, such as the G8 demonstrations in Genoa (Juris, 2005) and the G20 demonstrations in Edinburgh (Rosie and Gorringe, 2009) have explored the ways in which acts of protest designed to communicate particular political positions are decontextualised and reinserted into mainstream narratives which frame protesters as 'dangerous criminals or terrorists' (Juris, 2005, p. 451).

However the police force's standing within mainstream media narratives as the 'arbiters of citizenship' (Waddington, 1999, p. 41) has recently been undermined by a number of factors, one of which is the advent of new communications technologies. Thus, for example, the police's reputation as impartial upholders of the law was severely compromised by the mobile phone footage of Ian Tomlinson being pushed to the ground during a demonstration in 2009 by PC Harwood while he was trying to leave a 'controlled dispersal' area during a G20 demonstration (the report of the Hillsborough Independent Panel, p. 10). This two-minute video clip taken by a passing tourist quickly became embedded within mainstream news narratives and directly challenged the police's official record of events. Indeed the Metropolitan Police Authority eventually acknowledged its failure to tell the truth and offered Tomlinson's family a formal apology for this behaviour. This appears to support the view that new technologies are increasingly challenging the authorities' ability to control mainstream news narratives (Castells, 2007).

Consequent investigations into the police handling of the death of Ian Tomlinson have also exposed the closeness of the relationship between police and journalists. Thus, for example, the report into Tomlinson's death highlighted the 'seriously misleading press brief' (Independent Investigation into the Death of Ian Tomlinson on 1 April 2009, 2010, p. 11), which shaped mainstream news coverage until the release of Mr La Jaunie's mobile phone footage by the *Guardian* newspaper on 7 April

2009. It's worth noting that La Jaunie approached several media outlets with his footage before the *Guardian* eventually published this material on their website. In this instance I would suggest that the status of La Jaunie as a bystander rather than a participant in events enabled him to escape the good protester/bad protester dynamics that might otherwise have framed his representation with mainstream news narratives and therefore undermined his contribution to public debate.

This exposure of police violence during the G20 demonstrations and the subsequent cover-up unsettled the binary in which the police are law-abiding and protesters are not. The police's reputation in the UK has been further undermined by a series of highly critical reports and public inquiries. Thus for example while the Hillsborough Independent Panel[2] had yet to publish its findings at this time, it was clear within the wider public domain that unsolicited police briefings had been used to tarnish the reputation of Liverpool fans (Conn, 2009). The police force's use of such 'off-the-record briefings' has since been noted in the Leveson report which highlighted the 'lack of clarity' inherent in such a term (Leveson, 2012). As a result of these ongoing developments, the police's increasingly tarnished public image has undermined their ability to draw the invisible but all-important 'citizenship line' (Waddington, 1999, p. 61) that exists between protesters and publics. Having taken a little time to explore the dynamics between protesters and the police within a wider context, I will now focus on the implications raised by the advent of new and mobile communications technologies in more detail.

. . . Sukey take it off again

This section is written with particular reference to an 'anti-kettling' application called Sukey. Here I examine the aims and intentions of the app's creators, and compare these to those of the activists behind the creation of online platforms such as Indymedia and offline protest publications such as *Circus Free* and *The Greenham Factor*. These debates will be followed by an analysis of a backlash led by more experienced activists against the app. This backlash revolved around three interrelated issues, namely Sukey activists' use of closed rather than open networks, the use of commercial media platforms such as mobile phone carriers

---

2. This panel was set up to investigate the role of the South Yorkshire Police in the death of 96 Liverpool football fans during the FA semi-final in 1989. For more information visit www.bbc.uk/news/uk-19545126 .

and Google Maps and, finally, activists' willingness to connect and communicate with mainstream organisations such as newspapers and the police force.

Towards the end of 2009, the newly elected Conservative-Liberal Democrat coalition government announced their intention to cut spending on further education and to increase the cap on the tuition fees. This policy broke pledges made by the Liberal Democrat leader, Nick Clegg, during his election campaign and prompted a series of demonstrations in the UK. The first of these demonstrations took place in central London on 10 November 2009. Around 52,000 people attended this demonstration, which was largely peaceful. However, in the afternoon several hundred protesters broke away from the main demonstrations and occupied Millbank Tower, the building which houses the Conservative Party's campaign headquarters. This occupation was described as 'volatile': windows were broken and walls 'daubed with anarchist graffiti' (Blake, 2010). The mainstream media followed the lead of the National Union of Students' president, Aaron Porter, who 'absolutely condemned' the small minority of protesters who had 'hijacked' the demonstration, and London Mayor Boris Johnson, who claimed that these students had 'shamefully abused their right to protest' (*Guardian* Newsblog, 2009).

These demonstrations are of particular interest because participants were, on the whole, very young and new to the dynamics of protest. Thus the protesters inside Millbank were described by a *Guardian* columnist as 'fresh faced' and 'excited' (Smith, 10 November 2010). Even the columnists of papers that were usually highly critical of protests, such as the *Telegraph*, described the main demonstration as 'utterly dignified' (Mount, 2010). Thus, while the more seasoned activists protesting at anti-globalisation summit demonstrations in the late 1990s attended demonstrations in the knowledge that they were unlikely to experience a 'safe or peaceful struggle' (Starhawk, 2003, p. 340), many of the students at Millbank appear to have been genuinely surprised and shocked by the physicality of being kettled by the Metropolitan Police. Consequently, many young protesters (and some of their parents) were unexpectedly radicalised by the witnessing of the 'walking wounded staggering back [from Millbank] with blood dripping from mouths and noses, split lips, baton bruises on their face and arms' (Sam Gaus cited in Kingsley, 2011).

A small group of 'recently politicised computer programmers' (Kingsley, 2011) responded to these events by developing Sukey.[3] While Sukey is generally described as an app it is actually a 'multi platform news, communication and logistical support system which displays real time police and protester behaviour, combining validated information sourced directly from protesters combined with feed from twitter, facebook, SMS, RSS and others' (Sukey, 2011). Critics initially described the website as a tool for rioters. For example, Tory blogger Harry Cole tweeted 'there is something disgustingly ironic about a riot organising iPhone app. Just about says it all about this country's kids' (cited in Kingsley, 2011). However the Sukey team describe their website in very different terms. They maintain that the site aims 'to provide peaceful protesters with up to date news that will keep them informed, assist them in avoiding injury, help them keep clear of trouble spots and avoid unnecessary injury' (Sukey: live demo info service for saturday – ldn, 27 January 2011).

Sukey sets out to achieve this aim by gathering information from multiple sources as a demonstration unfolds on the ground. Information is crowd-sourced from members of the Sukey team embedded in the demonstration, protesters who have signed up to the site and non-protesting but interested parties such as parents, police, journalists. Once information has been gathered, it is verified, condensed and plotted onto a map, which is then fed back out to those on the streets via smartphone. Protesters on the ground can use Sukey in one of two ways. They can use it either to access a map that plots the movements of protesters and the police in real time or they can use it to access a compass which points to safe or hazardous protest zones. In this way protesters using Sukey can, in principle, avoid getting caught up in police kettles and other points of conflict.

Sukey gathers information from a combination of human and technological actors in a way which echoes Bruno Latour's work on actor network theory. Within this context Sukey can be read as a 'heterogeneous amalgamation of textual, conceptual, social and technological actors' which compose themselves into a rhizomatic network of nodes and links which are 'local, variable and contingent' (Crawford, 2005, p. 3). The way in which these networks extend beyond the technological can be illustrated by examining the ways in which information delivered

---

3. Sukey's name is taken from the well-known children's rhyme 'Polly Put the Kettle on', which ends with the lines 'Sukey take it off again / We all go home'.

via Sukey's digital infrastructure is subsequently spread through the face-to-face communications of those in proximity to one another during a demonstration. Thus, the Sukey team member responsible for sending information from the demonstration itself emphasised the way in which information was being passed through face to face as well as mediated forms of communications. The *Guardian* went even further, maintaining that the mere knowledge of Sukey's existence 'made people more aware of the need to share information and to keep in touch' (Kingsley, 2011).

McAdams maintains that the acts of civil disobedience which characterised the emergent civil rights movement in the United States could only have taken place within the context of the strong ties built through a 'personal connection' to the movement (Gladwell, 2010). The lack of such strong ties in an online environment has led both scholars and activists to question the rather more optimistic account offered by 'digital evangelists' and to doubt the depth of political potential offered by the internet (Gladwell, 2010: Morozov, 2011). However, Sukey is significant in that it appears to link up actors on the fringes of activism through pre-existing (non-political) friendship groups and to connect them with a strong network of activists at the heart of popular protest. In this way, the network benefits from both 'access to information and resources beyond their own social group' offered by weak ties and the 'motivation to be of assistance' afforded by the strong ties (Granovetter, 1983, p. 209).

The Sukey website draws upon these interlinked networks of strong and weak ties and maintains that the app fulfils the aims laid out in its mission statement by redressing the imbalance of information between police and protesters. Protesters with access to the app are able to maintain the flexibility and autonomy offered by rhizomatically-organised demonstrations and therefore actively engage in the construction of popular protest whilst also, and at the same time, being able to 'see what's going on around them' (Hardy, 2011). In this way Sukey enables protesters to occupy both an enmeshed, in-the-middle position 'below the threshold at which visibility begins' and an elevated, all-seeing 'solar eye' position (de De Certeau, 1984, p. 92). Thus, it creates an information network within which protesters can move smoothly through the city, occupying public space and evading the striating administrations of the police.

These types of communications networks are particularly significant when one compares them with flows which connect the on and offline world to the far more rigid and inflexible communications structures utilised by the police force. While the police enjoy access to a communications network that include aerial surveillance units, closed-circuit television cameras and forward intelligence teams, their communications systems remain distinctly hierarchical and organisational (Policing Public Order, 2011). It enables police commanders to communicate clearly with the police officers on the ground but does not facilitate horizontal communication between the latter or between the police and the wider public. As one student protester pointed out, whilst Sukey was crowd-sourcing information from a plethora of individuals and relaying summaries of that information back out to those occupying the city streets, the police were 'handing out little slips of paper' (Kingsley, 2011).

However, protesters against the rise in tuition fees were not the only audience anticipated by the creators of Sukey. Sukey's mission statement declares that it

[D]elivers maximum information to those participating in a demonstration so that they can make sensible and informed decisions, as well as to those following externally who might be concerned about friends and family at the demonstration or to those who may simply have a political or journalistic interest in the progress of the protest. (Sukey, February 2011)

In this way, Sukey offers a mediated space designed to be accessible to interested third parties, particularly the parents of young and potentially vulnerable protesters. However while the assumption is that these third parties will be the family and friends of students taking part in a demonstration, it is of course possible that other interested parties such as the police may also be offered a birds-eye view of proceedings.

While the technological possibilities offered by social networking sites and mobile technologies clearly contributed to the flow of information between activists, it's important to stress that I am not advocating a technologically deterministic view that ignores or downplays the importance of activism as a cultural practice. As argued in Chapter 3 of this book, new communications technologies have enabled activists to capitalise on the horizontal and participatory communication linkages that have always been an important feature of autonomous popular protest. After all, it should be remembered that Carnival Against Capitalism protesters overwhelmed the police's communication system just as effectively during the J18 demonstrations in London. Moreover, these protesters did so with nothing more technologically advanced than a selection of coloured streamers and cardboard masks.

Sukey as an Emblem of Organisation or Statement of Intent

> Sukey itself is both a nifty gadget and a kind of emblem of organisation, a statement of intent.
>
> (Fox, 2011)

I have reflected upon the way in which Sukey combines strong and weak ties in a communication network, which enables protesters to occupy an active and enmeshed position within city space whilst also, and at the same time, maintaining an overarching awareness of a demonstration as it unfolds around them. This analysis recognises the organisational potential of digital communication (Bennett and Segerberger, 2012) and appears to substantiate the more abstract accounts of networked power put forward by scholars such as Castells and Benkler (2007; 2006). As such, Sukey appears to be part of the empowering groundswell of technology-driven tools, which has transformed the nature of protest since the advent of the internet and framed popular debates around both the London riots and the Arab spring.

The mainstream narratives that have framed activists' use of social networking sites and mobile technologies have much in common with those that framed activists' use of the internet room and online pressrooms. As discussed in Chapter 3 Sukey, like Indymedia, emerged in response to a protest environment shaped by a particular moment in the unfolding dynamics of neo-liberal globalisation. Like Sukey, Indymedia developed the potential afforded by new technologies in such a way as to challenge traditional top-down flows of information. Like Sukey, Indymedia has attracted a considerable amount of interest from the mainstream. However Sukey is significantly different from Indymedia in a number of ways.

In the following section I will compare Sukey and Indymedia as emblems of organisation in order to pull out the political implications raised by the differences between Indymedia and Sukey, and their potential ramifications for the nature of protest. In doing so, I will argue that while Sukey appears to be fulfilling a radical role within the media ecology which contextualises political protest, it is actually occupying a far less challenging position than that which was occupied by Indymedia. I will begin by looking at the way in which both Indymedia and Sukey conceptualise the relationship between demonstrations as they unfold on the ground and as they unfold within protest narratives. As previously discussed, Indymedia perceives itself to be the teller of truths that are ignored by the corporate media providers. As such it is like *Circus Free* and *The Greenham Factor*, open to a multiplicity of alternative and sometimes conflicting perspectives. Its homepage therefore describes Indymedia as follows: 'The independent media centre is a network of collectively run media outlets for the creation of radical, accurate and passionate telling of truth' (About Indymedia).

The emphasis on accuracy implies that mainstream news narratives which frame wider public debate are currently misrepresenting the experiences and opinions of the radical left. Indymedia therefore recognises the ways in which information flows structure our understanding of the world, and offers explicitly alternative understandings in an attempt to instigate social and political change. However it does so by unsettling traditionally arborescent editorial structures and creating smooth spaces which can accommodate the articulation of non-hierarchical polyvocal dissent.

In comparison, Sukey has a far less passionate, more distanced sense of truth. Rather than recognising the existence of competing narratives that contribute unevenly to the construction of events, Sukey focuses its energies on creating an information flow which channels previously unavailable information into the pre-existing mainstream narratives.

In this way, Sukey aims to deliver information to members of the demonstrating public that will enable them to make informed decisions about the ways in which they engage with the legal limits previously specified by the police. This is not to say that Sukey is uninterested in redressing the imbalance of information between protesters and police, but to point out that they do so in a way which emphasises the veracity of narratives rather than challenging pre-existing narratives in such a way as to articulate alternative truths.

Consequently, Sukey places great emphasis on the ways in which information is gathered, condensed and *verified* before being released back out on to the street. Whereas as Indymedia sees the representation of events on the ground as something which can, and should, be contested in the discursive realm, Sukey presents events as something that can, and should, be independently verified by external observers before entering the discursive realm. According to this view, events are something that have either happened or not happened and Sukey perceives its role to be that of determining in which of these two categories a particular piece of information should fall. 'When you see something interesting, you tell us. When we're confident that something has actually happened we tell you' (www.opensukey.org).

Perhaps surprisingly, it is precisely this filtering role which has led commentators who are normally sceptical about the liberating potential of social networking, such as Tim Hardy (author of the blog Beyond Clicktivism), to argue that Sukey is a tool that 'is really being used to enable something to happen' (Hardy, 2011).

Sukey's conceptualisation of truth as something that has either happened or not happened (A/not A) is rooted within a very traditional emphasis on mutually opposed binaries. In doing so, Sukey backgrounds the structural inequalities which prompted the creation of Indymedia and implies that an approach which balances informational flows will provide users with a more complete understanding of events as they unfold upon the ground. The problem is that this balance depends upon an assumption of equality that many protesters of more longstanding experience do not perceive to exist (www.blowe.org.uk). Thus many protesters criticised Sukey for its failure to take into account the many ways in which the police enjoy symbolic and material resources that are unavailable to protesters.

Sukey's conceptualisation of information as true, verifiable and objective is an informational ethos, that Sukey team members acknowledge as having come straight from the mainstream newsroom. '"We're like a busy newsroom", says Bernie. "We have to get information in, check it makes sense, and then get it back out"' (Kingsley, 2011).

This ethos is built upon a traditionally Habermasian conception of the public sphere in which the media both inform the public, and constitute a neutral-power-free zone in which to agree upon what constitutes the greater good. Thus, while the sense of distanced objectivity which characterises Sukey is in keeping with the ethos of a mainstream newsroom, it is markedly different from the type of impassioned truth-telling you might find on Indymedia. Indymedia also aims to inform the public, but it perceives the space within which political participation takes place to be constructed very differently. Its commitment to horizontal communication flows and its refusal to act as an informational gatekeeper constitute a far more agonistic, and potentially antagonistic, public arena. Consequently, posts on Indymedia are frequently characterised by robust exchanges that usually (but not always) recognise the political other as an opponent rather than an enemy.

Although Sukey subscribes to a notion of truth as verifiable and objective, I should also point out that it is also aware of its ability to contribute to the construction of events on the ground. Thus, for example, one of Sukey's founding members describes a moment of doubt within the Sukey team when the demonstration on the ground split into three and began to wander off the route which had been pre-arranged with the police. There was some debate over whether the team should continue to produce information at this point as they felt that this might be 'instructing' rather than 'supporting' the flow of people upon the ground (Kingsley, 2011). Whilst the team agreed to continue working in order to 'protect people from trouble spots', they also made it clear that they, unlike Indymedia, did not see their role as that of leading 'people to the palace gates for the revolution' (Kingsley, 2011).

Sukey is upfront about its role as an informational gatekeeper and consequently its web pages exhibit none of the organisational soul-searching that accompanied Indymedia's decision to distinguish between different types of bottom-up comments. Since 2005, two contribution categories exist on the Indymedia South Coast website; 'additions' which are always on display and 'actually add useful information or make important factual corrections to something already posted' and 'Comments' which are listed by title only but which can be displayed by clicking on a reveal icon. This move was controversial – producing ten pages of additions/comments – but finally pushed through on the grounds that 'Indymedia is not a discussion forum, it is a news service' and therefore has an obligation to defend its 'credibility' (Blix bloc in Brighton, 22 March 2005).

In contrast Sukey does not aim to provide a conduit for information through which activists can communicate with each other, but to pass down compressed and verified information vertically. Thus, while Sukey occupies a smooth space which we routinely talk about as being characterised by empowering horizontal flows, we can see that it is actually rather didactic and hierarchical in its composition. This point can most easily be illustrated by looking at the visuals on its tutorial video (www.sukey.org), which feature a school master dinosaur, pointing stick in hand, forcefully instructing those below him.

Activist Critiques of Sukey

Having examined the ways in which Indymedia and Sukey function as 'emblems' (Fox, 2011) for two very different types of political organisation,

I will now focus briefly on the way in which Sukey has been received within the wider media environment. Sukey has garnered a considerable amount of (generally positive) mainstream media coverage. This is partly to do with the way in which social networking has become widely accepted as a mechanism through which global unrest can be better understood within popular narratives (Preston and Stelter, 2011). However, it also reflects the way in which Sukey, like activists from the Save Omar campaign, has issued press releases that engage effectively and enthusiastically, rather than cagily, with the mainstream. Articles prompted by Sukey's initial press release have appeared in *The Economist*, the *Star* and *New Scientist*. A far longer article, which also drew on a visit to the team's 'secret nerve centre', appeared in the *Guardian* shortly after the demonstrations on 29 January (Kingsley, 2011). All these articles outlined Sukey's basic aims and intentions and were cautiously optimistic about the opportunities offered by the new web application.

The response from the alternative media was initially similarly positive, with supportive articles and blogs appearing on sites such as Indymedia UK and Beyond Clicktivism. Sukey was recognised to be a 'nifty gadget' (Fox, 2011) with the potential to change the ways in which protesters and the police engaged with each other during public demonstrations. However a perceived reluctance to fully engage with alternative publics, coupled with a willingness to communicate with mainstream organisations such as the police, prompted a shift in activists' response to the web application. These doubts coalesced around a Sukey press release commenting on the Public Order Review published by Her Majesty's Inspectorate of Constabulary.

The initial press release was entitled 'Sukey comments on today's HMIC Report', and addressed the way in which the police force was struggling to 'cope with the increased volume and frequency of protest' in the wake of proposed cuts to their budget. It offered to 'step into that gap' by 'sharing information on planned kettles openly and honestly' and included the statement: 'Our work coincides entirely with the police goal of preserving public order, and the public's concern of staying safe at protests. It goes without saying that we are addressing concerns that we restrict criminals from exploiting it' (www.sukey.org).

This press release prompted a bitter and extended activist backlash manifesting itself through a flurry of frequently vitriolic outrage on Twitter and other social networking sites. Tweets included comments such as

Mirrorsandstuff #press release is poor; they seem proud that they are colluding with those that violate our rights. A useful tool, but come on . . .

boutmycolum@sukeyData right, the police are liars. We're not on the same side, their role is to 'faciliate' our ineffectuality so that we are ignored.

BrumProtest wtf?i thought #suky was a tool for protesters not 4 working with the police wonn't be contributing my data or my location to it in the future shame.

Activists' criticism unfolded over a range of social networking sites and quickly consolidated around three interwoven issues; Sukey's refusal to release the code behind the application, Sukey's reliance on commercial platforms and Sukey's willingness to engage with mainstream organisations. These issues will now be discussed in such a way as to reveal the unexamined givens which underpin Sukey's position in relation to both the margins and the mainstream.

The first criticism was technological in its nature. Unlike Indymedia, Sukey was not initially an open source project. While the Sukey team were prepared in principle to release the code to organisations that had expressed an interest in replicating the application in different locations, they claimed that 'usability issues' (Sukey: live demo info service for saturday – ldn, 27 January 2011) prevented them from doing so. The Sukey team maintained that the code would be 'meaningless to most without a decent and easy to use front and back end' (Gaus cited in Re: issues around Sukey the protest app, February 2011). When pushed, Sukey expressed its intention to release an annotated version of the code after the London demonstration 'then start working on Sukey 2 in a private fork' on the grounds that this would 'maximise both security and openness' (Sukey: live demo info service for saturday – ldn, 27 January 2011).[4]

However, activists from the Indymedia tradition, who are generally happy to throw 'messy code out into the public domain', felt that this was an act of technological gatekeeping (Harrison cited in Sukey sucks, 9 February 2011). At a pragmatic level, it was pointed out that refusing

---

4.   Sukey has as yet to release the code although it has been working with activists from Visionon TV. Following a period of silence on 3 August 2013 it tweeted about a forthcoming collaboration with 'the most intuitive hackers/developers'.

to release the code prevented Sukey from crowd-sourcing technical skills which would enable 'holes to be found and fixed a lot faster' (Harmon cited in Sukey sucks, 9 February 2011). On a more strategic level, it was argued that releasing the code would enable other activists to develop the code rhizomatically in any direction and so contribute to 'a diversity of strategies that is the building block of all successful social change projects' (Campell cited in Re: issues around Sukey the protest app, February 2011). The most critical commentators maintained that Sukey's refusal to release the code stemmed from a desire to remain in 'complete control' in order to 'collaborate with the police' (Harrison cited in Sukey sucks, 9 February 2011).

The second criticism stems from the web application's occupation of mainstream rather than alternative online spaces. In the past years there has been a move from explicitly radical sites such as Indymedia and Alternet to online spaces that are owned and controlled by commercial organisations such as Facebook and Twitter. The speed and intensity of technological change means that activists are frequently faced with a choice between remaining loyal to alt-tech and accepting 'the probably crippling effects of moving into a shadow world of limited usability/ effectiveness' (Campbell cited in Re: issues around Sukey the protest app, February 2011) or interacting with corporate sites which function 'on a scale and at a speed and with a user base that is huge compared to anything we ever did' (Indymedia London network cited in Askanius and Gustafsson, 2010, p. 36). In these circumstances protest organisations are increasingly 'hopping the fence' and moving into online spaces with greater technological affordances (Lodge cited in Re: issues around Sukey the protest app, February 2011).

These changes in the media practices of activism create hybrid spaces, which are characterised by 'the coexistence of subversive politics and commodified private communications' (Askanius and Gustafsson, 2010, p. 23). Within such spaces activists' passionate critiques of neo-liberalism are invariably bordered by banner ads promoting the very consumption patterns that ensure the continuance of neoliberal dynamics. Thus while activists may be radical in their intent, these spaces are often politically ambiguous in that the politics of collective action are being subsumed by those of connective action (Bennett and Segerberg, 2012).

Sukey's uncertain position within this hybrid space is highlighted by its own use of language. Sukey rarely echoes the vocabulary and tone of the radical left. Instead, it tends to mirror that of the consumption-orientated lexicon of the mainstream. For example, rather than describing itself as an 'international grassroots, activist network' (About Indymedia), the Sukey team describe it as a 'free product' (Sukey press release, 2011). Similarly, as well as distributing information about the movements of police and protesters, the web application also offers protesters information about nearby amenities such as coffee shops and payphones (Sukey press release, 2011). At times, their tone verges on the corporate. Thus its aims and intentions are outlined in 'an executive statement' and it carefully outlines its 'objectives' and 'Success Criteria' (Sukey: live demo info service for saturday – ldn, 27 January 2011).

Criticisms from the wider activist community were less concerned with overall control of these spaces and more alarmed by the security implications raised by the use of mainstream media platforms. The occupation of mainstream online space also raises a plethora of issues related to third-party management of data. As Morozov points out in relation to recent uprisings in the Middle East, the authorities now routinely use platforms such as Facebook and Twitter to maintain and/or increase socio-political control (2011). For many activists who may engage in more confrontational forms of protest and whose lives are already heavily policed, this is of course deeply problematic. According to Indymedia activist Yossarian, occupying mainstream online spaces, such as Twitter and Facebook, is 'like holding all your political meetings at McDonalds and ensuring that the police come and film while you do so' (cited in Askanius and Gustafsson, 2010 p. 34).

Despite these very real fears, the opportunities offered by mainstream service providers mean that activists simply cannot afford to ignore mainstream platforms such as Facebook or Twitter. Having decided to utilise mainstream platforms, Sukey took these issues seriously from the onset and all its data is 'anonymised using secure encryption that is known to be unbreakable in less than ten years using current computer technology' (Sukey – peaceful protest app without any mobile phone network communications data or traffic data anonymity, 29 January 2011). Unfortunately, these unsubstantiated reassurances were given late in the day and severely compromised the web application's 'reputation and credibility' (Gaus cited in Sukey: live demo info service for saturday – ldn, 27 January 2011) within the wider activist community.

Sukey's reluctance to release their coding, and their use of corporate platforms is indicative of the web application's ambiguous position on the boundary which both separates and connects the margins from the mainstream. This is interesting because it signals a shift away from the alternative/oppositional dichotomy outlined at the start of this book and towards a less explicitly critical view of the mainstream. Thus, while Sukey may well be critical of specific governmental policies, it is not critical of the mainstream per se. Indeed Sukey perceives itself *to be* the mainstream. Thus, for example, one of Sukey's responses to criticism reads: 'I think we have a different perception between our target audiences/readers . . . Sukey is about keeping peaceful protesters safe and informed and mobile. We're not part of the anarchist toolkit – and nor do we want to be . . . Sukey is designed to be predominately mainstream' (Re: issues around Sukey the protest app, February 2011).

This conceptualisation of protesters goes beyond challenging or unsettling the distinctions commonly drawn between protesters and publics. Indeed, Sukey relocates the boundary completely by redefining protesters as 'not full time activists' and re-conceiving them as '. . . just normal people who want to go about their normal lives and not be bundled in with those they see as crazies as a result of having attended the protest' (Re: issues around Sukey the protest app, February 2011).

This demarcation could be read as a precursor to Occupy's introduction of the phrase 'the 99%' which attempted to de-marginalise protest and, in doing so, presented its concerns as coinciding with those of the majority. However, whereas Occupy distinguishes between the 99 per cent who are disempowered by the process of neoliberalism and the 1 per cent who benefit from those processes (Chomsky, 2012), Sukey distinguishes between the majority who are characterised as 'normal people' and the minority who are characterised as the 'crazies'.

This is a distinction that ignores the possibility of solidarity between differently orientated protest clusters and is therefore entirely in keeping with more mainstream representations of activists. This is a view that was quickly taken up and articulated within the wider activist community. '[W]hat about those protesters who are not peaceful? What about solidarity with them? Your language is buying into the mass media and the government's line on what kind of protest is acceptable (Steven cited in Sukey sucks, 9 February 2011).

As such, one could argue that Sukey is contributing to, rather than resisting, the deligitimisation of certain more confrontational/effective forms of protest.

As discussed in Chapters 3, 4 and 5, the anti-globalisation and the anti-war movements have both attempted, with varying degrees of success, to maintain solidarity across the boundaries which have been used by the mainstream to distinguish good protesters from bad protesters. However Sukey, whose imagined audience is not explicitly radical but 'predominantly mainstream' (Gaus cited in Re: issues around Sukey the protest app, February 2011), has drawn this boundary very differently. Indeed Sukey is clear in its disavowal of protest forms which transgress the pre-established boundaries of the law. For them, activists who are prepared to engage in more confrontational forms of protest are crazy at best and criminal at worst. The reservations expressed by the wider activist community in response to these distinctions were compounded by what critics perceived to be Sukey's willingness to communicate and even collaborate with the police.

These critiques are rooted in two interrelated issues. Firstly, activists are hugely critical of Sukey's tendency to categorise police and protesters as equally powerful partners in dialogue. This point is best exemplified by an activist who criticised Sukey's willingness to engage with the police on the grounds that the police are a 'massive conservative and powerful state institution which can legally use force and coercion', and who argued that Sukey's emphasis on balance was failing to 'whole-heartedly take sides with those who hold the least power' (The curious case of Sukey and the bizarre press release, 10 February 2011). This view is rooted in the radical democratic understanding of the public sphere which sees debate within the public sphere as masking rather than challenging the processes of domination (Fraser, 1990).

Secondly, there was hostility towards the idea expressed by Sukey that the eradication of the communicative boundary between police and protesters was desirable as it would contribute to 'reducing the need for kettling' (www.openSukey.org). However, as an activist writing in the *Commune* puts it: 'Mass violence against the police is a necessary part of any social struggle' (On violence against the police, 10 December 2010).

This focus is indicative of a more fundamental difference in relation to Indymedia and Sukey's conceptualisation of the role of conflict within mass demonstrations. Whilst Sukey adopts a very mainstream position in which conflict is seen as evidence of a failure of the political system, the wider activist community sees conflict as a necessary element in the production of social and political change.

As discussed at the beginning of this chapter, Sukey is designed to enable ordinary people to avoid being kettled; it is designed to ease the friction between protesters and police. In collapsing the boundary between protesters and police it creates a new (and far more familiar) boundary between activists and protesters, normals and crazies, the mainstream and the margins. According to this view, Sukey could be read as dissipating resistance before it has even had time to form and, in doing so, one might argue that it is doing the police's job for them. This would require one to re-evaluate the usefulness of Sukey and to think of it as another means of administering popular protest.

Confrontation

> The brutality of the police is not incidental to the nature of the state, it is essential to it… someone has to say it.
>
>   (On violence against the police, 10 December 2010)

In this book I have opened up the binary distinctions that underpin classical models of the public sphere and explored the ways in which protest coalitions exist within a multiplicity of ideological and tactical distinctions. This chapter contrasts Indymedia's very ideologically embedded position with Sukey's almost entirely solution-orientated perspective. In doing so, I highlight the ways in which differently-orientated protest organisations communicate both with other co-aligned protest clusters and the mainstream. Thus, while Indymedia imagines its users to be a horizontally-organised group of like-minded radicals brought together by a shared informational endeavour, Sukey imagines its audience to be a group of disparate individuals who are in need of practical information but may not describe themselves as activists.

An ongoing consequence of the frictions outlined above is that protesters' positions on the legitimated side of the citizenship line are constantly being negotiated from a multiplicity of differing perspectives. A networked understanding of the public sphere which foregrounds the ways in which the agonistic friend/opponent relationships are perpetually in danger of tipping over into an antagonistic friend/enemy distinction, can more easily withstand the contestation and confrontation that necessarily characterises a fully functioning democracy (Mouffe, 2005). Such understandings can also accommodate the way in which the smooth and the striated, the rhizomatic and the arborescent, the alternative and the mainstream are both separated and connected by the boundaries that distinguish them. This enables one to better understand the way in which differently organised and ideologically orientated protest groups can communicate both with each other and with the mainstream.

In this book I have also explored some of the different ways in which clusters of protesters within wider coalition movements maintain political solidarity across tactical difference. This opening out is necessary in order to take into account the changes in an increasingly fractured and fractious protest environment as well as the changes in a media landscape provoked by both the unfolding processes of globalisation and the advent of new communications technologies. Within this context the boundary loses the static quality that characterises traditional conceptualisations of the public sphere and becomes dynamic and potentially transformative.

While scholars such as Benkler and Castells (2006; 2007) have proposed networked models of the public sphere, these models frequently lose or background the sense of nuance and contradiction offered by the work of scholars such as Fraser (1987; 1990). The model proposed in these pages offers an understanding of the public sphere that can accommodate the articulation of polyvocal dissent. Such a model has the capacity to account for both rhizomatic and arborescent communication systems on the one hand and smooth and striated public spaces on the other, and therefore constitutes a theoretical framework within which a multiplicity of differently-organized protest movements can be better understood.

This understanding requires one to foreground, rather than to eliminate, the boundary both between differently-oriented protest clusters and between wider coalitions and the mainstream. Within such a model, distinctions are central to the legitimation of political difference (Mouffe, 2005) and therefore the existence of boundaries becomes a necessary and productive part of the political process. Indeed, I would argue that the notion of the boundary is central to the notion of resistance. Resistance is something that happens in relation to something else. Thus we have the existence of the *anti*-globalisation movement, the *anti*-war movement and *anti*-austerity movements. It is the boundary, the sense of being against something, that creates friction and gives protest movements political traction. To lose the boundary entirely would be to lose the place where traction is created.

Consequently, this book does not follow the route suggested by scholars such as Hardt and Negri who advocate the eradication of the boundary. Instead it focuses on the need to challenge demarcations that move from a political register to a moral one. Within a moral register, the implications raised by the friend and opponent/enemy distinction become key, as opponents can so easily be cast as enemies and therefore deemed to exist beyond the realm of public debate. In this way, the necessary tension in agonistic relations that are an essential part of a fully-functioning democracy can slip into the antagonism that is so harmful to the democratic process.

The de-legitimisation of protesters is a way of justifying the use of state force. If protesters are criminals rather than citizens, bad rather than good, then any action against them becomes an action taken in the public interest. Moreover, and as Waddington points out, it is frequently the police (and, I would argue, in an increasingly mediated world, journalists) who position protesters on either side of this line. Thus, in our streets and on our screens we are confronted by protest narratives in which good peaceful protesters comply with the status quo and bad/mad protesters do not. These protesters are framed as a threat that must be contained in both actual and textual spaces in order to protect the interests of the wider public.

Conclusion

This does not merely allow us to hope for human improvement; it is already a form of improvement in itself.

(Kant, 1991, p. 182)

In this book I have attempted to address some of the questions which puzzled me as an idealistic young activist. How do political understandings move from the margins to the mainstream? What impedes their journey? How can these barriers be overcome? These issues have always been central to our understanding of political progress in mature western democracies and have been approached by scholars from a range of interconnected disciplines. Thus contributions have been made by sociologists, academics interested in new social movements, political communications scholars and alternative media theorists (McCurdy, 2012). This book is situated between these bodies of work and seeks to create a space in which different interrogative approaches can productively overlap.

The recent rise of coalition movements requires academics and activists to reflect again upon the way in which protesters contribute to the formation of public opinion. This book suggests that changes in the systems and structures which shape grass roots political communications require one to reconceptualise the theoretical models which traditionally frame an understanding of the public sphere within mature western democracies. Consequently it aims to re-examine the theoretical and empirical implications raised by the communicative strategies used in the articulation of polyvocal dissent and attempts to inflect them differently. It is particularly concerned with the role of the us/them divides within coalition politics and the role which protest methodologies play in managing the agonistic/antagonistic distinction.

In an attempt to better understand how the on-going relationship between the margins and the mainstream is altered by the articulation of polyvocal dissent, I have explored some of the ways in which a political system traditionally structured by clearly demarcated boundaries can accommodate articulations of dissent predicated on an entanglement of differences. Rather than focusing on one particular movement, I have chosen to examine the organisational systems which structure both alternative and mainstream public spheres and to analyse protest coalition movements' communication *across* a multiplicity of political differences. This has enabled me to move beyond an analysis of individual organisations and to comment on coalition movements as a communicative force within contemporary public spheres.

This book is distinctive in that it contributes, both theoretically and empirically to a number of interrelated themes. Firstly, it updates the work of Epstein by focusing on the ways in which social movements are characterised by a celebration of difference whilst at the same time recognising that the articulation of dissent has always been a surprisingly fractured and uncertain business (Calhoun, 2012). In doing so it situates contemporary protest coalitions within the specific context of a newly globalised world characterised by a self-reflexive awareness of risk (Beck, 1992; Giddens, 1991) in which activists are acutely conscious of the difficulties and potentials prompted by difference.

Secondly, it extends Mouffe's work by arguing that the need to combine solidarity and difference is of central importance to a notion of coalition politics. The need autonomously to manage political relationships on the brink of the antagonistic/agonistic divide is central to the well-being of democracy in an increasingly fragmented and fractured world. Similarly the need to refrain from overwhelming a plethora of 'minority' differences in the interest of establishing 'majority' interests is an increasingly pertinent political challenge. This book explores these issues in a number of political contexts and concludes by suggesting that protest coalitions emphasis on methodology over ideology holds the key to negotiating these democratic challenges.

Consequently the third theme developed in this book relates to the methodologies which underpin the communicative strategies of coalition protest movements. I focused on the ways in which very differently orientated activist groupings preserve solidarity as well as political difference, arguing that protest coalitions' use of experimental organisational structures and systems distinguishes them from more traditionally organised political groupings. I suggest that alternative modes of communication have enabled activists to side-step many of the divides which characterise arborescent inter-organisational relationships of both radical left and mainstream organisations. This methodological emphasis is an extension and development of Habermas's focus on communicative procedures (a theoretical position which has been recognised by Hands) and creates a space in which coalition movements use of innovative and challenging protest repertoires can be better understood.

Finally, I have concentrated on the ways in which coalition groups communicate nuanced and sometimes contradictory political positions in a frequently inhospitable mainstream. I have analysed coalition activists' deployment of communicative strategies which reveal power dynamics (which are under developed in the work of both Habermas and Benkler) in order to renegotiate the boundaries which exist between activists and non-activists. I have therefore focused on how political ideas travel through the complex system of connections which both bind and separate the margins and the mainstream. Thus, I have attempted to develop a more interconnected understanding of the ways in which protest coalitions contribute to the formation of public opinion.

The fluctuating dynamics under consideration in this book have been complicated by the ways in which the texture of coalition protests has evolved during the time it has taken to complete this research. When I began this book, the anti-globalisation movement was at its political peak. However, the attacks on the World Trade Center in 2001 transformed the political environment within which protest groups must function and redirected the energies of many grassroots campaigners. The end of the Bush administration combined with the global economic downturn at the end of 2008 has once again altered the relationship between public(s) and both political and economic powers. While the parameters of protest have always been challenged and redefined by the political, social and economic circumstances which surround them, there is a sense in which the last ten years *may* have fundamentally altered the ways in which dissent can be articulated.

While the contextual circumstances surrounding the articulations of dissent are constantly changing, the issues raised by this book are of ongoing relevance and concern. For example, while public debates around the practice of 'kettling' protesters have evolved considerably over the past ten years, the technique continues to reveal the power dynamics which exist between protesters, police and the public. 'Kettling' can be read as a metaphor for the many frictions which surround the constantly changing and competing needs for freedom and security. Thus I would suggest that while the inflections articulated in this book are historically specific, the issues they raise transcend the political moment.

In order to address the issues raised by activists' articulation of polyvocal dissent, I began this book by complicating traditional understandings of the public sphere (Habermas, 1974). Jürgen Habermas's conception of a space in which private individuals can gather in order to arrive at a reasoned understanding of what constitutes the public good is rooted in an enlightenment tradition. The enlightenment ideals of equality, reason, and transparency continue to underpin the political processes of most democracies in mature Western societies. Despite the many problems associated with these aspirational ideals the notion of the public sphere remains 'indispensable to critical social theory and to democratic political practice' (Fraser, 1990, p. 57). Democracy still is, as Winston Churchill famously declared, the least 'worst form of government' (1947, pp. 206–7).

However, the increasing complexities of our globalised world accentuate the gaps which have always existed between the ideal and the actuality of our democratic processes. The perceived (and actual) decline in political participation has prompted a re-evaluation of the notion of the public sphere. Academic responses to this fissure between theory and practice have tended to focus on the constitutive boundaries of the public sphere and on the democratic legitimacy of various communicative modes (Garnham, 2007, p. 207). This book develops both these strands of research in relation to the communicative strategies of protest coalitions. It has focused in particular on the ways in which binary thinking, which tends to structure our democratic systems, has been unsettled and re-negotiated by the often experimental communicative strategies of protest coalition movements.

In Chapters 1 and 2 I began by focusing on the implications raised by the articulation of polyvocal dissent in mainstream arenas still accustomed to the clear-cut boundaries offered by more modernist political understandings. I built upon the work of authors such as Nancy Fraser (1987; 1990; 2007) by trying to re-imagine the constitutive boundaries of an interconnected series of public spheres. I also drew on the work of Chantal Mouffe (2005) and attempted to envisage a model of the public sphere characterised by an unsettling sense of uncertainty but more able to accommodate forcefully felt political differences. Lastly, I utilised Deleuze and Guattari's notion of rhizomatic systems and smooth spaces (2004) in order to better conceptualise a model of the public sphere able to accommodate fully entangled articulations of dissent.

The connections between the fields of research outlined above are implicit but underdeveloped in much of the work being done by social movement theorists and alternative media scholars. In these pages I have attempted to foreground and highlight the connections which exist between the aspirational certainties of a classical approach to the public sphere and the fluctuating political potential inherent in rhizomatic models. In this way I have developed a model of the public sphere which, unlike Benkler, recognises the power dynamics at play in a networked public sphere and can therefore more easily accommodate the polyvocal articulation of dissent. I hope that the approaches outlined in this book will be of value not only to academics working within these theoretical fields but also to activists attempting to access mainstream public spheres.

An unanticipated element in this research has been the emphasis on boundaries. Unlike Hands I do not see boundaries as in themselves politically problematic, nor do I follow Michael Hardt and Antonio Negri (2000; 2006) in attempting to overcome or deny the existence of boundaries. Instead I endeavour to reconceptualise the ways in which the notion of the boundary is brought to bear on our understanding of political communications within the public sphere. Therefore I have argued that boundaries which are uncertain and can be renegotiated are an entirely necessary and politically productive element of our democratic system. In this way rather than striving to overcome boundaries, I endeavour to better understand the flexible connective boundaries which tend to characterise political life in general and the communicative strategies of coalition protest movements in particular. Ironically this book is therefore, in many ways, structured by the very boundaries and binaries it attempts to unsettle.

This emphasis on boundaries calls upon one to think about them differently. It requires one to view boundaries as a frontier with the potential to connect as well as separate differently constructed spaces. In this way boundaries stop being a barrier to be crossed and become an in-between space which can be productively occupied. As this book has illustrated, such 'in the middle' spaces are full of exciting and unexpected political possibilities. However the price of such a productively entangled position is that everything is in a state of unstable and perpetual renegotiation. Consequently one is denied the comfort of certainty. Such a position demands that academics relinquish the possibility of a theory to end all theories and accept instead that theoretical progress is uneven, fractured and fragmented.

This book went on to reflect on activists' interest in the relationship between political ideologies and strategic methodologies. This focus is of particular relevance to coalition movements because they are in a position where they must maintain solidarity whilst also preserving political difference. I therefore followed Habermas (1974) and Hands by making a connection between methodological systems (such as rational consensual deliberation) and ideological spaces (such as the liberal bourgeois public sphere). I also expanded this connection to include the non-textual strategies utilised by coalition activists frustrated by the limitations imposed by traditional political modes of communication. In this way I addressed protest movements' need to accommodate both and express difference by focusing on the communicative strategies of coalition activists.

This position challenges the work of commentators such as Daniel Boorstin (1992) and Neil Postman (1985), who attribute the (perceived) decline in the standard of public debate within the public sphere to a move away from traditional communication forms. In doing so I develop the work of scholars such as Jon Simons (2003) and Lisbet van Zoonen (2004) who celebrate the political potential offered by a more postmodern interpretation of political discourse and I examined the ways in which alternative discourses contribute to the production of mainstream print narratives. In this way I explored the political possibilities offered by alternative communicative forms, such as routes, bands and masks, and proposed a model of the public sphere which accommodates, rather than laments, changes in the systems and structures which constitute the contemporary public sphere.

It's important to note that the chapters in this book do not constitute the realisation of a pre-conceived plan or idea. In my view a methodological plan which determines one's route through the field limits the possibility of discovering anything other than what one was already expecting to find. In contrast an entry into the field without a map requires one to engage more thoroughly with one's environs and opens up the possibility of encountering ways in which to think about things differently. In keeping with the aspirational idea of an 'in the middle' position I have therefore adopted a methodological approach that prioritises reflexivity and enables the temporal and spatial rhythms of everyday political life to unfold.

Chapters 3, 4, 5 and 6 of this book are organised around a number of case studies which explore the protest strategies of grassroots coalition movements. Thus I have examined the way in which single issue organisations such as the women of Greenham Common and anti-Criminal Justice Bill coalitions metamorphosed into multi-issue groups such as the anti-globalisation movement, the anti-war movement and anti-austerity movements. This focus has allowed me to analyse the way in which specific coalition movements communicate with both each other and the mainstream, whilst also enabling me to develop a broader understanding of the systems and structures which connect these organisations across time.

Towards the end of the twentieth century the declining interest in traditional party politics led to a rise in single-issue politics. Each single-issue campaign was perceived as somehow discrete and distanced from those which ran alongside them. However, this fractured notion of protest has since led to a political environment in which previously separate campaign strands have coalesced into a shared multiplicity of differing positions. As a result, coalition movements are playing an increasingly important role in political life. It is therefore important to investigate the communicative strategies employed by protest coalition movements attempting to articulate polyvocal dissent.

By examining the ways in which protest coalitions unsettle and renegotiate the in-between or overlapping spaces between their different elements and between themselves and the mainstream, I have tried to develop a more flexible and nuanced account of the democratic potential offered by organisations which privilege the impassioned entanglement of differing political views. Such an understanding recognises the multiplicity of possibilities offered by an approach which refuses the constraints of the A not A dichotomy and celebrates rather than fears the energising forces of agonistically expressed difference.

I have been particularly concerned with the move away from organisations which seek to replace mainstream systems and structures and have focused on protest coalitions which offer a far more fragmented amalgamation of views both as an alternative to, and in opposition to, the mainstream. This replaces the traditional understanding of political progress as a revolutionary movement from black to white with a more complex ideologically inclusive area in uncertain shades of grey. Such a position requires activists, like academics, to let go of traditional assurances and to embrace the perils and pleasures of uncertainty.

Chapters 3, 4 and 5 were particularly interested in the ways in which protest coalitions stemming from a socialist-anarchist tradition capture and construct both textual and actual spaces. I extended the anarchist organisation's historical emphasis on capturing geographical or actual spaces to include symbolic or textual spaces, in the belief that such a move would open up the theoretical debate on the validity of alternative communicative approaches within the public sphere. I therefore reflected upon the relationship between democratic methodologies and ideologies in my attempt to further rehabilitate non textual forms of political communication.

Chapter 3 began by focusing on groups which can retrospectively be characterised as coalition movements such as the peace activists who protested against cruise missiles and free-party activists opposed to the introduction of the 1994 Criminal Justice Bill. These two protest coalitions are of particular relevance because while they were considered at the time to be examples of single issue politics, their organisational systems emphasised ideological flexibility and multiplicity which is now considered to be characteristic of contemporary coalition movements. Consequently these groups offer a particularly useful insight into the move from single-issue politics (which are more easily accommodated by communicative systems which are characterised by binaries and boundaries) to multi issue politics or coalition politics which require different systems and structures if they are to flourish.

I began Chapter 3 by focusing on *Socialist Worker*. I argued that *Socialist Worker* is characterised by arborescent organisational systems which tend to produce striated political spaces characterised by order, hierarchy and clearly defined boundaries. I compared these organisational systems and structures with an analysis of three more rhizomatically structured organisations/publications (*The Greenham Factor*, *Circus Free* and Indymedia) and argued that these experimental communicative strategies, which refused hierarchy and prioritised flexibility, enabled coalition movements to both generate and maintain a multiplicity of protest positions. Thus I extended rhizomatic models of media organisations to include the emergence of protest coalitions and suggested that there was a relationship between the rhizomatic organisational structures utilised by protest coalition movements and their occupation of vibrantly smooth spaces able to sustain the articulation of political differences.

I also challenged the commonly held view that coalition movements have flourished as a direct result of computer-mediated communication forms. I supported this view by analysing the rhizomatically produced web spaces of Indymedia and traced its smooth qualities back through the photocopied pages of the anti-Criminal Justice Bill publication *Circus Free* and into the printed pages of *The Greenham Factor* and argued that coalition movements' use of computer mediated technologies is rooted in historical rather than teleological arguments. I concluded by suggesting that the desire to capitalise on horizontal, participatory communication linkages has always been an important feature of the smooth political spaces which foster the prioritisation of polyvocal dissent.

Chapter 4 extended and developed the text based analysis of Chapter 3 by exploring how rhizomatically organised mass demonstrations occupy city spaces in such a way as to challenge and unsettle previously unnoticed boundaries. I drew a parallel between the ways in which political texts and political marches are consumed by the reader/viewer and widened my focus to include non-textual communicative modes. I focused on how differently orientated anti-globalisation protest groupings interact during large-scale summit demonstrations by utilising non-textual communicative strategies in order to articulate a multiplicity of complex, but more or less unified, protest positions.

This chapter was particularly interested in the protest repertoires which exist on the very brink of the agonistic/antagonistic divide. Confrontational protest actions are of particular relevance to this book because they illuminate the way in which the inter-organisational systems of coalition movements are predicated, not on an absence of boundaries, but on the notion of boundaries in a state of perpetual flux. I argued that the confrontational communicative strategies of some protest groupings highlight the ways in which coalition movements have developed strategies which enable them to both foreground and then overcome potentially divisive political differences. In doing so I examined the ways in which conflicting protest repertoires, particularly those which advocate radical confrontations, were assimilated into more generally cautious and reformist political movements.

Chapter 4 examined the agonistic relationship between coalition movements and the mainstream. However it is also necessary for both activists and academics to reflect upon the point at which agonistic relations between the margins and the mainstream become antagonistic. A second interrelated series of questions was raised in Chapter 5 which focused on the tendency of some politically marginal organisations to advocate an absolute withdrawal from mainstream systems and structures. Both these scenarios recast the relationship between alternative and mainstream publics and raise a new series of questions about the articulation of dissent in mature western democracies. While these issues are worthy of consideration they sadly fall beyond the confines of this book.

Chapter 5 reflected on the classification and management of public demonstrations. This chapter focused on the anti-war movement in Brighton and Hove and examined the internal and external pressures on the boundaries which both separate and connect the margins from the mainstream. It looked at the contradictory dynamic between some activists' desire to preserve alternative spaces and the need felt by other activists to access mainstream spaces. This chapter was therefore primarily concerned with the connections which lie between the protest coalition movements and the way in which these connections continue to unsettle the boundaries between alternative and mainstream spaces. It looked at how the spaces between differently organised groupings are maintained, clash and occasionally overlap. In this way it foregrounds the political potential inherent in the boundaries which both separate and connect the alternative and the mainstream, the activist and the non-activist, us and them.

Chapter 5 developed many of the issues raised in Chapter 4 by further exploring the distinctions drawn between 'good' and 'bad' coalition protesters. In doing so it examined the political potential of the deliberately awkward and uncertain position chosen by coalition protesters, exploring the implications raised by occupying such an enmeshed position in 'the fabric of the rhizome' (Deleuze and Guattari, 2004, p. 27). It also analysed the ways in which differently orientated protest clusters can combine into a more articulate and polyvocal whole and examined how coalition relationships with both journalists and the police contribute to the ever changing relationship between activists and the wider public. Thus Chapter 5 attempted to collapse many of the distinctions drawn in the previous chapters in an attempt to better understand the issues raised by the communicative strategies of protest coalition movements.

This chapter could have expanded to become an entirely new book. The temporal and spatial proximity of both the Smash EDO and the Save Omar campaigns offered many opportunities for participant observation which, due to the constraints of time and space, could not be more fully developed. For example a more extensive and precise survey of the organisational structures which shape activists' interactions away from the mainstream would have offered many insights into the ways in which polyvocal dissent is actively constructed by individual activists. However this research focus would not have addressed the questions laid out in this book and must therefore wait for another day!

Chapter 6 developed and extended the discussions around the police practice of kettling in a number of ways. Firstly it built upon De Certeau's notion of walking/reading the city in relation to the routes of public demonstrations, discussed in Chapter 4. It also developed the connection introduced in Chapter 5, regarding the way in which demonstrations are enacted upon the ground, with particular reference to the police practice of kettling. This chapter did so with a specific emphasis on the way in which social networking sites and mobile technologies have contributed to the dynamic between police and protesters; protesters and publics; 'good' protesters and 'bad' protesters. It differed from Chapters 3, 4 and 5 in that it did not look at explicitly anarchist/autonomist publics, or indeed even alternative publics but looked instead at demonstrators as 'ordinary people'.

This chapter addresses the recent UK demonstrations against cuts in the public sector in general and rises in student fees in particular. It focused on the ways in which the mobile application Sukey combines the strong ties of activism and the weaker ties of online participation to create a resilient network of texts, tweets and Google Maps offering protesters a solar eye view of the demonstration they constitute as it unfolds upon the ground. It reflected upon the implications raised by Sukey's occupation of mainstream corporate spaces rather than explicitly alternative spaces that have traditionally had both technological and political connotations. In doing so it focused in upon the nature of Sukey's imagined audience and the ramifications of their understanding for activists more generally in their attempts to resist the totalising administrations of the state.

Like the coalition movements these pages investigate, this book occupies a position between a plethora of very differently constructed spaces. As such I have attempted to explore some of the possibilities offered by multiplicity and flux whilst also maintaining a commitment to the aspirational ideals that constitute the democratic process. As a result I have combined very different critical and methodological approaches. I have also tried to blur the distinctions between concepts which are frequently understood in opposition to each other, such as reason and passion, the real and the unreal, the smooth and the striated, the textual and the actual, the alternative and the mainstream. In doing so I have offered a model that can account for the hugely diverse range of organisations that constitute contemporary responses to the dynamics of neoliberalism by foregrounding, rather than eradicating the boundaries which exist between protesters and publics, the online and the offline, the margins and the mainstream.

Despite the difficulties and complications I have encountered, I firmly believe that an emphasis on the 'lines' between coalition movements rather than the 'points' which isolate them (Deleuze and Guattari, 2004,

p. 9) has much to offer the understanding of democracy in an increasingly complex and fractured world. Moreover such a focus foregrounds issues and concerns such as the balancing of us/them distinctions, the use of innovative protest methodologies and their role in renegotiating the boundary between the political margins and the mainstream. These are concerns which are of ongoing practical relevance both to protest coalition movements and to media policy-makers which future research projects could develop in more empirical detail. Such understandings may soon become particularly pertinent within mainstream British arenas as forthcoming elections might well necessitate changes in political communication systems which currently find it difficult to recognise and interact with more fractured forms of politics.

The political spaces produced by coalition movements are uncomfortable in that they foreground and unsettle many of the binary distinctions which have traditionally structured communication within the public sphere. The mainstream's current lack of familiarity with the organisational strategies of coalition movements, particularly those stemming from a socialist-anarchist tradition, has resulted in a tendency to perceive a different type of order as a complete lack of order. Partly as a result of this misrecognition, the communicative strategies of coalition movements have frequently been viewed as evidence of an ongoing decline in the quality of public debate. In these pages I have therefore tried to makes visible the systems and structures which shape this 'disorder'.

However, in these pages I have argued that, far from being evidence of a terrible and somehow inevitable deterioration in the democratic processes which shape our society, the communicative strategies of coalition movements are innovative and effective contributors in the wider debate over what constitutes the public good. This view requires one to re-envisage both the parameters of public debate and the modes of communication which take place within and between differently orientated publics. While there are undoubtedly many problems associated with these differently organised in-between positions, this book maintains that they are also hugely productive political spaces.

Consequently this book has focused on the perpetually shifting, fluctuating and contradictory dynamics which characterise these in-between political spaces and analysed the ways in which these spaces interact with both the alternative and mainstream spaces which surround them. It has argued that coalition activists' commitment to rhizomatic organisational structures creates spaces in which there are far fewer limitations on thinking differently. These spaces are characterised by an emphasis on innovation and participation which has revitalised the communicative strategies of grassroots campaigning. So, whilst in the past protesters waited in optimism or despair for the day everything changed, now protesters concentrate on the small but endless opportunities for contestation. Thus I would like to conclude by following Kant and suggesting that this sense of political enthusiasm 'does not merely allow us to hope for human improvement; it is already a form of improvement in itself' (1991, p. 183).

Bibliography and Sources

Books and Journals

Abel, R. (1997) 'An alternative press: why?' *Publishing Research Quarterly* Vol. 12(4), pp. 78–84.

Adorno, T. and Horkheimer, K. (1979) *Dialectic of Enlightenment*, London: Verso.

Aldridge, M. (2007) *Understanding the Local Media*, London and New York: Open University Press.

Allen, P. (1985) 'Socialist Worker – paper with a purpose', *Media, Culture and Society* Vol. 7, pp. 205–32.

Amad, P. (1994) *Radical Inauthenticity and Cultural Anxiety: The Benetton Advertising Phenomenon*, MA thesis, Department of English: University of Melbourne.

Aronowitz, S. (1996) *Techno Science and Cyber Culture*, London and New York: Routledge.

Askanius, T. and Gustafsson, N. (2010) 'Mainstreaming the alternative: the changing media practices of protest movements', *Interface: a Journal for and About Social Movements* Vol. 2, pp. 23–41.

Atkinson, R. (1998) Review of Soja, E. Third space: Journeys to Los Angeles and other real and imagined places, Capital and Class, Vol. 64, pp. 237.

Atton, C. (1999) 'A reassessment of the alternative press', *Media Culture and Society* Vol. 21(1), pp. 51–76.

Atton, C. (2002) *Alternative Media*, London: Sage.

Bailey, O. Cammaerts, B. and Carpentier, N. (2008) *Understanding Alternative Media*, Maidenhead: Open University Press.

Bakhtin, M. (1941) *Rabelais and his World*, Bloomington: Indiana University Press.

Barry, R. MacRury, I. Botterill, J. (2000) *The Dynamics of Advertising*, Amsterdam: Harwood Academic Publishers.

Bartholomew, A. and Mayer, M. (1992) 'Nomads of the present: Melucci's contribution to "New Social Movement"', *Theory, Theory Culture and Society* Vol. 9, pp. 142–9.

Baudrillard, J. (1983) *Simulations*, New York: Semiotext.

Bauman, Z. (1998) *Globalisation: The Human Consequences*, Cambridge: Polity Press.

Bauman, Z. (2004) *Wasted Lives*. Cambridge: Polity Press.

Beck, U. (1992) *Risk Society: Towards a New Modernity*, Ritter, M. (trans), London: Thousand Oaks, New Delhi: Sage.

Benhabib, S. (1992) *Situating the Self: Gender, Community and Postemodernism in Contemporary Ethics*. Cambridge: Polity Press .

Benjamin, W. (1982) 'The author as producer', Frascina, F. and Harrison, C. (eds), *Modern Art and Modernism: A Critical Anthology*, London: Paul Chapman Publishing.

Benkler, Y. (2006) *The Wealth of Networks: How Social Production Transforms Markets and Freedoms*, New Haven CT: Yale University Press.

Bennett, L. (2003) 'New Media Power: The Internet and Global Activism', Couldry N. and Curran J. (eds), *Contesting Media Power*, New York: Rowman and Littlefield.

Bennett, L. and Segerberg, A. (2012) 'The logics of connective action: digital media and the personalisation of contentious politics', *Information Communication and Society* Vol. 15, pp. 739–68.

Bentham, J. (1995) *Panopticon Letters* Bozovic, M. (ed.) London: Verso pp. 29–95.

Berger, S. (2005) 'From Aldermaston marcher to internet activist', de Jong, W. Shaw, M. and Stammers, N. (eds), *Global Activism Global Media*, London: Pluto Press, pp. 84–93.

Berry, D. (2008) *Copy, Rip, Burn: The Politics of Copyleft and Open Source*, London: Pluto Press.

Billig, M. (1995) *Banal Nationalism*, London: Sage.

Birchall, I. (1981) *The Smallest Mass Party in the World*, London: Socialist Workers Party pamphlet.

Blake, H. (2010) 'Student tuition fee protest turns violent as Tory headquarters evacuated', 10 November 2010, *Telegraph*.

Blunt, A. and Wills, J. (2000) *Dissident Geographies: An Introduction to Radical Ideas and Practice*, Singapore: Prentice Hall.

Boje, D. and Rosilie, G. (2003) 'Life imitates art: Enron's epic and tragic narration', *Management Communication Quarterly* Vol. 17, p. 87.

Boorstin, D. (1992) *The Image: A Guide to Pseudo-Events in America*, New York: Vintage Books.

Bostdorff, D.M. (1994) *The Presidency and the Rhetoric of Foreign Crisis*, Columbia: University of South Carolina.

Bruner, M.L. (2005) 'Carnivalesque protest and the humourless state', *Text and Performance Quarterly* Vol. 25 pp. 136–55.

Bryan, C. and Tatam, J. (1999) 'Political participation and the internet', Liberty (ed.), *Liberating Cyberspace: Civil Liberties, Human Rights and the Internet*, London: Pluto Press.

Burbules, N. (1998) 'Rhetorics of the web: hyper-reading and critical literacy', Snyder, I. (ed.) *Page to Screen: Taking Literacy into the Electronic Era*, London: Routledge.

Calhoun, C. (1992) *Habermas and the Public Sphere*, Cambridge MA: MIT Press.

Calhoun, C. (2012) *The Roots of Radicalism*, Chicago: University of Chicago Press.

Cammaerts, B. (2012) 'Protest logics and the mediation opportunity structure', *European Journal of Communication*, 27(2), pp. 117–34.

Carrigan A. (2001) Afterword to Marcos, Subcomandante Insurgente, *Our Word is Our Weapon: Selected Writings*, Ponce de Leon, J. (ed.), London: Serpent's Tail.

Castells, M. (1996) *The Rise of the Networked Society*, The Information Age: Economy Society and Culture Vol. 1, Oxford: Blackwell.

Castells, M. (2007) 'Communication, power and counter power in the networked society', *International Journal of Communication*, pp. 238–66.

Chatterton, P. (2006) '"Give up activism" and change the world in unknown ways: or learning to walk with others on uncommon ground', *Antipode* Vol. 38, pp. 259–81.

Chomsky, N. (1997) *The Spectacular Achievements of Propaganda*, New York: Seven Stories Press.

Chomsky, N. (2012) *Occupy*, London: Penguin.

Cleaver, H. (1998) 'The Zapatista effect: the internet and the rise of an alternative political fabric', *Journal of International Affairs* Vol. 51, pp. 621–40.

Conboy, M. (2008) 'Carnival and the popular press', Biressi, A. and Nunn, H. (eds), *The Tabloid Culture Reader*, Maidenhead: Open University Press.

Corner, J. (2007) 'Mediated politics: promotional culture and the idea of "propaganda"', *Media Culture and Society* Vol. 29, pp. 669–77.

Cottle, S. (2012) 'Demonstrations, riots and uprisings: mediated dissent in a changing communication environment', public lecture given at London School of Economics and Political Science, January 2012.

Couldry, N. (2000) *The Place of Media Power: Pilgrims and Witnesses of the Media Age*, London and New York: Routledge.

Couldry N. and Curran J. (2003) 'The Paradox of Media Power', Couldry N. and Curran J. (eds), *Contesting Media Power*, New York: Rowman and Littlefield.

Coyer K. (2005) 'If it leads it bleeds: the participatory news making of the Independent News Centre', de Jong, W. Shaw, M. and Stammers, N. (eds), *Global Activism Global Media*, London: Pluto Press.

Crawford, C. (2005), 'Actor network theory', in Ritzer, G. (ed.), *Encyclopedia of social Theory*, pp. 1–4, Thousand Oaks CA: Sage.

Cubitt, S. (1998) *Digital Aesthetics*, London: Sage.

Cupers, K. (2005) 'Towards a nomadic geography: rethinking space and identity for the potential of progressive politics in the contemporary city', *International Journal of Urban and Regional Research* Vol. 29 (4), pp. 729–39.

Curran, J. (1991) 'Re-thinking the media as a public sphere', Dahlgren, P. and Sparks. C. (eds), *Communication and Citizenship*, London: Routledge.

Curran, J. (2000) *Media Organisations in Society*, London: Arnold.

Curran, J. Fenton, N. and Freeman, D. (2012) *Misunderstanding the Internet*, London and New York: Routledge.

Dahlberg, L. (2007) 'Rethinking the fragmentation of the cyberpublic: from consensus to contestation', *New Media and Society* Vol. 9, pp. 827–47.

De Certeau, M. (1984) *The Practice of Everyday Life*, Berkeley: University of California Press.

Deleuze G. and Guattari F. (2004) *A Thousand Plateaus: Capitalism and Schizophrenia*, London and New York: Continuum.

Diani, M. (2010) *Social Movements and Networks: Relational Approaches to Collective Action*, Oxford: Oxford University Press.

Dinan, W. and Miller, D. (2007) *Thinker, Faker, Spinner, Spy*, London: Pluto Press.

Doherty, B. (2000) 'Manufactured vulnerability', Benjamin, S. Paterson, M. and Doherty, B. (eds), *Direct Action in British Environmentalism*, London and New York: Routledge.

Donald, J. and Donald S. (2000) 'The publicness of cinema', Gledhill, C. and Williams, L. (eds), *Reinventing Film Studies*, London: Arnold.

Donson, F. Chester, G. Welsh, I and Tickle, A. (2004) 'Rebels with a cause, folk devils without a panic: press jingoism, policing tactics and anti-capitalist protest in London and Prague', *Internet Journal of Criminology*.

Downing, D.H. (2003) 'New media power: the internet and global activism', Couldry, N. and Curran, J. (eds), *Contesting Media Power*, New York: Rowman and Littlefield.

Downing J. (1984) *Radical Media: The Political Experience of Alternative Communication*, Boston MA: South End Press.

Downing, J. (1995) 'Alternative media and the Boston Tea Party', Downing, J. Mohammad, A. and Sreberny-Mohammad, A. (eds), *Questioning the Media*, London: Sage.

Downing J. (2001) *Radical Media, Rebellious Communication and Social Movements*, London: Sage.

Duncombe, S. (1997) *Notes from the Underground: Zines and the Politics of Alternative Culture*, London: Verso.

Eglin, J. (1987) 'Women and peace: from the suffragists to the Greenham women', Taylor, R. and Young, N. (eds), *Campaigns for Peace: British Peace Movements in the Twentieth Century*, Manchester: Manchester University Press.

Epstein, B. (1993) *Political Protest and Cultural Revolution: Non-violent Direct Action in the 1970s and 1980s*, Berkley and Los Angeles: University of California Press.

Escobar, A. (1996) 'Welcome to cyberia: notes on the anthropology of cyberculture', Sardar, Z., and Ravets, J. (eds), *Cyberfutures: Culture and Politics and the Information Superhighway*, London: Pluto Press.

Ess, C. (1994) 'The political computer: hypertext, democracy and Habermas', Landow. G. (ed.), *Hyper/Text/Theory*, London: Johns Hopkins University Press.

Feher, M. (2007) *Non Governmental Politics*, New York: Zone Books.

Foucault, M. (1985) *The Use of Pleasure*, Hurley, R. (Trans.), New York: Vintage.

Foucault, M. 1995 *Discipline and Punish: The Birth of the Prison*. New York: Vintage Books.

Foley, D. and Valenzuela, A (2005) 'Critical ethnography: the politics of collaboration', Denzin, N. and Lincoln, Y. (eds), *The Sage Handbook of Qualitative Research*, London: Sage.

Fournier, V. (2002) 'Utopianism and the cultivation of possibilities: grass roots movements of hope', M. Parker (ed.), *Utopia and Organisation*, Oxford: Blackwell.

Franklin, B. (1994) *Packaging Politics: Political Communication in Britain's Media Democracy*, London: Arnold.

Fraser, N. (1987) 'What's critical about critical theory? The case of Habermas and gender', Benhabib, S. and Cornell, D (eds), *Feminism as Critique: On the Politics of Gender*, Cambridge: Polity Press, pp. 31–56.

Fraser, N. (1990) 'Re-thinking the public sphere: a contribution to the critique of actually existing democracy', *Social Text* Vol. 8–9, pp. 56–80.

Fraser, N. (2007) 'Transnationalizing the public sphere: on the legitimacy and efficacy of public opinion in a post-Westphalian world', *Theory, Culture and Society* Vol. 24 (4), pp. 7–30.

Garnham, N. (2000) *The Media and Politics: Emancipation, the Media and Modernity*, Oxford: Oxford University Press.

Garnham, N. (2007) 'Habermas and the public sphere', *Global Media and Communication*, Vol. 3 pp. 201–14.

Gerbaudo, P. (2011) *Tweets from the Street* London: Pluto.

Giddens, A. (1991) *Modernity and Self-Identity: Self and Society in the Late Modern Age*, Oxford: Polity Press.

Gitlin, Todd (2003) *The Whole World is Watching: Mass Media in the Making and the Unmaking of the New Left*, Berkeley: University of California Press.

Gilbert, J. (2008) *Anticapitalism and Culture: Radical Theory and Popular Politics*, Oxford and New York: Berg.

Gilroy, P. (2004) *After Empire: Melancholia or Convivial Culture?*, London: Routledge.

Gladwell, M. (2010) 'Small change: why the revolution will not be tweeted', *New Yorker*.

Goode, L. (2005) *Jürgen Habermas and the Public Sphere*, London: Pluto Press.

Graeber, D. (2004) 'The new anarchists', Mertes, T. (ed.), *A Movement of Movements: Is Another World Really Possible?* London and New York: Verso.

Granovetter, M. (1983) 'The strength of weak ties: a network theory revisted', *Sociological Theory* Vol. 1, pp. 201–133.

Habermas, J. (1974) 'The public sphere: an encyclopaedia article', *New German Critique*, Vol. 3, pp. 49–55.

Habermas, J. (1992) 'Further reflections on the public sphere', Calhoun, C, (ed.), *Habermas and the Public Sphere*, Cambridge MA: MIT Press.

Habermas, J. (1999) *The Structural Transformation of the Public Sphere: An Inquiry into a Category of Bourgeois Society* (trans. Burger, T.), Cambridge MA: MIT Press.

Halloran, J. Elliott, P. and Murdock, G. (1970) *Demonstrations and Communications: A Case Study*, London: Penguin.

Hammersley, M. and Atkinson, P. ([1983] 1995) *Ethnography Principles in Practice*, 2nd edition, London: Routledge.

Hands, J. (2011) @ is for Activism: Dissent, Resistance and Rebellion in a Digital Culture, London: Pluto Press.

Hansen, Tom and Civil, Enlace (2001) 'Timeline' to Marcos, Subcomandante Insurgente, Our Word is Our Weapon: Selected Writings, Ponce de Leon, J. (ed.), London: Serpent's Tail.

Hardt, A. and Negri, M. (2000) Empire, Cambridge MA: Harvard University Press.

Hardt, A. and Negri, M. (2004) Multitude: War and Democracy in the Age of Empire, London: Penguin Books.

Hartley, J. (1996) Popular Reality: Journalism, Modernity, Popular Culture, London: Arnold.

Herbert, D. (2005) 'Media Publics, Culture and Democracy', in Media Audiences, Gillespie, M. (ed.), Oxford: Open University Press.

Herman, E. and Chesney, B. (1997) The Global Media, London and Washington: Cassell.

Herngren, Pat (1993) Path of Resistance: The Practice of Civil Disobedience (trans. Margaret Rainey), Philadelphia, New Society Publishers.

Hetherington, K. (1998) Expressions of Identity: Space, Performance, Politics, London: Sage.

Hollingsworth, M. (1986) The Press and Political Dissent, London: Pluto Press.

Holmes, B. (2003) 'Touching the violence of the state', in Notes from Nowhere (ed.), We are Everywhere: The Irresistible Rise of Global Anti-Capitalism, London: Verso.

Iacono, S. and Kling, R. (1996) 'Computerising and controversy: value conflicts and social choices' Iacono, S. and Kling, R. (eds) Computerization Movements and Tales of Technological Utopianism, San Diego CA: Academic Press.

Jameson, F. (1984) Postmodernism or the Cultural Logic of Late Capitalism, Durham: Duke University Press.

Johnson, J.H. (2001) 'Versailles, meet les Halles: masks, carnival and the French revolution', Representations, Vol. 73 pp. 89–116.

Juris, J. (2005) 'Violence performed and imagined: militant action, the black block and the mass media in Genoa', Critique of Anthropology, 25(4), pp. 413–32.

K (2001) 'Being Black Bloc', On Fire: The Battle of Genoa and the Anti-capitalist Movement, London: One Off Press.

Kant, I. (1991) 'The contest of faculties', Reis, H. (ed.), Kant: Political Writings, Cambridge: Cambridge University Press.

Kingsnorth, P. (2003) One No, Many Yeses: A Journey to the Heart of the Global Resistance Movement, London: Free Press.

Kinny, J. (1996) 'Is there a New Political paradigm lurking in Cyberspace?', Sadar, Z. and Ravets, J. (eds) CyberFutures: Culture and Politics and the Information.

Klein, N. (2000) No Logo, London: Flamingo.

Klein, N. (2004) 'Reclaiming the commons', Metres, T. (ed.), A Movement of Movements: Is Another World Really Possible?, London and New York: Verso.

Kling, R. (ed.) (1996) *Computerization and Controversy: Value Conflicts and Social Choices* (Second Edition), San Diego CA: Academic Press.

Kofman, E. and Lebas, E. (1996) 'Introduction', *Writings on Cities*, Lefebvre, H., Oxford: Blackwell.

Kripps, H. (1990) 'Power and resistance', *Philosophy and the Social Sciences* Vol. 20, pp. 170–82.

Krøvel, R. (2008) 'The war in Chiapas: a revenge for critical journalism? The end of journalism?', Technology, Education and Ethics Conference, University of Leeds.

Landow, G. (1994) *Hyper/Text/Theory*, Baltimore and London: Johns Hopkins University Press.

Landry, C. Morley, D. Southwood, R. and Wright, P. (1985) *What a Way to Run a Railroad: An Analysis of Radical Failure*, London: Comedia.

Leavis, F.D. (1930) *Mass Civilisation and Minority Culture*, Cambridge: Minority Press.

Lee-Treweek, G. and Linkogle, S. (2000) *Danger in the Field: Ethics and Risk in Social Research*, London: Sage.

Lefebvre, H. (1996) *Writing on Cities*, Kofman, E. and Lebas, E. (trans), Oxford: Blackwell.

Leveson (2012), An Inquiry into the Culture, Practices and Ethics of the Press: Report, London: The Stationery Office.

Lovatt, A. and Purkis, J. (1996) 'Shouting in the street: popular culture, values and the new ethnography', O'Connor, J. and Wynne, D. (eds), *From the Margins to the Centre: Cultural Production and Consumption in the Post-industrial City*, Aldershot: Ashgate.

Maeckelbergh M. (2009) *The Will of the Many*, London: Pluto Press.

Martin, M. (2004) 'New social movements and democracy', Tod, M. and Taylor, G. (eds) *Democracy and Participation: Popular Protest and New Social Movements*, London: Merlin Press.

Marcos, Subcomandante, (2001) *Our Word is Our Weapon: Selected Writings*, Ponce de Leon, J. (ed.), London: Serpent's Tail.

Marcos, Subcomandante (2004) '"The hour glass of the Zapatistas", interview by Gabriel Garcia Marquez and Robert Pombo', Mertes, T. (ed.), *A Movement of Movements: Is Another World Really Possible?* London and New York: Verso.

Marshall, P. (1993) *Demanding the Impossible: A History of Anarchism*, London: Freedom Press.

Massey, D. (1993) 'Politics and space/time', Keith, M. and Pile, S. (eds), *Place and The Politics of Identity*, London and New York: Routledge.

Massumi, B. (2004) 'Translator's foreword: pleasures of philosophy', Deleuze G. and Guattari F., *A Thousand Plateaus: Capitalism and Schizophrenia*, London and New York: Continuum.

McChesney, R. (1997) *Corporate Media and the Threat to Democracy*, New York: Seven Stories Press.

McCurdy, P. (2012) 'Social Movements, Protest and Mainstream Media', *Social Compass* Vol. 6 No. 3, pp. 244–55.

McGee, M. C. (1975) 'In search of 'the people': a rhetorical alternative', *Quarterly Journal of Speech* Vol. 61 (3), pp. 235–49.

McGuigan, J. (1998) 'What price the public sphere?', Thussu, Daya Kishan (ed.), *Electronic Empires: Global Media and Local Resistance*, London: Arnold.

McKay, G. (1998) *DiY Culture: Party and Protest in Nineties Britain*, London: Verso.

McLaughlin, C. (1998) 'Gender, privacy and publicity in "Media event space"', Carter, C. Branston, G. Allan, S. (eds) *News, Gender and Power*, London: Routledge.

McNair, B. (1998) 'Journalism, politics and public relations: an ethical appraisal', Kieran, M. (ed.), *Media Ethics*, London and New York: Routledge.

Melucci, A. (1989) 'Nomads of the present: social movements and individual needs in contemporary society', Keane, J. and Mier, P (eds), Philadelphia, PA: Temple University Press.

Mertes, T. (2004) 'Grass-roots globalism', Mertes, T. (ed.), *A Movement of Movements: Is Another World Really Possible*, London and New York: Verso.

Mills. J.S. (1989) *On Liberty and other writings* Collini, S. (ed.) Cambridge: Cambridge University Press.

Moles, K. (2008) 'A Walk in Thirdspace: Place, Methods and walking', *Sociological Research Online* Vol. 13(4)2.

Moreiras, A. (2001) 'A line of shadows: metaphysics in Counter Empire', in *Rethinking Marxism* Vol. 13, pp. 216–24.

Morozov, E. (2011 [2012]) *The Net Delusion: How not to Liberate the* World, London: Penguin.

Mouffe, C. (2005) *On the Political*, London and New York: Routledge.

Moulthrop, S. (1994) 'Rhizome and resistance: hypertext and the dreams of a new culture', Landow, G. (ed.) *Hyper/Text/Theory*, Baltimore and London: Johns Hopkins University Press.

Neale, J. (2002) *You are G8, We are 6 Billion: The Truth Behind the Genoa Protests*, London: Vision Paperbacks.

Negt, O. and Kluge, A. (1993) *Public Sphere and Experience: Towards an Analysis of the Bourgeois and Proletarian Public Sphere* (trans, Labanyi, P. et al.), Minneapolis: University of Minneapolis.

Newburn, T. (2011) *Reading the Riots: Investigating England's Summer of Disorder*, Guardian Shorts.

Notes from Nowhere (ed.) (2003) *We Are Everywhere: The Irresistible Rise of Global Anti- Capitalism*, London: Verso.

Olesen, T. (2004) 'Globalising the Zapatistas: from third world solidarity to global solidarity', *Third World Quarterly*, Vol. 25, pp. 255–67.

Ong, W. (1982) *Orality and Literacy: The Technologising of the Word*, London and New York: Methuen.

Passavant, D and Dean, J. (2004) *Empire's New Clothes: Reading Hardt and Negri*, London and New York: Routledge.

Patton, P. (2000) *Deleuze and the Political*, London and New York: Routledge.

Peters J.D. (1993) 'Distrust of representation: Habermas on the public sphere', *Media, Culture and Society* Vol. 15, pp. 541–72.

Peters, J.D. (2001) 'Witnessing', *Media Culture and Society*, Vol. 23 pp. 707–23.

Plant, S. (1992) *The Most Radical Gesture: The Situationist International in a Postmodern Age*, London: Routledge.

Plato, (1995) *The Statesman*, Cambridge: Cambridge University Press.

Ponce de Leon, J. (2001) 'Travelling back for tomorrow', Marcos, Subcomandante Insurgente, *Our Word is Our Weapon: Selected Writings*, Ponce de Leon, J. (ed.), London: Serpent's Tail.

Poster, M. (1990) *The Mode of Information: Poststructuralism and Social Context*, Chicago: University of Chicago Press.

Postman, N. (1985) *Amusing Ourselves to Death: Public Discourse in the Age of Show Business*, London: Penguin.

Purkis, J. (1996) 'The city as a site of ethical consumption and resistance', O'Connor, J. and Wynne, D. (eds), *From the Margins to the Centre: Cultural Production in the Post-Industrial City*, Aldershot: Ashgate.

Purkis, J. (2000) 'Modern millenarians'. Benjamin, S. Paterson, M. and Doherty, B. (eds), *Direct Action in British Environmentalism*, London and New York: Routledge.

Rantanen, T. (2005) *The Media and Globalisation*, London: Sage.

Reiner, R. (1998) 'Policing, protest and disorder', Della Porta, D. and Reiter, H. (eds) *Policing Protest: The Control of Mass Demonstrations in Western Democracies*, Minneapolis: University of Minnesota Press.

Rheingold, H. (1994) *The Virtual Community: Finding Connections in a Computerised World*, London: Minerva.

Ritzer, G. (2007) (5th revised edn) 'The Starbuckisation of society', *The MacDonaldisation of Society*, London: Sage.

Roake, H. (2009) *Weekly Worker: Paper of the Communist Party of Great Britain*, No. 777, 9 July 2009, p. 5.

Rootes, C. (2000) 'Environmental protest in Britain 1988–1997', Benjamin, S. Paterson, M. and Doherty, B. (eds), *Direct Action in British Environmentalism*, London and New York: Routledge.

Rosello, M. (1994) 'The screener's maps: Michael de Certeau's "wandersmaenner" in Paul Auster's hypertextual detective', Landow, G. (ed.), *Hyper/text/theory*, London: Johns Hopkins University Press.

Rosie, M. and Gorringe, H. (2009) 'What a difference a death makes: protest, policing and the press at the G20', *Sociological Research Online*, 4(5), p. 4.

Routledge, P. (1996) 'The third space as critical engagement', *Antipode* Vol. 28 (4), pp. 399–419.

Ruiz, P. (2005) 'Bridging the gap', de Jong, W. Shaw, M. and Stammers, N. (eds), *Global Activism Global Media*, London: Pluto Press.

Ruiz, P. (2013) 'Revealing power: masked protest and the public sphere', *Cultural Politics*, Dukes Journals.

Ryan, R. (2003), 'Genoa: the new beginnings of an old war', Notes from Nowhere (ed.), *We Are Everywhere: The Irresistible Rise of Global Anti-Capitalism*, London: Verso.

Sadar, Z. (1996) 'Alt.civilisation.fac: cyberspace as the dark side of the west', Sadar, Z. Ravets, J. R (eds) *Cyberfuture; Culture and Politics on the Information Superhighway*, pp. 14–41.

Sakolsky R. and Dunifer, S. (eds) (1998) *Seizing the Airways: A Free Radio Handbook*, Oakland: AK Press.

Sardar, Z., and Ravets, J. (eds) (1996), *Cyberfutures: Culture and Politics and the Information Superhighway*, London: Pluto Press.

Shields, R. (1992) *Places on the Margin: Alternative Geographies of Modernity*, London and New York: Routledge.

Shields, R (1996) *Cultures of Internet: Virtual Spaces, Real Histories, Living Bodies*, London: Sage.

Silverstone, R. (2007) *Media and Morality: On the Rise of the Mediapolis*, Cambridge: Polity.

Simons, J. (2003) 'Popular culture and mediated politics: intellectuals, elites and democracy', Corner, J. and Pels, D. (eds), *Media and the Restyling of Politics*, London: Sage.

Smith, N. and Katz, C. (1993) 'Grounding metaphor: towards a spatialised politics', Keith, M. and Pile, S. (eds), *Place and The Politics of Identity*, London and New York: Routledge.

Soja, E. and Hooper, B. (1993) 'The space that difference makes: some notes on the geographical margins of the new cultural politics', Keith, M. and Pile, S. (eds), *Place and the Politics of Identity*, London and New York: Routledge.

Soja, E. (1996) *Thidspace: Journeys to Los Angeles and Other Real-and-Imagined Places*, Oxford: Basil Blackwell.

Sparks, C. (1985) 'The working class press: radical and revolutionary alternatives' *Media Culture and Society*. Vol. 7 pp. 132–46.

Stafford, B. (1996) *Good Looking: The Virtue of the Image*, Cambridge MA: MIT Press.

Starhawk (2003) 'The bridge at midnight trembles', Notes from Nowhere (ed.), *We Are Everywhere: The Irresistible Rise of Global Anti-capitalism*, London: Verso.

Stein, L. (2009) 'Social movement web use in theory and practice; a content analysis of US movement websites', *New media and Society* Vol. 11, pp. 749–71.

Stokes (2009) *Digital Copyright: Law and Practice*, Oxford and Portland OR: Hart Publishing.

Szerszynski, B. (1999) 'Performing politics: the dramatics of environmental protest', Ray, L. and Sayer, A. (eds) *Cultural Economy: After the Cultural Turn*, London: Sage.

Szerszynski, B. (2003) 'Marked bodies: environmental activism and political semiotics', Corner, J. and Pels, D. (eds), *Media and the Restyling of Politics*, London: Sage.

Taylor, C. (2003) *Modern Social Imaginaries*, Durham and London: Duke University Press/Public Planet Books.

Thornton, S. (1994) 'Moral panic, the media and British rave culture', Rose, A. and Rose, T. (eds), *Microphone Fiend: Youth Music and Youth Culture*, London and New York: Routledge.

Thu Nguyen, D. and Alexander, J. (1996) 'The coming of cyber space-time and the end of polity', R. Shields, (ed.) *Cultures of Internet: Virtual Spaces, Real Histories, Living Bodies*, London: Sage.

Triggs, T. (2006) 'Scissors and glue: punk fanzines and the creation of the DiY aesthetic', *Journal of Design History* Vol. 19 (1), pp. 69–83.

Tumber, H. (2000) *Media Power, Professionals and Policies*, London and New York: Routledge.

Tyler, W. (2003) Notes from Nowhere (ed.), *We Are Everywhere: The Irresistible Rise of Global Anti-Capitalism*, London: Verso.

Van Zoonen, L. (2004) *Entertaining the Citizen: When Politics and Popular Coverage Converge*, New York: Rowman and Littlefield.

Villa, D.R. (1992) 'Postmoderism and the public sphere', *American Political Science Review* Vol. 86 (3), pp. 712–21.

Virilo, P. (1995) 'Red alert in cyberspace!', *Radical Philosophy*, No. 74, Nov/Dec.

Vitaliano, Don (2003) Notes from Nowhere (ed.), *We Are Everywhere: The Irresistible Rise of Global Anti-Capitalism*, London: Verso.

Warner, M. (2002) 'Publics and Counter Publics', *Public Culture* Vol. 14, pp. 49–90.

Waddington, P.A.J. (1998) 'Controlling protest in contemporary, historical and comparative perspective', Della Porter, D. and Reiter, H. (eds) *Policing Protest: The Control of Mass Demonstration in Western Democracies*, Minneapolis: University of Minnesota.

Waddington, P.A.J. (1999) *Policing Citizens*, London and New York: Routledge.

Walch, J. (1999) *In The Net: An Internet Guide for Activists*, London and New York: Zed Books.

Ward, C. (1972) *Anarchy in Action*, London: George Allen and Unwin.

Whitney, (2003) 'Infernal noise: the soundtrack to insurrection', Notes from Nowhere (ed.), *We Are Everywhere: The Irresistible Rise of Global Anti-Capitalism*, London: Verso.

Williams, R. (1983) *Towards 2000*, London: Chato and Windus.

Wolfsfeld, G. (1997) *Media and Political Conflict: News From the Middle East*, Cambridge: Cambridge University Press.

Woodcock, G. (1962) *Anarchism: A History of Libertarian Ideas and Movements*, London: Penguin.

Online Sources

About Indymedia
https://www.indymedia.org/or/static/about.shtml

Account of pink and silver march
www.action-samba-berlin.so36.net/site/network.html
[8 October 2009]

Anti-Terrorism, Crime and Security Act (2001) HMSO
www.opsi.gov.uk/Acts/acts2001/ukpga_20010024_en_1
[14 December 2009]

Anti-war girl 'silly' – judge, *Sun*, 3 May 2003 www.thesun.co.uk/sol/homepage/
news/article77908.ece
[21 July 2009]

Anti-war protesters converge on city, *Argus*, 11 June 2007 www.archive.theargus.
co.uk/2005/10/6
[2 July 2009]

Anti-war yob jailed for attack, *Mirror*, 24 October 2006 www.mirror.co.uk/news/
top-stories/2006/10/24/anti-war-yob-jailed-for-attack- 115875–17981027/
[21 July 2009]

Archbishop of Canterbury: UK debt culture straining fabric of society', *Daily
Telegraph*, 25 April 2008
www.telegraph.co.uk/news/1903558/Archbishop-of-Canterbury-UK-debt-culture-
straining-fabric-of-society.html
[11 November 2008]

Barker, J., Carnival against capitalism, *Vangaurd*
www.vanguard-online.co.uk/archive/politicsandculture/1103.htm
[1 October 2009]

Barker, R. The lost voice of protest, *Guardian*, 21 September 2001. www.guardian.
co.uk/education/2001/sep/25/students.studentpolitics
[30 October 2001]

BBC internet plans will kill off local newspapers, *Daily Telegraph*, 14 August
2008 www.telegraph.co.uk/news/2552609/BBC-internet-plans-will-kill-off-local-
papers.html
[7 November 2008]

Beware of white dressed cops,
www.insurgentdesire.org.uk
[1 October 2009]

Black Bloc participant interview by Active Transformation, 26 January 2000
http://ainfos.ca/00/jan/ainfos00446.html
[14 March 2014]

Black Bloc protester, With love from a black bloc activist … 3 June 2003
https://www.nadir.org/nadir/initiativ/agp/free/evian/reports/0603blackbloc.htm
[14 March 2014]

Black, M., Letter from inside the Black Bloc
www.alternet.org/story/11230/letter_from_inside_the_black_bloc
[1 October 2009]

Blix bloc in Brighton, 22 March 2005
www.indymedia.org.uk/en/regions/southcoast/2005/03/307464.html
[11 August 2005]

Bowcott, O., Met Police kettled pupils aged 11 during fee protests, court told,
Guardian, 5 July 2011
www.guardian.co.uk/uk/2011/jul/05/met-police-kettling-children-high-court
[1 July 2013]

Bruno, K., After Calio Giulian, peaceful protests must continue, 25July 2001
www.corpwatch.org/article.php?id=400
[14 March 2014]

Bush you're either with us or against us, 6 November 2001
http://archives.cnn.com/2001/US/11/06/gen.attack.on.terror/
[8 august 2013]

Can the coffee, *Argus*, 31 May 2006
http://archive.theargus.co.uk/2006/5/31/211319.html
[2 July 2009]

Chaos fears over rally, *Argus*, 3 December 2005 http://archive.theargus.
co.uk/2005/12/3/205805.html
[2 July 2009]

Churchill, W. (1947), Official Report, House of Commons 5 Series, Vol. 444,
pp. 206–7, www.official-documents.gov.uk
[17 December 2009]

Cliff, T. (1974), The use of Socialist Worker as an organiser, *IS International
Bulletin*, www.marxist.org/archive/cliff/works/1974/04/spcworker.htm
[22 January 2006]

Criminal Justice and Public Order Act (1994) HMSO
www.opsi.gov.uk/acts/acts1994/ukpga_19940033_en_1
[14 December 2009]

Coffee chain bid scares traders, *Argus*, 26 May 2006 http://archive.theargus.co.uk/2006/5/26/211213.html
[2 July 2009]

Conn, D., Hillsborough police guilty of cover-up, says minister Maria Eagle, *Guardian*, 13 April 2009
www.guardian.co.uk/football/2009/apr/13/hillsborough-south-yorkshire-police
[1 July 2013]

The curious case of Sukey and the bizarre press release, Random Blowe, 10 February 2011
www.blowe.org.uk/2011/02/curious-case-of-sukey-and-bizarre-press.html
[1 July 2013]

Evans, R. and Lewis, P. (2013) Judge to rule on whether spy case should be held in open, 17 January 2013
www.theguardian.com/uk/2013/jan/17/judge-police-spy-case-open
[8 August 2013]

Famous faces back the fight to free Omar, *Argus*, 6 April 2006 http://archive.theargus.co.uk/2006/1/23/207209.html
[2 July 2009]

Fox, D., Double lyric, 10 February 2011
http://codepoetics.com/octoblog/blog/2011/02/10/double-lyric/
[1 July 2013]

Genoa beyond the hype
http://flag.blackened.net/revolt/freeearth/genoa_hype.html
[1 October 2009]

Guardian News Blog
www.guardian.co.uk/uk/blog/2010/nov/10/demo-2010-student-protests-live
[1 of July]

Hardy, T., Polly put the kettle on, Sukey take it off again, 27 January 2011
http://beyondclicktivism.com/2011/01/27/polly-put-the-kettle-on-sukey-take-it-off/
[1 July 2013]

Interview with Luca Casarini, spokesperson for the *Tute Bianche* (2001)
http://greenhouse.economics.utah.edu/pipermail/rad-green/2001-September/000259.html
[14 March 2014]

Independent Investigation into the Death of Ian Tomlinson on 1 April 2009 (2010) Independent Police Complaints Commission.

www.ipcc.gov.uk/sites/default/files/Documents/investigation_commissioner_
reports/inv_rep_independent_investigation_into_the_death_of_ian_tomlinson.
pdf
[14 January, 2014]

Inside Stories, BBC, 29 September 2008
www.bbc.co.uk/radio4/factual/newspapers.shtml
[2 October 2008]

J18 1999: Our resistance is as transnational as capital
www.network23.nologic.org/trapese/cdrom/contents/context/txts/past%20
mobilisations/j18 .htm
[1 October 2009]

Kingsley, P., Inside the anti-kettling HQ, *Guardian*, 3 February 2011
www.guardian.co.uk/uk/2011/feb/02/inside-anti-kettling-hq
[1 July 2012]

Klein, N. (2001) The unknown icon, *Guardian*, 23 March 2001 www.guardian.
co.uk/books/2001/mar/03/politics
[30 October 2001]

Make your voices heard for justice, *Argus*, 10 July 2006 http://archive.theargus.
co.uk/2006/7/10/212494.html
[2 July 2009]

Monbiot, G. (2001) Raising the temperature, 24 July 2001 www.theguardian.
com/politics/2001/jul/24/greenpolitics.globalisation
[11 March 2014]

Monbiot, G., The activists' guide to exploiting the media, no date
www.urban75.com/Action/media.html
[13 June 2004]

Moore, A., Riots in Tottenham after Mark Duggan shooting protest, BBC,
7 August 2011
www.bbc.co.uk/news/uk-england-london-14434318
[8 August 2013]

Mount, H., The students and police I saw today were utterly dignified, *Daily
Telegraph*
http://blogs.telegraph.co.uk/culture/harrymount/100048723/the-students-and-
police-i-saw-today-were-utterly-dignified/
[1 July 2010]

MP's fearing decline of local news, BBC, 19 March 2009 http://news.bbc.co.uk/1/
hi/uk_politics/7953778.stm
[9 April 2009]

The Newbury Roundhats outflanked, *Daily Telegraph*, 10 January 1996 http://
newburybypass.ukrivers.net/factfile.html
[22 January 1999]

Non criminalizziamo il Black Bloc!
www.barcelona.indymedia.org).
[1 October 2009]

NY police spied on anti Bush protesters, *Guardian* 6 March 2007 www.guardian.
co.uk/world/2007/mar/26/usa.suzannegoldenberg1
[15 May 2009]

Off side, Spiked Online, 7 April 2005
www.spiked-online.com/index.php?/site/article/1132
[11 November 2008]

On violence against the police, 10 December 2010
http://thecommune.co.uk/2010/12/10/on-violence-against-the-police/
[1 July 2013]

Online emails between activists and Starbucks, May 2006
www.business-humanrights.org/Links/Repository/587011,
www.reports-and-materials.org/Further-exchange-between-Starbucks-Quilty-
about- Guantanamo-May-2006.doc
[18 October 2006]

Person of the year, *Time*, December 2011
www.time.com/time/person-of-the-year/2011/
[8 August 2013]

Perryman, M., Fantasy Politics, *Guardian*, 11 July 2000,
www.guardian.co.uk/theguardian/2000/jul/12/guardianletters2
[22 January 2006]

Pink and Silver protester, Genoa: pink and silver on 'actions day' – report,
30 July 2001
www.nadir.org/nadir/initiativ/agp/free/genova/pinksilver.htm
[14 March 2014]

Police caught on tape trying to recruit Plane Stupid protester as spy, *Guardian*,
21 April www.guardian.co.uk/uk/2009/apr/24/strathclyde-police-plane-stupid-
recruit-spy
[15 May 2009]

Police paid informants £750 000 in four years, *Guardian*, 8 May 2009 www.
guardian.co.uk/politics/2009/may/08/strathclyde-police-informant-payments
[15 May 2009]

Policing Public Order, 2011
www.hmic.gov.uk/media/policing-public-order-20110208.pdf
[1 June 2013]

Police try to 'negotiate' EDO march Indymedia, 2 December 2005
www.indymedia.co.uk/en/regions/southcoast/2005/12/329002.html
[2 July 2009]

Postman, N. (1998) Five things we need to know about technological change,
speech given in Denver Colorado, March 27. www.mgi.polymtl.ca/marc.
bourdeau/InfAgeTeaching/OtherLinks/Postman.pdf
[7 November 2009]

Preston, J. and Stelter, B., Cellphones become the world's eyes and ears on
protests, *New York Times*, 18 February 2011.
www.nytimes.com/2011/02/19/world/middleeast/19video.html?_r=0
[1 July 2012]

Random Blowe, February 2011
www.blowe.org.uk/2011_02_01_archive.html
[1 July 2013]

Re: issues around Sukey the protest app, February 2011
http://visionon.tv/forum/-/message_boards/view_message/45270
http://visionon.tv/forum/-/message_boards/message/46202
[1 July 2013]

Redwood, J., Political blog, 10 October, 2007
www.johnredwoodsdiary.com/2007/10/10/postal-strikes
[11 November 2008]

Religious leaders back detainee, *Argus*, 29 September 2005 http://archive.
theargus.co.uk/2005/9/29/203518.html
[2 July 2009]

Report of the Hillsborough Independent Panel
http://hillsborough.independent.gov.uk/
[14 January 2014]

A response to press misinformation,
http://ludd.net/retort/msg00200.html)
[1 October 2009]

Roy, H., Speech to Rotary, 11 September, 2008
www.roy.org.nz/content/territorial-soldier-speech-rotary
[11 November 2008]

Royal Commission on the Press (1977) HMSO
http://library-2.lse.ac.uk/archives/handlists/CollMisc0610/CollMisc0610.html
[14 December 2009]

Second Declaration of La Realidad (1996)
www.cuauhtemoc.org/danza%20website/Zapatista%20docs/2%20Declaration
%20of%20La%20Realidad.htm
[14 December 2009]

Shirky C., This much I know, *Observer*, 15 February 2009 www.guardian.co.uk/
lifeandstyle/2009/feb/15/this-much-i-know-clay-shirky- technology
[17 February 2009]

Sometimes we have to stand up to the state, *Argus*, 6 September 2005 http://
archive.theargus.co.uk/2005/9/6/202732.html
[2 July 2009]

Stormont bomb was art says Stone, BBC, 22 September 2008 http://news.bbc.
co.uk/1/hi/northern_ireland/7629417.stm
[3 November 2008]

Smith, P., Student protest: the NUS lobby wasn't enough for us, *Guardian*,
10 November 2010
www.guardian.co.uk/commentisfree/2010/nov/10/student-protests-nus-lobby-
anarchists
[1 July]

Starbucks Action in Brighton, 3 March 2006
www.indymedia.org.uk/en/2006/06/341924.html

Sukey (2011)
http://web.archive.org/web/20130513134039/http:/www.opensukey.org/about/
[14 March 2014]

Sukey: live demo info service for saturday – ldn, 27 January 2011
http://london.indymedia.org/articles/7065

Sukey: peaceful protest app without any mobile phone network communications
data or traffic data anonymity, 29 January 2011
https://p10.secure.hostingprod.com/@spyblog.org.uk/ssl/spyblog/2011/01/29/
sukey--protest-app-without-any-mobile-communications-data-anonymity.html
[1 July 2013]

Sukey sucks, 9 February 2011
http://libcom.org/forums/general/sukey-sucks-09022011
[1 July 2011]

Sussex MP campaigns for Omar, *Argus*, 7 May 2007 http://archive.theargus.co.uk/2007/5/15/234191.html
[2 July 2009]

Sweden defends EU summit policing, BBC, 17 June 2001 http://news.bbc.co.uk/1/hi/world/europe/1392839.stm
[21 August 2001]

Three guilty of bomb conspiracy, BBC, 8 September 2008 http://news.bbc.co.uk/2/hi/uk_news/7528483.stm
[3 November 2008]

Tonks, Francis
www.youtube.com/watch?v=xZP1eXYM940
[5 July 2008]

Tripod tactics that work on bypass, *Guardian*, 10 January 1996 http://newburybypass.ukrivers.net/factfile.html
[22 January 1999]

Union backs Guantanamo detainee, *Argus*, 6 January 2006 http://archive.theargus.co.uk/2006/4/3/209488.html
[2 July 2009]

USA Patriot Act (2001) Congress
http://frwebgate.access.gpo.gov/cgi- bin/getdoc.cgi?dbname=107_cong_public_laws&docid=f:publ056.107.pdf
[14 December 2009]

Unnamed protester, the pink and silver bloc does Prague www.nadir.org/nadir/initiative/apg/S26/prague/pinkrephtm
[1 October 2009]

Universal Declaration of Human Rights
www.un.org/en/documents/udhr/
[8 August 2013}

Veil should not be worn says Muslim peer, *Guardian*, 20 February, 2007 http://politics.guardian.co.uk/homeaffairs/story/0,,2017271,00.html
[6 September 2007]

Vidal, J., Blair attacks 'spurious' May Day protests, *Guardian*, 1 May 2001 www.guardian.co.uk/uk/2001/may/01/mayday.immigrationpolicy1 [21 August 2001]

Vidal, J., Anatomy of a very nineties revolution, *Guardian*, 13 January 1999 www.guardian.co.uk/technology/1999/jan/13/internet2
[4 February 2004]

Viner, K., 'Luddites' we should not ignore, *Guardian*, 29 September 2000
www.guardian.co.uk/Archive/Article/0,4273,4069644,00.html
[4 February 2004]

Welch, J., Getting it printed: London in the 1970s, *Jacket Magazine*, Issue 29
http://jacketmagazine.com/29/welch-print.html
[22 January 2007]

Wells, M., A local paper takes on the Pentagon, *New Statesman and Society*,
31 October 2005
www.newstatesman.com/200510310005
[2 July 2009]

Whitaker, B., How a man setting fire to himself sparked an uprising in Tunisia,
28 December 2010
www.theguardian.com/commentisfree/2010/dec/28/tunisia-ben-ali
[8 August 2013]

Why we do it, Rhythms of Resistance
www.rhythmsofresistance.co.uk/?lid=52
[1 October 2009]

Wray, S. (1998), Rhizomes, Nomads, and Resistant Internet Use
www.thing.net/~rdom/ecd/RhizNom.html
[5 July 2008]

Interviews

Dagostino, L. – Defence lawyer (2006)
Dickinson, A. – *Argus* journalist (2007)
Tanyar, R. – *Circus Free* activist (2005)
Trice, I. – Samba Master (2004)
Unnamed activists – Save Omar activists (2006)
Unnamed activists – Smash EDO activists (2005 and 2006)
Unnamed activist – Sussex Action for Peace activist (2007)
Wells, M. – *Argus* journalist (2006)

Index

Compiled by Sue Carlton